Lecture Notes in Computer Science 10036

Commenced Publication in 1973
Founding and Former Series Editors:
Gerhard Goos, Juris Hartmanis, and Jan van Leeuwen

More information about this series at http://www.springer.com/series/7409

Ching-Hsien Hsu · Shangguang Wang
Ao Zhou · Ali Shawkat (Eds.)

Internet of Vehicles – Technologies and Services

Third International Conference, IOV 2016
Nadi, Fiji, December 7–10, 2016
Proceedings

Springer

Editors
Ching-Hsien Hsu
Department of Computer Science
Chung Hua University
Hsinchu, Taiwan
Taiwan

Ao Zhou
Beijing University of Posts
and Telecommunications
Beijing
China

Shangguang Wang
Beijing University of Posts
and Telecommunications
Beijing
China

Ali Shawkat
The University of Fiji
Suva
Fiji

ISSN 0302-9743 ISSN 1611-3349 (electronic)
Lecture Notes in Computer Science
ISBN 978-3-319-51968-5 ISBN 978-3-319-51969-2 (eBook)
DOI 10.1007/978-3-319-51969-2

Library of Congress Control Number: 2017930212

LNCS Sublibrary: SL3 – Information Systems and Applications, incl. Internet/Web, and HCI

Printed on acid-free paper

This Springer imprint is published by Springer Nature
The registered company is Springer International Publishing AG
The registered company address is: Gewerbestrasse 11, 6330 Cham, Switzerland

Preface

This volume contains the proceedings of the Third International Conference on Internet of Vehicles (IOV 2016), which was held in Nadi, Fiji during December on 7–10, 2016. IOV is different from telematics, vehicle ad hoc networks (VANET), and intelligent transportation (ITS), in which vehicles, like phones, can run within the whole network, and obtain various services by swarm intelligent computing with people, vehicles, and environments. IOV 2016 intended to provide an opportunity for researchers and industry practitioners to exchange information regarding advancements in the state of art and practice of IOV architectures, protocols, services, and applications, as well as to identify emerging research topics and define the future directions of IOV.

This year, we received a total of 55 paper submissions for IOV 2016 from 26 countries and regions. All papers were rigorously and independently peer-reviewed by the Technical Program Committee members. After a thorough review process, in which each paper was evaluated by at least three reviewers, 22 papers were selected for presentation and publication. We believe that the program and this volume present novel and interesting ideas.

The organization of conferences requires a lot of hard work and dedication from many people. It would not have been possible without the exceptional commitment of many expert volunteers. We would like to take this opportunity to extend our sincere thanks to all the authors, keynote speakers, Technical Program Committee members, and reviewers. Special thanks go to the entire local Organizing Committee for their help in making the conference a success. We would also like to express our gratitude to all the organizations that supported our efforts to bring the conference to fruition. We are grateful to Springer for publishing the proceedings.

Last, but not least, we hope that the participants enjoyed the technical program during this prestigious conference and discovered a lot of unique cultural flavors in Fiji to make their stay unforgettable.

December 2016

Mohammed Atiquzzaman
Chung-Ming Huang
Reinhard Klette
Raouf Boutaba
Peng Cheng
Der-Jiunn Deng

The original version of the book was revised:
For detailed information please see Erratum.
The Erratum to this Book is available at
https://doi.org/10.1007/978-3-319-51969-2_23

Organization

2016 International Conference on Internet of Vehicles (IOV 2016)

General Co-chairs

Mohammed Atiquzzaman	University of Oklahoma, USA
Chung-Ming Huang	Nat' l Cheng Kung University, Taiwan
Reinhard Klette	Auckland University of Technology, New Zealand

General Executive Chairs

Yang Xiang	Deakin University, Australia
Shawkat Ali	The University of Fiji, Fiji

Program Chairs

Raouf Boutaba	University of Waterloo, Canada
Peng Cheng	Zhejiang University, China
Der-Jiunn Deng	National Changhua University Education, Taiwan

Steering Committee

Robert Hsu	Chung Hua University, Taiwan
Shangguang Wang	BUPT, China
Victor C.M. Leung	The University of British Columbia, Canada

Award Chair

Robert Hsu	Chung Hua University, Taiwan

International Liaison and Publicity Chairs

Neal Xiong	Georgia State University, USA
Bibhya Sharma	The University of The South Pacific, Fiji
Zibin Zheng	Sun Yat-sen University, China

Publication Chairs

Ao Zhou   Beijing University of Posts and Telecommunications,
                                    China
Raghavendra S.   University Visvesvaraya College of Engineering, India

Demo/Poster Chair

Fuu-Cheng (Admor) Jiang   Tunghai University, Taiwan

Special Session Chair

Huan Zhou   China Three Gorges University, China

Local Arrangement Chairs

Rohitash Chandra   The University of The South Pacific, Fiji
Jesmin Nahar   The University of Fiji, Fiji

Technical Program Committee

Miguel López-Benítez   University of Liverpool, UK
Jeremy Blum   Penn State University, USA
Abdelmadjid Bouabdallah   Université de Technologie de Compiègne, France
Yu Cai   Michigan Technological University, USA
Carlos Calafate   Universidad Politecnica de Valencia, Spain
Juan-Carlos Cano   Technical University of Valencia, Spain
Luca Caviglione   CNR – ISSIA, Italy
Mehmet Celenk   Ohio University, USA
Ing-Chau Chang   National Changhua University of Education, Taiwan
Yao-Chung Chang   National Taitung University, Taiwan
Mu-Song Chen   Dayeh University, Taiwan
Tzung-Shi Chen   National University of Tainan, Taiwan
Zhe Chen   Northeastern University, China
Thomas ChenWoong Cho   Jungwon University, Korea
Massimiliano Comisso   University of Trieste, Italy
François-Xavier Coudoux   IEMN DOAE UVHC, France
Jana DittmannOscar   Universitat Politècnica de Catalunya, Spain
  Esparza
Esa Hyytiä   Helsinki University of Technology, Finland
Yiming Ji   University of South Carolina Beaufort, USA
Han-Shin Jo   Hanbat National University, Korea
Aravind Kailas   Algorithms, Models, and Systems Solutions,
                                LLC, USA
Sokratis Katsikas   University of Piraeus, Greece
Georgios Kambourakis   University of the Aegean, Greece

Contents

V2V and M2M Communications

Miscellaneous Issues

IOV Architectures and Applications

Advanced Road Vanishing Point Detection by Using Weber Adaptive Local Filter

Xue Fan$^{(\boxtimes)}$, Yunfan Chen, Jingchun Piao, Irfan Riaz, Han Xie, and Hyunchul Shin

Department of Electronics and Communication Engineering,
Hanyang University, Ansan, Republic of Korea
{fanxue,chenyunfan,kcpark,irfancra,
xiehan}@digital.hanyang.ac.kr, shin@hanyang.ac.kr

Abstract. Variations in road types and its ambient environment make the single image based vanishing point detection a challenging task. Since only road trails (e.g. road edges, ruts, and tire tracks) would contribute informative votes to vanishing point detection, the Weber adaptive local filter is proposed to distinguish the road trails from background noise, which is envisioned to reduce the workload and to eliminate uninformative votes introduced by the background noise. This is possible by controlling the number of neighbors and by increasing the sensitivity for small values of the local excitation response. After road trail extraction, the generalized Laplacian of Gaussian (gLoG) filters are applied to estimate the texture orientation of those road trail pixels. Then, the vanishing point is detected based on the adaptive soft voting scheme. The experimental results on the benchmark dataset demonstrate that the proposed method is about 2 times faster in detection speed and outperforms by 1.3% in detection accuracy, when compared to the complete texture based gLoG method, which is a well-known state-of-the-art approach.

Keywords: Vanishing point · Weber adaptive local filter · Generalized Laplacian of Gaussian (gLoG) filter · Voting map

1 Introduction

Over the past decade, the road vanishing point detection has been widely adopted for Autonomous Navigation Systems (AVNS) [1] and for perspective rectification [2]. It is a challenging problem owing to different road types and variations in background, color, texture, and illumination condition. For the unstructured or ill-structured roads, it is quite challenging to achieve robust vanishing point detection due to the lack of clear road boundaries and lane markings. However, it was found that the trails left by previous vehicles on the road surface, such as ruts and tire tracks, commonly tend to converge to the vanishing point. Thus, the texture based vanishing point detection methods [3–5] have been proposed to utilize these road trails for excellent detection accuracy in both of the well-paved roads and unstructured off-roads.

Among all the texture based vanishing point detection approaches, the generalized Laplacian of Gaussian (gLoG) filter based method [6] achieves the most promising

© Springer International Publishing AG 2016
C.-H. Hsu et al. (Eds.): IOV 2016, LNCS 10036, pp. 3–13, 2016.
DOI: 10.1007/978-3-319-51969-2_1

performance. It adopted two types of detection strategies: (1) the complete texture map based gLoG method, which achieves the state-of-the-art detection accuracy; (2) the blob based gLoG method, which obtains extremely fast detection speed. In complete texture map based gLoG method, a set of gLoG filters are generated to perform texture orientation estimation, and the voting map is obtained by the pixel-wise soft voting scheme. However, this method leads to high computation complexity because both road trails and background noise can be regarded as voters and vanishing point candidates. In blob based gLoG method, the vanishing point is detected by only using the texture orientations estimated at road blob regions. Fast detection speed is achieved at the expense of detection accuracy.

In this paper, a novel framework is proposed for road vanishing point detection, through which both the detection accuracy and computation time are improved compared to the gLoG filter based method. The Weber adaptive local filter (WALF) is proposed to extract the road trails and to eliminate background noise. This can reduce the complexity of pixel-wise texture orientation estimation and optimize the following voting. Compared to the complete texture map based gLoG method, the proposed WALF based vanishing point detection method can improve the detection speed about two times while increasing the detection accuracy by about 1.3%.

This paper is organized as follows. A brief review of the related works about the road vanishing point detection is presented in Sect. 2. The proposed WALF is explained in Sect. 3. The experimental results and analysis are described in Sect. 4. Finally, the conclusions and discussions are summarized in Sect. 5.

2   Related Works

Road vanishing point detection can be generalized into two main categories: edge based method [7, 8] and texture based method [3–6, 9]. Edge based vanishing point detection approaches depend on the utilization of dominant line segments to detect the vanishing point. In [7], the vanishing point is estimated through calculating the intersection points of line segments selected by a temporal filtering. In [8], real time vanishing point detection is achieved by utilizing adaptive steerable filter banks. These approaches can be applied to real time applications for structured road images, but the performance is seriously degraded for unstructured roads.

The texture based vanishing point detection approaches have been proposed to overcome the drawback of edge based methods. In [3], multi-scale Gabor wavelet and hard voting scheme are used to estimate the vanishing point. Nevertheless, it suffers from high computational complexity and tends to favor the points in the upper part of the image. To compensate this drawback, Kong et al. [4, 5] used Gabor filters to estimate every pixel's texture orientation and also assign confidence value to each estimated orientation, and then the local soft voting scheme is adopted to detect the vanishing point. In [9], the Weber local descriptor (WLD) [10] and line voting scheme are used to detect the location of vanishing point. To better utilize the texture information, Kong et al. [6] proposed gLoG filter based vanishing point detection method, which achieves the-state-of-the art performance.

In this paper, to improve the performance of gLoG filter based method, the Weber adaptive local filter is developed to distinguish road trails from background noise, which can be used to reduce the workload of texture orientation estimation and to optimize the following voting stage. As a result, our proposed method achieves desirable detection accuracy as well as fast computation time compared to the complete texture map based gLoG method.

3   Proposed Vanishing Point Detection Approach

In this section, our proposed method is explained in detail. For an input image, the Weber adaptive local filter is used to extract road trails, and the gLoG filters [6, 11] are used to estimate the texture orientation of these road trails. Then, the adaptive soft voting scheme is adopted to generate the voting map. The location with the maximum voting score is detected as the vanishing point. Figure 1 shows the flowchart of the proposed method and the shaded blocks are the new contributions of our work.

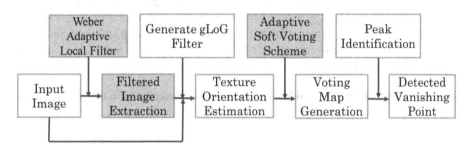

Fig. 1. The framework of our proposed method

3.1   Weber Adaptive Local Filter for Road Trail Extraction

In previous methods [3–6], all pixels that come from either road trails or background region have the same influence during the voting stage, which results in the degradation of the vanishing point detection accuracy. The differential excitation of WLD is introduced to distinguish the road trails from background noise in [9]. However, it is not robust and adaptive to different road conditions and a large percent of informative votes from valid road region are also removed. To solve these problems, a new road trail extraction method, which we call a Weber Adaptive Local Filter (WALF) is proposed.

Weber local descriptor. Weber's law [12] states that the ratio of the just noticeable change of stimulus (such as sound, lighting) to the original stimulus is a constant. It means that a human being would consider the new stimulus as background noise rather than a valid signal if its change is smaller than this constant ratio of the original stimulus. This law can be defined as

$$\frac{\Delta I}{I} = k \tag{1}$$

where ΔI denotes the increment threshold, I is the initial stimulus intensity, and the constant k is called Weber fraction, which signifies that the proportion on the left side of the equation remains constant despite of the variations in the term I.

Motivated by Weber's law [12], a simple yet quite robust local descriptor WLD is proposed in [10], which is robust to noise and illumination change and has powerful ability for texture representation. The WLD consists of two components: differential excitation (ξ) and orientation (θ). The differential excitation is calculated using the ratio between the relative intensity differences of its neighbors p_i against a current pixel p_c and the current pixel itself:

$$\xi(p_c) = \arctan(\sum_{i=1}^{n} \frac{p_i - p_c}{p_c}) \tag{2}$$

where n is the number of current pixel's neighbors. The orientation θ is the gradient orientation of current pixel p_c. Intuitively, the excitation response is positive value at dark pixels, where "dark" denotes that the pixel is relatively darker than its surroundings. On the contrary, it is negative at bright pixels, where "bright" means the pixel is relatively lighter than its surroundings.

Proposed Weber adaptive local filter.   Given an input image, after transforming it into grayscale space, the local excitation response is calculated for every pixel at a block level by using:

$$\xi_{loc}(p_c) = \sqrt[3]{\arctan(\sum_{i=1}^{n} \frac{p_i - p_c}{n \times p_c})} \tag{3}$$

where the cubic root function is utilized to make ξ_{loc} more sensitive to small values, n denotes the number of neighbors within the $N_k \times N_k$ kernel centred at p_c, which is used to reduce the effects of the number of neighbors. In our experiment, the kernel size is experimentally set to be 7×7. The kernel size N_k is an important factor, using larger kernel size, we can extract more texture information. Using smaller kernel size, more locally representative texture can be obtained.

Considering that the road images exhibit large variations in illumination, texture, color, and ambient environment, extracting road trails of different images by directly comparing the local excitation response with a specific threshold as in [9] is not robust and effective. Hence, we first calculate the global excitation response ξ_g of the input image based on every pixel's response value ξ_{loc}:

$$\xi_g = \frac{1}{W \times H} \sum_{i=1}^{W \times H} |\xi_{loc}(p_i)| \tag{4}$$

Then each pixel's excitation response is normalized by this global excitation response ξ_g:

$$\xi_{norm}(p_i) = \frac{\xi_{loc}(p_i)}{\xi_g} \tag{5}$$

where $\xi_{norm}(p_i)$ denotes pixel's normalized excitation response. If the absolute value of a pixel's ξ_{norm} is larger than T_f, which is experimentally set to be 0.8, it will be regarded as a valid pixel and preserved in the filtered image I_f. Otherwise, it will be filtered out. Figure 2 shows the examples of road trail extraction with the WLD and the proposed WALF on different types of road image. It illustrates that the proposed WALF is more robust and adaptive than the WLD to different road conditions.

(a)   (b)   (c)   (d)   (e)

Fig. 2. Examples of road trail extraction by the proposed WALF and the WLD. (a) Input images. (b) Extracted road trails by the proposed WALF. (c) Filtered images by the proposed WALF. (d) Extracted road trails by the WLD. (e) Filtered images by the WLD.

3.2 Texture Orientation Estimation of Road Trails

After road trail extraction, we need to estimate the texture orientation of the road trails. The gLoG filter proposed in [6, 12] is adopted to perform texture orientation estimation considering that it achieves the best performance among all related works [3–5].

To perform texture orientation estimation, the generated gLoG kernels are divided into $n_\theta(n_\theta = 12, in\ the\ current\ implementation)$ groups, where within each group $F_i(i = 1, \ldots, n_\theta)$ all the kernels have the same orientation. For any valid pixel p in filtered image I_f, a local patch I_p around p is extracted from the original input image. The patch I_p is used to convolve with every kernel of each group F_i, and the integrated response value is calculated as follows:

$$R_{F_i}^{I_p} = \sum_{K_t \in F_i} K_t \times I_p, \quad i = 1, \dots, n_\theta \tag{6}$$

where K_t denotes a gLoG kernel belonging to group F_i. It is noteworthy that $R_{F_i}^{I_p}$ tends to be positive value when convolving the gLoG kernels with dark patch regions, where 'dark' means that the patch is relatively darker than its surroundings. On the contrary, it tends to be negative value at bright patch regions, where 'bright' means that the patch is relatively brighter than its surroundings. The texture orientation of pixel p is determined by the group of kernels that can produce the maximum convolution response, which is computed as follows:

$$\theta_p = (\arg_i \max \left| R_{F_i}^{I_p} \right| - 1) \frac{180°}{n_\theta}, \qquad i = 1, \dots, n_\theta \tag{7}$$

where θ_p is the estimated texture orientation of pixel P.

Figure 3 displays the texture orientation of road trails estimated by the gLoG filters. Normally, the road texture orientation changes gradually form left to right. From Fig. 3(c) we can see that the estimated orientation maps illustrate a similar change in pixel intensity, which means that the major trend of the estimated texture orientation is correct, although the texture orientations of some pixels are not accurately estimated, which can be observed from Fig. 3(d).

(a)	(b)	(c)	(d)

Fig. 3. Examples of estimated texture orientation based on extracted road trails. (a) Input images. (b) Filtered images with extracted road trails. (c) Texture orientation maps. (d) Visualization of the estimated texture orientations.

3.3   Voting Map Generation

After estimating the texture orientation of the extracted road trail, the adaptive soft voting scheme proposed in [6] is used to perform voting map generation, which is as follows:

$$V(p, v) = \begin{cases} \exp(-\dfrac{d(p, v) \times |\gamma_i|}{l}), & if \, |\gamma_i| \leq \delta \\ 0, & otherwise \end{cases} \tag{8}$$

where $d(p, v)$ is the Euclidean distance between p and the vanishing point candidate v, γ_i is the angle difference, l is the normalization factor, and δ denotes the angular resolution. A voting map is generated through aggregating votes from the road trails. The location with the maximum votes is detected as the road vanishing point. Figure 4 illustrates the sample results obtained by the proposed WALF based vanishing point detection method.

Fig. 4. Examples of detected vanishing points.

4   Experimental Results

The performance of the proposed method is mainly compared with the gLoG filter based method [6] and the Gabor filter based method [3, 4]. The dataset used to evaluate the performance of different approaches is a standard evaluation set, which is utilized in other related literatures [4–6]. It consists of 1003 general road images with ground truth, and all images are normalized to the same size of 180×240.

4.1   Performance Comparison and Analysis

For every image, the normalized Euclidean distance is calculated, where the Euclidean distance between the detected vanishing point and the ground truth is normalized by the diagonal length of the input image. If the distance is not bigger than a specific threshold, the detected vanishing point is regarded as a correct detection. As shown in Fig. 5, the horizontal axis shows the normalized Euclidean distance D_{norm}, and the vertical axis shows the percentage of correct vanishing point detection under specific threshold. It can be seen that the WALF based method achieves the best result among all. It is around 1.3% better than the complete texture map based gLoG method, 8.3% better than the blob based gLoG method, and 5.0% better than the Gabor filter based method, when the threshold is set to 0.05.

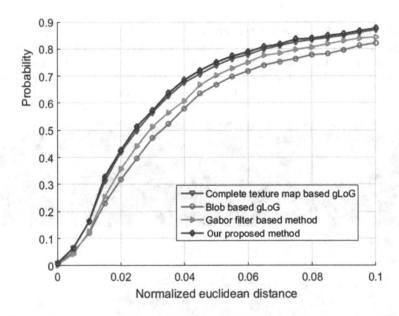

Fig. 5. Performance comparison of different vanishing point detection approaches.

The approaches are also compared on computation time and average normalized Euclidean distance $\overline{D_{norm}}$, which is the average of D_{norm} on the whole dataset, as shown in Table 1. It is obvious that the proposed method achieves the best performance on the whole dataset. In addition, it is more than 2 times faster than the complete texture map based gLoG method, but computationally expensive than the blob based gLoG method.

Table 1. Comparison of average normalized Euclidean distance and average computation time

Method	$\overline{D_{norm}}$	Average computation time
Gabor filter based method [4, 5]	0.064	36.3 s
Complete texture based gLoG [6]	0.057	56.2 s
Blob based gLoG [6]	0.071	3.1 s
Our proposed method	0.055	32.3 s

To provide a visual comparison, the detection results of related works [4–6] are illustrated and compared with our results on a set of complex road images. In Fig. 6, each column shows a comparison of the vanishing point detection results on desert roads, rural roads, snow roads, muddy roads, and structured roads. This visual comparison demonstrates that our proposed method works well on these different road type images.

| desert road | rural road | snow road | muddy road | structured road |

Fig. 6. Examples of road vanishing point detection results on different road types. The green crosses show the ground truth, the red stars denote the detection results of our proposed method, the blue circles are the detection results of the complete texture map-based gLoG method, the yellow diamonds are the detection results of the blob-based gLoG method, and the magenta squares represent the detection results of Gabor filter-based method (Color figure online)

The influence of various choices for parameters on performance is systematically investigated. First of all, the parameters used in the proposed WALF are analyzed. As plotted in Fig. 7, experiments are conducted with different kernel size N_k and threshold value T_f. The x axis is the threshold T_f which is ranging from 0.7 to 1.0, and the y axis represents the kernel size which is changed by setting N_k to 3, 5, 7, 9, 11, and 13, respectively. The z-axis shows the difference of the detection accuracy, which is obtained by subtracting the detection accuracy of the complete texture map based gLoG method from that of our method, where the normalized Euclidean distance threshold is set to 0.05.

It can be observed that 7×7 kernel size with threshold $T_f = 0.8$ works best, the detection accuracy is 3.6% better than the complete texture map based gLoG method. It will decrease the detection accuracy by using larger or smaller kernel size, and the threshold T_f affects the detection accuracy in the same way.

4.2 Limitation of the Proposed Method

Though the proposed method achieves state-of-the-art detection accuracy and faster detection speed, there are still some cases where it does not perform well, as shown in Fig. 8. Our method follows the line of texture based vanishing point detection approaches. The strong texture noise contained in the background, such as trees or mountains, is a serious distraction to the textures of road region. This distraction results in performance degradation, which

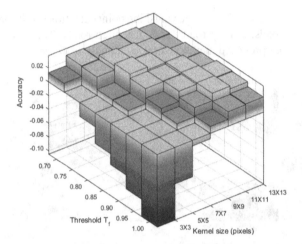

Fig. 7. Detection accuracy with the different parameters used in WALF

is the common limitation with the works of [3–6, 9], but could be solved by combining multiple road relevant features in a learning framework to distinguish the road region form the surrounding noise.

Fig. 8. Failure cases of our proposed vanishing point detection method. The green crosses show the ground truth, the red stars denote the detection results of our proposed method, the blue circles are the detection results of the complete texture map-based gLoG method, the yellow diamonds are the detection results of the blob-based gLoG method, and the magenta squares represent the detection results of Gabor filter-based method (Color figure online)

5   Conclusion

A novel framework for vanishing point detection has been proposed in this paper. The gLoG filter based method is improved by making full use of the new Weber adaptive local filer, through which the road trails can be distinguished from background noise. The experimental results demonstrate that the detection accuracy and computation time of our proposed method are improved by 1.3% and 2 times, respectively, when compared to the other state-of-the-art methods.

References

1. McCall, J.C., Trivedi, M.M.: Video based lane estimation and tracking for driver assistance: survey, system, and evaluation. IEEE Trans. Intell. Transp. Syst. **7**(1), 20–37 (2006)
2. Nieto, M., Salgado, L., Jaureguizar, F., et al.: Stabilization of inverse perspective mapping images based on robust vanishing point estimation. In: IEEE Conference on Intelligent Vehicles Symposium, pp. 315–320 (2007)
3. Rasmussen, C.: Grouping dominant orientations for illstructured road following. In: IEEE Conference on Computer Vision and Pattern Recognition, pp. 470–477 (2004)
4. Kong, H., Audibert, J.Y., Ponce, J.: Vanishing point detection for road detection. In: IEEE Conference on Computer Vision and Pattern Recognition, pp. 96–103 (2009)
5. Kong, H., Audibert, J.Y., Ponce, J.: General road detection from a single image. IEEE Trans. Image Process. **19**(8), 2211–2220 (2010)
6. Kong, H., Sarma, S.E., Tang, F.: Generalizing Laplacian of Gaussian filters for vanishing-point detection. IEEE Trans. Intell. Transp. Syst. **14**(1), 408–418 (2013)
7. Suttorp, T., Bucher, T.: Robust vanishing point estimation for driver assistance. In: IEEE Conference on Intelligent Transportation Systems, pp. 1550–1555 (2006)
8. Nieto, M., Salgado, L.: Real-time vanishing point estimation in road sequences using adaptive steerable filter banks. In: International Conference on Advanced Concepts for Intelligent Vision Systems, pp. 840–848 (2007)
9. Luo, X.S., Fang, B., Yang, W.B.: Road vanishing point detection using Weber local descriptor. J. Comput. Appl. **34**(S1), 219–222 (2012)
10. Chen, J., Shan, S.G., Chen, X.L., et al.: WLD: a robust local image descriptor. IEEE Trans. Pattern Anal. Mach. Intell. **32**(9), 1705–1720 (2010)
11. Hui, K., Akakin, H.C., Sarma, S.E.: A generalized Laplacian of Gaussian filter for blob detection and its applications. IEEE Trans. Cybern. **43**(6), 1719–1733 (2013)
12. Jain, A.K.: Fundamentals of Digital Image Processing, pp. 51–60. Pearson Education India (1989)

A Mobile Cloud Framework for Deep Learning and Its Application to Smart Car Camera

Chien-Hung Chen, Che-Rung Lee[⊠], and Walter Chen-Hua Lu

National Tsing Hua University, Hsinchu 30013, Taiwan
cherung@cs.nthu.edu.tw

Abstract. Deep learning has become a powerful technology in image recognition, gaming, information retrieval, and many other areas that need intelligent data processing. However, huge amount of data and complex computations prevent deep learning from being practical in mobile applications. In this paper, we proposed a mobile cloud computing framework for deep learning. The architecture puts the training process and model repository in cloud platforms, and the recognition process and data gathering in mobile devices. The communication is carried out via Git protocol to ensure the success of data transmission in unstable network environments. We used smart car camera that can detect objects in recorded videos during driving as an example application, and implemented the system on NVIDIA Jetson TK1. Experimental results show that detection rate can achieve four frame-per-second with Faster R-CNN and ZF model, and the system can work well even when the network connection is unstable. We also compared the performance of system with and without GPU, and found that GPU still plays a critical role in the recognition side for deep learning.

1 Introduction

Deep learning has become the most promising machine learning approach. From LeCun's LeNet [1] to Khrizevsky AlexNet [2] and recent GoogleNet [3], deep learning has shown its capability of solving difficult computer vision problems. Its detection performance surpasses other artificial classifiers which reply on the hand-crafted features. With the success in vision work, deep learning also attracts attentions from other fields, such as sentiment analysis [4], language processing [5], region of interest localization and description [6], and medical use [7].

The success of deep learning is brought off by three factors: the advance of numerical optimization methods, growth of data volume, and fast computational hardware. New numerical methods solved the convergence problems, which are more and more critical when the number of layers goes deeper and deeper. Large enough training data sets make the extracted features by deep learning sufficiently representative. These required data can be continuously collected by the sensors equipped in modern embedded systems and mobile devices.

© Springer International Publishing AG 2016
C.-H. Hsu et al. (Eds.): IOV 2016, LNCS 10036, pp. 14–25, 2016.
DOI: 10.1007/978-3-319-51969-2_2

Last, the accelerators, such as Graphic Processing Units (GPUs), provide strong computing power to support the training of deep learning model.

In the era of Internet of Things (IOT), the deployment of deep models to mobile devices is a nature request. One the one hand, the mobile devices can be smarter with the deep learning ability. Moreover, they also help the data gathering from various sources. On the other hand, the limited power, storage, and computational resources of mobile devices prevent the complex computation, like deep learning, from being practical. Therefore, the mobile cloud computing model, which combines the mobility of mobile devices and the computational resources of cloud platforms via ubiquitously accessible network, becomes a practical solution for mobile applications that utilize deep learning.

Mobile cloud computing has three types of models to coordinate the works between mobile devices and cloud platforms. The first one is to off-load all the work to the cloud platforms, and the mobile devices take care of data input and output only. However, such model usually require frequent data communication, which is not suitable for heavy data transmission. In addition, when the network is unstable, mobile devices cannot work alone. The second model relies on mobile devices to handle most of the works. Such model is only limited to light weighted works that can be processed on mobile devices. The last one splits the works to mobile devices and cloud platforms. This model could balance the computation and communication, but requires good synergy from both sides.

Most of the current solution of mobile deep learning utilizes the first solution since the computation of deep learning is heavy. In this paper, we utilized the third model for deep learning, which puts the training and model repository on the cloud platform, and recognition and data gathering on the mobile devices. Such architecture cuts the storage and computation requirement of mobile devices and the data transmission between cloud and end users. In addition, we employed the Git protocol for data communication data so that the transmissions can be resumed even the network connection is not available sometimes.

We used the smart car camera as an example application to demonstrate how the framework works. The smart car camera can select suitable deep learning models for video recognition, decide which part of video clips contain important information and send them to cloud platform, and update the deep learning models when necessary. We have implemented the system on NVIDIA Jetson TK1 embedded development board. Experimental results show that detection rate can achieve 2.8 to 4 FPS (frame-per-second) with Faster R-CNN and ZF model, and the system can work well even when the network connection is unstable. We also compared the performance of system with and without GPU, and found that GPU still plays a critical role in the recognition side for deep learning.

The rest of this paper is organized as follows. Section 2 introduces background knowledge and related works. Section 3 presents the framework and the implementation details of the smart car camera. Section 4 shows the experimental results of system performance. The conclusion and future directions are given in the last section.

2   Background

2.1   Mobile Cloud Computing

In the last decade, mobile devices have been widely used to provide various services, such as gaming, video streaming, health-care, and position-based services. However, mobile devices are still limited by storage capacity, battery life and computing power. As a result, Mobile Cloud computing (MCC) came up not long after cloud computing. Mobile cloud computing can be considered as a combination of mobile services and cloud computing which communicate through wireless network. The key concept of both cloud computing and MCC is offloading heavy tasks to cloud platforms so that users can access a variety of services without complicate computation on their devices.

Mobile Cloud Computing (MCC) architectures possess many desired advantages, as well as many critical issues. In [8], authors listed three merits of MCC: extending battery life, improving data storage capacity and processing power, and improving reliability. On the other hand, MCC has issues to overcome. Wireless network is less reliable and has lower bandwidth compared to wired network. Other than bandwidth issue, network for mobile devices is usually unstable, which could result service unavailable sometimes. Discussion of issues includes offloading, security, heterogeneity are remained in [8].

2.2   Deep Learning

Deep learning, or deep neural network, refers to a neural network that consists of one input layer, one output layer and multiple hidden layers. The earliest appearance of deep neural network can be traced to late 1960s in the work published by Alexey Grigorevich and V.G. Lapa. However, deep learning grows at a slow pace due to immature training scheme and architecture in the next few decades. In the 1990s, LeCun trained LeNet, a deep neural net with convolution and pooling layers, with back-propagation algorithm for digit recognition [1]. Stochastic gradient descent was invented in the 1970s to train artificial neural networks.

LeNet is the earliest work to take deep learning into recognition task. In 2006, layer-wise unsupervised pre-training was proposed for parameter initialization [9]. The new training method has two phases. In the pre-training phase, every two consecutive hidden layers are considered a restricted Boltzmann machine and weights are adjusted with an unsupervised learning manner. After pre-training, the whole model is fine-tuned with an additional supervised layer in the second phase. Pre-training makes layer parameters get better values compared to random initialization. As a result, trained models reach more sensible local minimum and quality gets more stable. In 2012, Krizhevsky et al. developed the eight-layer AlexNet and won the ILSVRC 2012 prize with about 85% classification and 66% location accuracy [2]. AlexNet won their competitors who used linear classifier over ten percentage. And the winners of ILSVRC classification task in the following years all used deep neural networks. Instead of using hand-crafted classifiers, deep neural network learns high level features during training time. And the ILSVRC challenge results prove its high performance.

With big success in image classification, deep learning attracts focus from other fields. Beside from classification, deep learning is also used in object detection [10–12], speech recognition [13,14], language processing [5], sentiment analysis [4], and many other works. Recent deep learning bloom can be ascribed to new optimization methods, appearance of more powerful processor and rapid growing data volume. With more powerful CPU and multi-core processor, especially general purpose GPU, training time can be cut down from months to days. With growing of various data, under-fitting can be prevented and makes deep learning be applied to solve different types of problem. Latest publications not only improve accuracy but boost performance. PReLU activation function pushes classification accuracy over 95% and saves time for deriving gradient [15]. Dropout prevents training from over-fitting [16]. Also, new initialization schemes make pre-training phase unnecessary [17].

2.3   Git Version Control System

Git is an open source version control system. The designated work space to be managed is called repository. The system would manage files added to tracked list in the repository. Users can copy files from remote directory through clone command. Cloned repository would be managed by Git system and repository status be kept consistent with remote if git pull command is called. Push command would be used in the situation that a user makes some modification and wants to update file in original repository. Modification of tracked file would not be send back to remote after a commit is created. And according to the official report, Git is faster than many other version control systems.

3   Framework and Implementation

3.1   Mobile Cloud Framework for Deep Learning

Our design of mobile cloud computing framework for deep learning is based on two facts. The first one is about deep learning processes, and the second one is for mobile network. Deep learning approach has two phases: training and recognition. In the recognition phases, deep learning application only needs to go through forward propagation with input data. After getting output data, some post-processes are required to retrieve desired information. On the contrary, the training phase needs both forward and backward propagation and a large amount of training data. As a result, training process usually takes days or weeks.

For mobile network, according to 4GTest [18], LTE network has a median of 5.64 Mbps upload bandwidth. Take image process for consideration, common car cameras have 1080p resolution, which also indicates that a raw image can have size overs 6 megabytes. Retrieving results after uploading and processing an image on the cloud becomes infeasible. Even we compress files first, unstable wireless network may prevents users some services.

Our design offloads the training phase to the cloud platforms and keeps trained models to the mobile devices for recognition. In addition, the mobile devices collect received data and feed back to cloud. Various data collected from users can help to improve accuracy of deep learning models. Also, the server side can evaluate how the model performs by analyzing prediction result.

3.2   Smart Car Camera System

We used car camera object detection as an example application. Many cars have equipped cameras to record videos during driving. However, the capacity of device storage is limited, and many parts of the recorded videos do not have interested objects. With the object detection ability, the car camera can find out the video segments that possibly have objects of interests. Those interested video segments can be uploaded to cloud platforms for further analysis, and the unwanted video segments can be deleted to save storage space. We designed a deep learning object detection system which not only provides detection service but handles model maintenance.

The designed system is presented in Fig. 1. When the system starts, version checker is executed first. If the client does not have model files in local disk storage, it will connect to server and get the desired model. Otherwise the system would check whether an updated version is available. In the second phase, the system has two threads: update thread and detection thread. The update thread keeps checking new model released periodically. This thread is only responsible for model checking and downloading. Models would not be replaced with the updated version until system restarts for safety concern. The detection thread handles data collection. Detection thread would collect network inputs and outputs if possible object appears in the input images. Meanwhile, it keeps a counter to control collected file size. Once the counter hits a designated threshold, the detection thread creates another thread for uploading data. The collected data after upload would be destroyed to save local storage space.

3.3   Detection Task

We have surveyed some object detection works, and chose Faster R-CNN as our detection approach. We have re-produced the C version Faster R-CNN using Caffe [19] and openCV. Figure 2 introduces the workflow of Faster R-CNN. Although Faster R-CNN can take any size of input, we cropped and resized every input image to a fixes size: 224×224 pixels to make it faster. The following section describes Faster R-CNN implementation in details.

Faster R-CNN trains RPN by sliding a small network over the feature map from the last shared convolutional layer. At each location on the feature map, RPN predicts 3 scales and 3 aspect ratios (the ratio of width to height). Centers and sizes of each box is encoded based on a reference box, called anchor box.

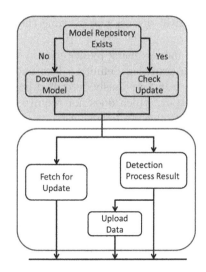

Fig. 1. Designed system

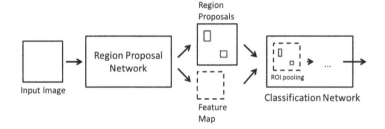

Fig. 2. Faster R-CNN workflow

At detection time, region proposal network (RPN) outputs two data blobs, predicted boxes and box scores, after a series of convolutional and pooling processes. Prediction box is represented by four elements (N, C, H, W), where N represents the batch size, C stores proposed boxes, and H and W correspond to the height and the width of feature map. After extracting proposal regions, we drop boxes that are too small and crop the remaining boxes for ensuring that the box size does not exceed input image size. Next, we sort the boxes by confidence c from score blob and apply non-maximal suppression to filter out highly overlapped boxes with lower confidence score.

Classification net takes n filtered regions and feature map generated by the last convolutional layer of region proposal network (RPN) as inputs, and outputs two blobs. Predicted boxes are stored in the same fashion as RPN's output in the first blob. The second blob contains prediction scores of background and desired object classes. If the number of region proposals from RPN exceeds the batch size N, the classification net will run more than one time. The batch size N is adjustable. In Sect. 4.2, we will discuss how to tune the batch size to optimize performance.

Besides, we trained the models using py-faster-rcnn with VOC2007 dataset. We trained ZF model with provided definition files and using the alternating optimization [20]. Different from previously described Faster R-CNN, the model takes over intermediate output, which does not require coordinate transformation between RPN and the following layers. Also, the output predicted boxes information are not related with anchor boxes. Instead, it retrieves coordinates of box vertices from the output blob. As to box regression, refined information can be calculated in the same manner with original Faster R-CNN.

3.4   Model Maintenance

We chose Git version control protocol for model transmission. By using Git, we save the effort to manage modifications. Also, Git provides the basic authentication service, by which users need account and password to access remote repository.

First time download and follow-up model update can be achieved by Git clone and Git pull functions. And the feedback part can be implemented by Git push. We created two Git repositories on our device: one for storing model files and the other for feedback data. When starts, the system checks whether the model repository exists. If files in need have not been downloaded, Git clone would be triggered to get the latest files from server. Otherwise, the system calls update function to keep version be consistent with the server. In the detection phase, update-thread calls Git fetch constantly and push-thread starts to push feedback repository once collected data reaches a threshold.

4   Performance Evaluation

We have implemented the smart car camera system using Nvidia Tegra K1, the processor and GPU designed for mobile device. Tegra K1 has four plus one core ARM Cortex-A15 CPU with upto 2.3 GHz frequency and a Kepler GPU. The experimental board has a 2 GB memory, and is connected to wired network. Data can be transmitted through WAN. We chose relatively light weight ZF model provided by origin work to do the detection task. ZF net has 5 convolutional layers and 3 fully connected layers. The trained model can be obtained from [20].

We evaluated out work on the trained dataset PASCAL VOC 2007 test data. In addition, we used pedestrian detection database from University of Pennsylvania and the clips downloaded from Youtube, which are videos recorded by car camera on highway.

We have four sets of experiments. The first set of experiments compares the performance with and without GPU. The second one is to tune the batch size for the best performance of the model. The third one compares the system performance for different data sets and different batches. The last one uses simulation to demonstrate how our system works under unstable network environments.

4.1   CPU and GPU Performance Comparison

We evaluated CPU and GPU performance for recognition process. Figure 3 shows average CPU and GPU forward pass time. As can be seen, GPU accelerates the forward propagation and performs over 20 times faster than CPU only version, both for RPN and classification net. The significant difference indicates the importance of accelerator. For the rest of our experiments, we only showed the performance results with GPU.

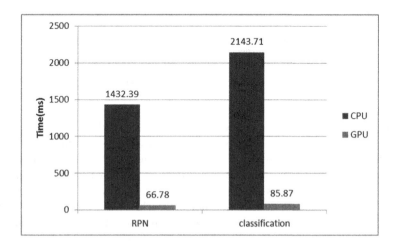

Fig. 3. CPU and GPU performance

4.2   Batch Size Tuning

In the recognition phase, the batch size, which is the number of Region Of Interests (ROI) to be processed at the same time, influences the performance significantly. In this experiment, we evaluated the time (seconds) of forward pass of classification net for different batch size. As Fig. 4 shows, execution time of one iteration grows as the batch size gets larger. This is not a surprised results since larger batch size means more work to do. However, if we normalized the execution time for 180 frames, the time decreases first and then curves up later. This is because when the batch size grows, the number of iterations to process the ROIs of 180 frames decreases, but the time of each iteration increases. The experimental results show the best performance falls around batch size 60, which is the parameter we used in the later experiments.

4.3   System Performance

We evaluated the system performance for different number of batches to be processed for the classification net. Since we resized and cropped input images,

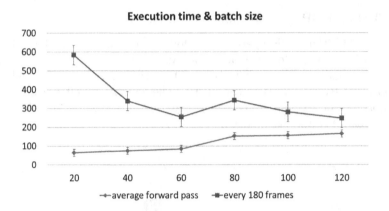

Fig. 4. Performance and batch size

execution time only relates to the number of candidate Region of Interests (ROI) per image. We can accelerate the system performance by dropping the ROIs with lower scores. The influence of dropping is that some of the objects may not be detected. But experiments show the dropping of low score ROIs does not alter the results much (less than 1%). Each frame usually has 60 to 180 ROIs. Since we let batch size be 60, the number of batches per frame is ranged from 1 to 3. Figure 5 shows the performance result, measured by frame-per-second, for different number of batches. The 1 batch means that we only keep at most 60 ROIs per frame; the 2 batch means each frame can have up to 120 ROIs; and the 3 batch means 180 ROIs are detected for each frame. The results show that the detection task could process over 4 frames per second for 1 batch. When the number of batches grows, the performance drops to around 3 frames per second. The results of two test data have similar behaviors.

4.4   Network Transmission

Our smart car camera system can dynamically download and update the required models from cloud platform. According to [18], the downlink of current LTE network is much faster than that of the uplink. However, the model files of deep learning usually are usually very large, around hundred megabytes, even with compression. In unstable network environments, transmission of such files could cause a problem, because file transmission needs to restart after re-connection. One solution to reduce the duplicate transmission is to split whole model into chunks with smaller file size. With this approach, duplicate transmitted data size would be limited to the chunk size. On the other side, it needs longer preparation time for file splitting, but that can be done in advance on cloud platform.

We used the Markov chain model, proposed in [21], to simulate the package loss to evaluate the performance of the file splitting strategy. The maximum number of retransmission in the simulation is 15, after which the file chunk is required to retransmit. The bandwidth of uplink in simulation is 15 Mbps and

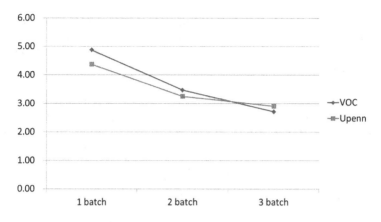

Fig. 5. Performance measured by frames per second

the model file size is 224 MB, which is a real data size of ZF model for 20 categories. The latency of each split file transmission is 0.1 s. The performance of three chunk sizes (number of chunks) are compared: 1 (no slitting), 20, and 100. The evaluated package drop rates are 0.1, 0.4. 0.5, and 0.6.

Table 1. The transmission time (seconds) of different chunk sizes for different package drop rates.

Drop rate\No. chunks	1	20	100
0	120	121	130
0.1	133	134	143
0.4	208	202	210
0.5	4382	271	256
0.6	(unable)	2877	451

Table 1 summarizes the transmission time of each method in seconds for different package drop rate. The result is the average of 10 times of simulation. It shows when the package drop rate is small, which means the network environment is stable, the splitting method takes longer time owing to the overhead of file transmission latency. However, for larger package drop rate, the time of un-split file grows rapidly. For drop rate 0.6, the un-split file cannot be completed in hours. On the other hand, for chunk number 100, the time grows much slower even when the network is extremely unstable.

5   Conclusion

In this paper, we proposed a mobile cloud computing framework for deep learning. The architecture leaves training on the cloud and performs recognition in the client side with some post processing. The advantage is that the mobile devices can still work under unstable network environment without huge storage and computing capacity. Experiments show that GPU is still critical for the recognition of deep learning, since it can accelerate the computation over 20 times.

Limited storage space and computing power remain a challenge for embedded systems using deep learning. S. Han et al. proposed DeepCompression [22], which reduces storage space by learning only important connections, quantize weights and apply Hoffman encoding. They reduced size of AlexNet from 240 MB to 6.9 MB without accuracy loss. With deeper models applied on mobile devices. For future work, we will integrated their work to the system, and investigate further optimization of storage and computation for deep learning.

Acknowledgment. This study is conducted under the The Core Technologies of Smart Handheld Devices (3/4) of the Institute for Information Industry; which is subsidized by the Ministry of Economy Affairs, Taiwan. The authors thank the Institute for Information Industry for the financial support under grant number 105-EC-17-A-24-0691.

References

1. LeCun, Y., Jackel, L., Bottou, L., Brunot, A., Cortes, C., Denker, J., Drucker, H., Guyon, I., Muller, U., Sackinger, E., et al.: Comparison of learning algorithms for handwritten digit recognition. In: International Conference on Artificial Neural Networks, vol. 60, pp. 53–60 (1995)
2. Krizhevsky, A., Sutskever, I., Hinton, G.E.: Imagenet classification with deep convolutional neural networks. In: Advances in Neural Information Processing Systems, pp. 1097–1105 (2012)
3. Szegedy, C., Liu, W., Jia, Y., Sermanet, P., Reed, S., Anguelov, D., Erhan, D., Vanhoucke, V., Rabinovich, A.: Going deeper with convolutions. In: Proceedings of the IEEE Conference on Computer Vision and Pattern Recognition, pp. 1–9 (2015)
4. Socher, R., Perelygin, A., Wu, J.Y., Chuang, J., Manning, C.D., Ng, A.Y., Potts, C.: Recursive deep models for semantic compositionality over a sentiment treebank. In: Proceedings of the Conference on Empirical Methods in Natural Language Processing (EMNLP), vol. 1631, p. 1642. Citeseer (2013)
5. Collobert, R., Weston, J.: A unified architecture for natural language processing: deep neural networks with multitask learning. In: Proceedings of the 25th International Conference on Machine Learning, pp. 160–167. ACM (2008)
6. Johnson, J., Karpathy, A., Fei-Fei, L.: Densecap: fully convolutional localization networks for dense captioning. arXiv preprint arXiv:1511.07571 (2015)
7. Fakoor, R., Ladhak, F., Nazi, A., Huber, M.: Using deep learning to enhance cancer diagnosis and classification. In: Proceedings of the International Conference on Machine Learning (2013)
8. Dinh, H.T., Lee, C., Niyato, D., Wang, P.: A survey of mobile cloud computing: architecture, applications, and approaches. Wirel. Commun. Mob. Comput. **13**, 1587–1611 (2013)

9. Bengio, Y., Lamblin, P., Popovici, D., Larochelle, H., et al.: Greedy layer-wise training of deep networks. Adv. Neural Inform. Process. Syst. **19**, 153 (2007)

10. Girshick, R., Donahue, J., Darrell, T., Malik, J.: Rich feature hierarchies for accurate object detection and semantic segmentation. In: Proceedings of the IEEE Conference on Computer Vision and Pattern Recognition, pp. 580–587 (2014)

11. Redmon, J., Divvala, S., Girshick, R., Farhadi, A.: You only look once: unified, real-time object detection. arXiv preprint arXiv:1506.02640 (2015)

12. Sermanet, P., Eigen, D., Zhang, X., Mathieu, M., Fergus, R., LeCun, Y.: Overfeat: integrated recognition, localization and detection using convolutional networks. arXiv preprint arXiv:1312.6229 (2013)

13. Hinton, G., Deng, L., Yu, D., Dahl, G.E., Mohamed, A.R., Jaitly, N., Senior, A., Vanhoucke, V., Nguyen, P., Sainath, T.N., et al.: Deep neural networks for acoustic modeling in speech recognition: the shared views of four research groups. IEEE Sig. Process. Mag. **29**, 82–97 (2012)

14. Dahl, G.E., Yu, D., Deng, L., Acero, A.: Context-dependent pre-trained deep neural networks for large-vocabulary speech recognition. IEEE Trans. Audio Speech Lang. Process. **20**, 30–42 (2012)

15. He, K., Zhang, X., Ren, S., Sun, J.: Delving deep into rectifiers: Surpassing human-level performance on imagenet classification. In: Proceedings of the IEEE International Conference on Computer Vision, pp. 1026–1034 (2015)

16. Srivastava, N., Hinton, G.E., Krizhevsky, A., Sutskever, I., Salakhutdinov, R.: Dropout: a simple way to prevent neural networks from overfitting. J. Mach. Learn. Res. **15**, 1929–1958 (2014)

17. Sutskever, I., Martens, J., Dahl, G.E., Hinton, G.E.: On the importance of initialization and momentum in deep learning. ICML **28**(3), 1139–1147 (2013)

18. Huang, J., Qian, F., Gerber, A., Mao, Z.M., Sen, S., Spatscheck, O.: A close examination of performance and power characteristics of 4G LTE networks. In: Proceedings of the 10th International Conference on Mobile Systems, Applications, and Services, pp. 225–238. ACM (2012)

19. Jia, Y., Shelhamer, E., Donahue, J., Karayev, S., Long, J., Girshick, R., Guadarrama, S., Darrell, T.: Caffe: convolutional architecture for fast feature embedding. arXiv preprint arXiv:1408.5093 (2014)

20. Ren, S., He, K., Girshick, R., Sun, J.: Faster R-CNN: Towards real-time object detection with region proposal networks. In: Advances in Neural Information Processing Systems, pp. 91–99 (2015)

21. Sanneck, H.A., Carle, G.: Framework model for packet loss metrics based on loss runlengths. In: Proceedings of the SPIE, Multimedia Computing and Networking 2000, vol. 3969 (1999)

22. Han, S., Mao, H., Dally, W.J.: Deep compression: compressing deep neural network with pruning, trained quantization and huffman coding. CoRR, abs/1510.00149 **2** (2015)

iParking – Real-Time Parking Space Monitor and Guiding System with Cloud Service

Ching-Fei Yang, You-Huei Ju, Chung-Ying Hsieh, Chia-Ying Lin,
Meng-Hsun Tsai[✉], and Hui-Ling Chang

Department of Computer Science and Information Engineering,
National Cheng Kung University, Tainan, Taiwan
jingfei@imslab.org, tsaimh@csie.ncku.edu.tw

Abstract. By the popularization of cars, average number of vehicles owned by one person grows with passing days. However, the number of parking areas is out of proportion. In order to satisfy the requirements of parking space and reduce illegal parking, we propose iParking, a real-time parking space monitoring and guiding system, in this paper. We lay emphasis on roadside parking. The system determines and records empty parking spaces through cloud computing, wireless technology between vehicles, and image analysis. It tells you the nearest location of empty parking space while drivers have requests. We expect the system to cause attention to more people and government while it solves relative problems about parking space.

Keywords: Cloud computing · Image recognition · Parking space management · Wireless technology

1 Introduction

Recently, parking problem has become people's harassment. It is shown from statistical data in Ministry of Transportation, Taiwan that the number of registered vehicles is 7,554,319 until December 2014 [1]; However, it is also mentioned that the number of legal parking space is about four million in total. Furthermore, it will cause several problems such as the extremely slow speed while finding parking space, scrambling for roads with scooters, parking temporarily in dangerous part, or driving U-turn illegally. The behavior will not only break the safety and regular of transportation but also make noise and consume resource. It is easy to observe that some vehicles need to find parking space by themselves while roadside parking spaces are not enough. The situation will bring out arbitrary parking, and it is also the main reason of illegal parking.

Over the last few years, LBS (Location-Based Service) [2] is getting noticed along with the appearance of smartphones. LBS can apply broadly to different area like health, job, daily life, and etc. Thus, how to use LBS to help different users find the appropriate parking space is vital. The usage of monitoring parking space now is to provide roadside parking space's locations at best, but it will not

C.-H. Hsu et al. (Eds.): IOV 2016, LNCS 10036, pp. 26–33, 2016.
DOI: 10.1007/978-3-319-51969-2_3

tell drivers where the vacant space is. Thus, we would like to develop a monitor and guiding system focus on roadside parking to provide the information of nearby parking space and help drivers park with the fastest way.

We will introduce the system in four parts. First of all, know what is the demand of our work and compare with other techniques. Next, show the details, especially features and structure of our service. In addition, demonstrate how we implement and design the system. Finally, make a conclusion, discuss more about future work.

2   Related Work

2.1   Demand of Parking Space

In the statistical table of important indicators from Ministry of Transportation, Taiwan [1], it is pointed out that parking space is one of the important indicators in addition to the number of vehicles.

It is shown that the difference between supply and demand of parking space is about two million. In addition, it is pointed out from trend of line that the growth rate of vehicles and parking spaces is closed. However, it is not simple to add parking spaces because it involves road network planning. In this knotty situation, it becomes vital and urgent to solve the management of parking space in order to make good use of limited resource.

Furthermore, some recent researches verify that people would rather spend more time finding roadside parking space than off-street parking even if there are vacant spaces in the off-street parking lot [3]. Take Tainan City for example, service in parking lot does not meet drivers' expect, such as high parking fee, mess surroundings, or etc. Hence, the situation results in low usage rate of parking lot and shortage of roadside parking space. Thus, to solve the problem of roadside parking is necessary.

2.2   Existing Parking Space Monitored Technique

All of existing parking space monitored techniques are limited to parking lot and only supported by sensors. For instance, intelligent parking lot uses wireless sensor network, ZIBEE, pressure sensors [4,5]. They update database by sensors to know if it is empty. The another instance is Eco-Community plan developed by several schools [6]. Its main method is using the sensitivity of the sensor, Octopus II, updating changes to database. Therefore, the changes will tell users information about parking spaces. However, the two techniques have a big constraint when it comes to downtown area. It is a huge challenge to set up sensors for all parking spaces in downtown due to the fee of building and maintenance. That is to say, both of them are not suitable to roadside parking in comparison with our system.

As regards other apps in the market, they are connected to nearby parking lot, offering real-time information. However, only few of them mention payment information about roadside parking. In conclusion, none of the apps in the market provide function to find roadside parking spaces until now.

3   Service and System Structure

3.1   Software Platform

We choose smartphone and related device to complete mobility, driving recorder, and Network communication by reason of the target users, people with mobile vehicle. We build the application base on Android, using Java to implement code structure and GUI design.

3.2   Features

Cloud Storage and Computing. Cloud Storage is an online service which can save data on virtual server through Internet. The service become more and more popular due to the popularity of Internet and the increasing demand of data storage. That is to say, simply save data in actual hard dick is getting insufficient. Therefore, limited storage devices will bring more benefit by Internet and storage virtualization technique.

In order to improve the efficiency of driving records, and reduce the capacity of mobile device. We will refer to existing cloud storage service, analyzing data through servers in cloud, and send the parking information to users who have request.

Static Image Streaming. Streaming media is a process to compress a series of media data, send through network section, and offer real-time media service on the Internet [7]. By the technique, media data are able to watch without downloading whole media. Therefore, it is called "streaming" because data in the process behaves like running water.

We can say that static image streaming is to connect images, record the event over the next period of time. Under the premise that analyzing driving records accurately, we will use static image streaming to lessen the burden instead of sending whole driving record.

Analyzing Vacant Parking Space. In the reference [8], the author has proposed solutions to detect if parking spaces are vacant. Its technique includes Hough line detection and Canny edge detection, implementing by OpenCV library. The original method has two limitations. The first one is that it can only identify one photo at a time while the another is that only the parking space at bottom right corner can be identified. We breakthrough them by using static image streaming.

3.3   Efficacy

Monitoring Parking Space. The situation of parking space is different from area, timing, and location. Therefore, the key point is how to monitor the specific parking space immediately. Besides, if there are many people use this service at the same time, it will be fairly accurate with steadily update.

Saving and Analyzing Driving Recorder. In the process of detecting vacant parking space's condition, it is necessary to analyze big data and use large storage. Hence, we use cloud service and client-server model to handle and send all the requests in order to reduce the usage of memory, storage, and workload.

Data Transmission. If the goal is to keep high accuracy and immediacy, the system will bring out high Internet usage because it continuing transfers driving recorder. Therefore, we will capture driving image with a fixed distance according to speed of the vehicle. Coordinating with GPS position, it will become image streaming instead of video. That is to say, capacity and the time of data transmission can be saved.

3.4   Structure

We mainly focus on car owners. Besides, we will use our own approach to detect driving record automatically and communicate between vehicles. The application is built on Android, expected to run the program on driving recorders. We will limit to a specific road section while testing and developing the system.

Four steps are supposed to proceed. First, determine the specific road section, and collect data; Next, sort out the collected data. Start to plan the structure of program; Then, begin to develop the program, add GUI, do simulation, and test system. Finally, analyze and present whole the research.

Building Cloud Service and Algorithm Design. The main usage of cloud service is to implement each operated function, handle users' request, and provide storage to save driving records. The operated function includes receiving image data from users, analyzing images, building database, searching database, and etc. Hold time is the first concern because of massive calculation. The other factor is the availability of data, for example, we will not use old data and data which has been analyzed in the same location. This algorithm will help reduce repeated operations, furthermore, it helps us make sure that we are analyzing real-time image in every data.

Program Structure in Device and UI Design. We will plan our service with relation to different characters. For example, it is necessary for users to search nearby parking space, it is required for devices to send image information to servers in cloud, and it is important for servers to analyze and collect data. As for UI design in app, in order to realize convenient searching function and interface, it need to be designed from the view of users.

The error of GPS measurement is about 5 to 10 m. We can say that it is about 1 or 2 roadside parking spaces. In order to enhance the accuracy, we will combine Google Maps API, take the advantage of its navigation and distance matrix service. Besides accessing the speed and distance of vehicles, the API can also help send GPS location to keep loading and operating fast in the device.

When it comes to clients, we will check whether there is anyone else sending the same information of specific location at the same time or not. It will not send information if anyone else is sending the data. However, if there is not anyone else sending the data, we plan to capture image immediately after moving a small and appropriate distance before sending to servers in cloud (Fig. 1).

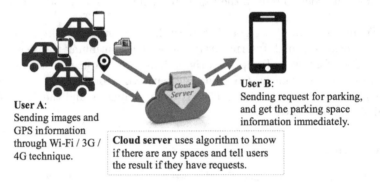

User A:
Sending images and GPS information through Wi-Fi / 3G / 4G technique.

User B:
Sending request for parking, and get the parking space information immediately.

Cloud server uses algorithm to know if there are any spaces and tell users the result if they have requests.

Fig. 1. System flow chart

4   Implementation

The system is divided into three parts - image recongization, cloud server, and client's application. At first, the three parts will be implemented separately. They will be combined and operate after they all make a certain proportan.

4.1   Image Recognition of Roadside Parking Space

Image recognition and analysis of roadside parking space is implemented by C++ with OpenCV library. The program will return if the image of parking space is vacant after received an image.

Setting ROI (Region of Interest). First, the program will convert the image into gray scale. The reason is that the perspective of image will affect the degree of image recognition. Moreover, the image will be divided into four equal parts. Only the right-bottom part will be reserved because the spaces are usually located in the right hand side (Fig. 2).

(a) Gray scale image

(b) ROI image

Fig. 2. Setting ROI

Sides Detection and Noise Reduction on Image. The program uses Canny edge detection in OpenCV to find each side of parking space. Afterward it reduces noise by the way, Median Blur. (Fig. 3)

Fig. 3. Detect each side   **Fig. 4.** Draw parking space

Find Out Parking Spaces. First, find out straight line with Hough line detection. Detect which one is the line of parking space by angle and intersection of lines (Fig. 4).

If the appropriate space is not found, the program will return the result of no vacant space (equals to occupied by vehicle). However, if the space is found, it will continue to next to detect if the space is able to use.

Detect if the Parking Space Is Able to Use. If the ratio between the side of parking space and its shelter is more than a certain number, it means that the space has been occupied. Therefore, the program will return no vacant spaces. On the contrary, it will return there is a vacant parking space (Fig. 5).

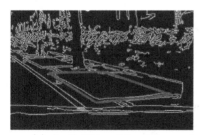

(a) Available parking space   (b) Unavailable parking space

Fig. 5. Detect parking space

4.2   Cloud Analyzing Server

After passing image recognition of roadside parking space testing, the program mentioned above will be moved to cloud service. Moreover, it will coordinate with the open data offered by government. The data will provide the information about roadside parking space. Therefore, we are able to know which road sections do not have spaces, prevent analyze the images from those sections. We implement the server by nodejs action hero framework; In addition to offering API with http, we will provide interface for webpages in order to let users find parking spaces directly. Non-relational database, Mongo, is also used to accelerate access and operated speed.

Servers in cloud will translate longitude and latitude into address information while receiving GPS information and images by users. Next, it will compare the road section with open data to confirm if the section provides parking spaces. After successful analysis, the result with address will update to database for other users.

4.3 Mobile APP (Client Side)

It is divided into several steps to implement, mainly separated into user (device) and server side. First, we use Android platform with Android Studio and Android SDK, which are based on JAVA, to develop client's application.

| (a) Home | (b) Record | (c) Setting | (d) Result | (e) Map |

Fig. 6. User interface

Figure 6 is our main interface and function. Figure 6(a) is the first screen of the system. You can choose the function of both recording and searching. Figure 6(b) is recording screen. It will use device's camera automatically, temporarily save the records in iParking folder. The purpose is to let users check the record, choose if they want to provide it to other users or delete it. After uploading the record, it will be deleted. Figure 6(c) is the setting page. Users can change their sending rate (network flow) and searching range while finding parking space. Figure 6(d) is the result of searching. Users will know how many parking spaces nearby. After choosing the one user prefers, the location will be shown on the map like Fig. 6(e). Therefore, user can be navigated to the space combined with Google API.

5 Conclusion

The goal of this system is to offer users a practical and useful application. Users are able to find parking spaces while having requests. In addition, traffic problem, air pollution problem, and the behavior of illegal parking will decrease.

We have a simple but completed system until now. The system includes cloud service, the technique to analyze images, and an application for Android. We expect to develop more applications on iPhone and Windows Phone. Besides, we look forward to doing more research on accuracy of image recognition, server load balance, and Vehicular ad hoc network.

Acknowledgement. This work was sponsored in part by Ministry of Science and Technology (MOST), Taiwan, under the contract number MOST 105-2221-E-006-186- and MOST 104-2815-C-006-029-E.

References

1. Statistical chart of important indicators in Taiwan, Ministry of Transportation (2014). http://www.motc.gov.tw/uploaddowndoc?file=reference/g004.pdf&filedisplay=g004.pdf&flag=doc. (in Chinese)
2. Kupper, A.: Location-Based Services: Fundamentals and Operation. Wiley, New York (2005)
3. Huang, Z.T.: Simulating the On-Street Parking Behavior of Commercial Consumer Based on Agent-Based Model. Master's thesis, National Cheng Kung University (2014)
4. Hsu, C.J.: Intelligent roadside parking payment system. Urban Traffic **22**, 97–105 (2007). (in Chinese)
5. Cui, Y., Zhao, J.: Real-time location system and applied research report. In: Hsu, C.-H., Xia, F., Liu, X., Wang, S. (eds.) IOV 2015. LNCS, vol. 9502, pp. 49–57. Springer, Heidelberg (2015). doi:10.1007/978-3-319-27293-1_5
6. Yi, C.W.: Eco-Community: Building an Intelligent Cyber-Physical Community Using Wireless Sensor Networks. Technical report NSC100-2218-E009-002, Government of Taiwna (2011)
7. Kanter, T., Rahmani, R., Li, Y., Xiao, B.: Vehicular network enabling large-scale and real-time immersive participation. In: Hsu, R.C.-H., Wang, S. (eds.) IOV 2014. LNCS, vol. 8662, pp. 66–75. Springer, Heidelberg (2014). doi:10.1007/978-3-319-11167-4_7
8. Lin, C.Y., Su, J.T., Tsai, W.P., Tsai, M.H.: Finding nearby available roadside parking spot. In: The Proceeding of IPPR Conference on CVGIP (2014)

Predictive Assessment of Response Time for Road Traffic Video Surveillance Systems: The Case of Centralized and Distributed Systems

Papa Samour Diop[✉], Ahmath Bamba Mbacké[✉], and Gervais Mendy[✉]

Laboratoire d'Informatique et de Réseaux Télécoms (LIRT), Département Génie Informatique, École Supérieure Polytechnique de Dakar (ESP/UCAD), Dakar, Senegal
{papasamour.diop,ahmathbamba.mbacke, gervais.mendy}@esp.sn

Abstract. In this paper, we propose mathematical models for predictive assessment of response times of road traffic video surveillance systems. Their performances depend highly on the ability to perceive mobiles within a certain radius of networked sensors, then distinguish their potential trajectory for further decision making. Most QoS measurements and evaluations used within actual literature are hardware based, and do not consider the influence of the technical architecture. We therefore proposed a process based decomposition of video surveillance systems to obtain functions approximating each ones time consumption. The integration of these components guided us to generic mathematical models validated through experimentations. The comparison between them shows a considerably lower response time for a distributed architecture over a centralized.

Keywords: Data · Transmission · Mobile · Monitoring · Forecasting · Perception · Distributed learning

1 Introduction

Nowadays, smart cameras are almost designed to mimic eyes and brains. These devices are capable of capturing a large amount of information and give them a meaning.

They are integrated into intelligent transport systems [20], video surveillance [1] to better manage road traffic, supervising public or private places. Research efforts and the reduction of material costs opened the possibility of using these systems to a wider range of applications (automatic recognition and object tracking [10], the interpretation of the scene [5] and the extraction or indexing special events [9]...).

There are also applications in the monitoring of industrial fields (access control or the production quality control), in the supervision of highly frequented public places (train stations, subway, [2] businesses [3]), in monitoring and analysis of elderly activities (indexing activities [4] or fall detection [5]), in sport (football, golf, ...)

© Springer International Publishing AG 2016
C.-H. Hsu et al. (Eds.): IOV 2016, LNCS 10036, pp. 34–48, 2016.
DOI: 10.1007/978-3-319-51969-2_4

These systems generally operate according to the following process:

- Motion detection,
- Extraction and classification of objects,
- Monitoring of objects over time,
- Behavior analysis and incident detection [6]
- Transmission of information (events related to objects) to decision making unit.

However, the real-time management of this mass of data is problematic. Indeed, the cameras must have a significant computing power to process it, or be connected to a central collection and processing unit, engendering transmission duration issues, and this in order to identify objects for example, before they go out of their reach.

Technologies have been developed to implement smart and powerful cameras [11] and solutions have been proposed to better control the flow of information between intelligent cameras and a central collection and treatment [11]. In the case of smart cameras, solutions are now available to equip them with analysis capacities [7.8]. In the field of prediction, more work was done: Road pedestrian path prediction in a normal environment [7], arrival time estimation of the bus considering several routes [8], a system of the destination and estimated future prediction according to the [9] trajectory. In these systems, most of the evaluations are based on an assessment of an event [15] and the cameras are not equipped with learning abilities, nor collaboration.

Given these limitations, we propose two types of road CCTV system architectures resulting in two formal evaluation models detection performance by focusing on the time of the response of the system following a picture taking.

The first case studied is based on a forecast model using distributed learning and a shared knowledge base. The second case used evaluate distributed systems with intelligent cameras working capacity.

In both cases an assessment of the potential response time between when an image is captured, and the time a decision is made by the system, is proposed.

This work is presented through the following 5 sections:

- Section 2 presents the state of the art in performance assessment models in a network video surveillance,
- Section 3 presents various deployment architectures,
- In Sect. 4 we divide and describe each architecture treatments via sub-processes,
- Section 5 provides the evaluation and comparison of centralized and distributed data processing time models,
- Section 6 presents the conclusion and perspectives for future work.

2 State of the Art of Video Surveillance Network Performance Assessment Models

2.1 Network Performance Measurement

Much work has been mentioned on network performance in terms of throughput, delay and jitter [23–25].

In [24] they proposed a model to identify flow variations and time in order to optimize the system design with the correct configuration settings. A number of simulations were conducted to demonstrate the performance of the model. However, these studies were limited to the WiMax network wireless mesh. Mahasukhon et al. [26] have established a platform in which they measured the flow based on RSSI for each of the mobile nodes in a mobile WiMax network operating on the IEEE 802.16e standard. A method for improving performance in terms of throughput, end to end delay, and the jitter of a WiMax network (carrying voice calls) was proposed in [27].

Kafhali et al. [28] presented a performance analysis for the frequency band allocated to the IEEE 802.16 for wireless broadband access. In this analysis, the rate was compared to the intensity of traffic. They noticed an increase in traffic intensity was associated with an increase in flow to a point of saturation.

The authors [29], among others, have led throughput tests in TCP and UDP for the downlink channels and amount of WiMax networks. Flow tests were conducted under different types of modulations and varying distances. Reference [25] shows the work done to determine the minimum value of the signal-noise attribute to ensure acceptable levels in terms of throughput and quality of service in the WiMax networks.

2.2 Performance Measure to CCTV

PRISMATICA [31] is one of the most sophisticated monitoring systems developed to detect relevant situations in complex environments. The architecture consists of a set of devices that perform local monitoring on a small area. The obtained information can be sent to a central manager. The authors conclude their work by talking about the need to integrate expert knowledge and machine learning to provide more advanced monitoring. Detmold et al. [32] discussed a middleware as a deployment mechanism of intelligent video surveillance systems based on the topologies described as the activity of the monitored objects. One of the contributions is the use of a distributed table to increase flexibility and scalability of the communication model. In this same line of research, IBM introduced an alternative (Tian et al.) [33] based on the intelligent management of the data collected by the safety device and open standards. For measurements of performance applied to video surveillance, [30] talks about the flow characteristics for video surveillance systems with WiMax with variations on the nodes, frame rate and size of the MSDU to check their performance. The obtained results show that, in similar circumstances, the HWW video surveillance system surpasses the legal system in terms of throughput in a factor of 1.75.

All these works do not make a formal assessment of the response time of treatment centers based on the architecture of the video surveillance system and thus relativize these studies. In this article, we propose a predictive model assessment of the response time of road traffic video surveillance systems in the case of centralized and distributed systems.

3   Presentation of the Different Architectures

The significant problem in the design of urban traffic monitoring system is the ubiquity of detection points, the quality and reliability of the communication system and the establishment of the processing system. A widely distributed network cameras requires infrastructure so vast that granting energy supply to the cameras and establish a communication channel between devices [21] is problematic. The implementation of such infrastructure involves high costs and relevant policy choices that often undermine the feasibility of the entire project. Installation and network infrastructure maintenance costs for both the cameras and infrastructure are of great importance for better system performance. We proposed two generic architectures with video surveillance for each specific treatment possibility.

3.1   Centralized Architecture

In this architecture the cameras are placed at the roadside and each covers a clearly defined vision ray. A processing device is located at the remote monitoring center and cameras are connected to the latter via a wireless system. As in a centralized system, the processing unit is located at the monitoring center and handles the processing of the transmitted video stream from the cameras, followed by the treatment of video meta-data. Each camera, detecting the presence of a mobile in his field of vision, sends its flow to the monitoring center where metadata are processed.

The example of prediction we consider is the anticipation of the direction of the mobile through a learning system. The goal is to predict the path that the mobile will take. Monitoring of the mobile and the prediction (activation of the next camera) will be handled at this level (see Fig. 1).

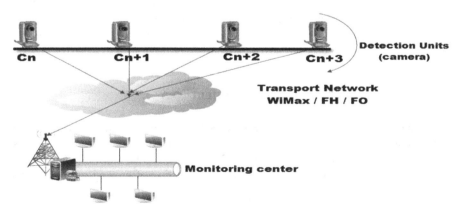

Fig. 1. Centralized architecture

3.2 Distributed Architecture

In this architecture the cameras are placed at each side of the road and has an embedded processor. A wireless link connects the cameras together and each camera is connected to the monitoring center via a wireless transmission system. Each camera that detects the presence of a mobile in its scope follow it up and analyze until the activation of the next camera using the onboard processor. Data processed and results will be transmitted to the monitoring center to be displayed and stored (Fig. 2). The prediction process will be triggered before the camera loses the mobile. Therefore, the current Cn camera sends a signal to the next camera Cn + 1 so that it prepares for the detection and monitoring.

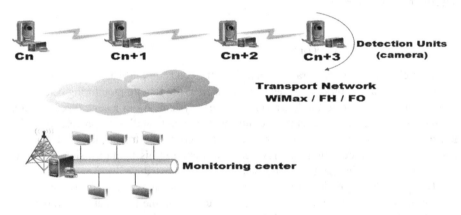

Fig. 2. Distributed architecture

Note that the average distance between the cameras is not significant because they will be positioned according to the routes and the coverage area.

The description of the processing system and activation of the cameras to the prediction will be outlined in the next section.

4 Description of the Processing System

The captured images transmission delay depends on several factors such as the transmission rate, the weight of the images, the number of pictures etc. More images weight, the higher the transfer time is long. [29] In our case, the transmission rate will be calculated from the initial node, i.e. since the detection of moving up to the activation of the next camera.

4.1 How a Camera Works?

This diagram outlines the different behaviors of a camera during the monitoring process to the activation of the next camera. Detecting a mobile to the prediction for the next camera to activate, there are a set of processes between the different components of the video surveillance system. The conditions for a camera to be involved in the process are: whether it detects the presence of a mobile in his field of vision, or another sends a signal that she is preparing for a mobile that is in his direction. The different states taken by a camera system are: standby activation, detection and follow-up (Fig. 3).

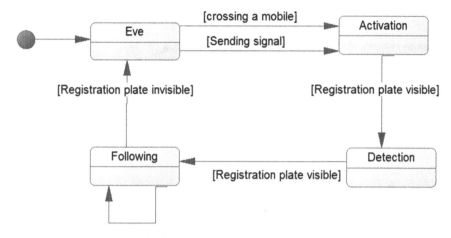

Fig. 3. State/Transition diagram of a camera

4.2   System Sub-processes Modeling

In the system, a set of processes occur as soon as a camera detects a mobile in his field of vision. This action arises a set of processes that induce communication between the various system components (camera processing unit) depending on the architecture of the video surveillance system (centralized or distributed architecture). These processes can be grouped into processing block: launch detection, identification of the license plate of the mobile, treatment and enrichment of metadata, enabling the next camera (Fig. 4).

For a mobile to be detected, it must be in the field of view of a camera that is to say at a range of 15 m (experimental data taken on the basis of available material). At this level, a set of variable comes into play in the treatment process (Fig. 5).

It is well known that the speed $= \frac{\text{distance}}{\text{time set}}$

Let:

T_{ti} = processing time of an image
T_i = size image file
P_c = camera range
D_a = next camera activation time
D_p = time decision
V_m = speed mobile
T_m = time taken
D_b = actual flow rate of the transmission medium

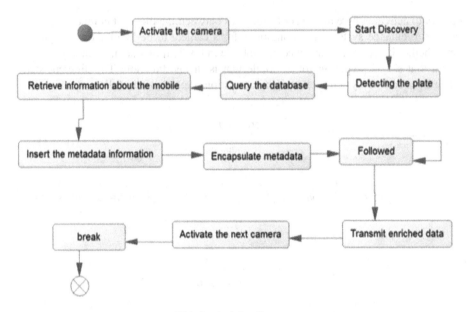

Fig. 4. Activity diagram

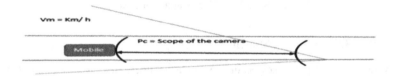

Fig. 5. Monitoring system of the mobile

D_t = Duration of treatment
T_{cf} = propagation delay information
N_{it} = Number processed image

In our case, the processing is done every 10 ms (Tt). So we will have 20 ms to create a displacement vector for tracking mobile 10 ms and a centralized architecture for a distributed architecture. With an image size of 30 kb = 0.029296875 MB and a camera that covers a 15 m field of view, we have:

The number of images processed by the system during a mobile is in its field of action is $N_{it} = \frac{T_m}{T_{ti}}$.

With this system, we can offer the speed evaluation models of transmission at different available architectures (centralized and distributed). An example of mobile tracking system (Fig. 5).

After a description of our system, the evaluation of the treatment time between the two systems will be outlined in the next section.

5 Evaluation of Centralized Data Processing Time or Distributed in a Predictive Video Surveillance Architecture

The evaluation consists in determining the time required for various processes to be realized. Depending on the speed of the mobile, we have the possibility to determine the time required for a mobile to be out of the camera's field of view. Therefore, we can determine the number of images to be processed by the processing unit. The number of processed images allow us to determine the processing duration depending on the transmission media for each architecture. By adding this result to the duration of decision making and the activation duration of the next camera, we will be able to evaluate the data processing times for our different cases (centralized and distributed processing).

Alias	Name	Reference value with the hardware
P_c	Scope of the camera	15
T_{ti}	Processing time	0.01
C_{te}	Constant	2
T_i	Image File Size	0,029296875
D_a	Time to next camera activation	0.01
D_p	Time decision making decision	0.01

5.1 For a Centralized Architecture

- With Time taken $= \frac{\text{distance}}{\text{speed}}$ (1) and
- Number of images processed $= \frac{\text{Time put}}{\text{processing time of an image}}$ (2). $\Rightarrow$
- $T_m = N_{it} * T_{ti}$
- If we replace 1 in 2, we have:
- $N_{it} = \frac{P_c}{V_m * T_{ti} * \text{cte}}$
- $D_t = \frac{T_i}{D_b} * 8 * N_{it}$
- $T_{pi} = D_t + D_p + D_a$

$$Y = -13\ln(x) + 62,541$$
$$R^2 = 0,9843$$

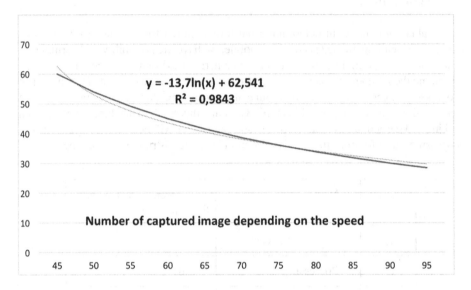

Fig. 6. Number of images processed

Analysis of this curve shows the variation in the number of images processed according to the mobile's movement speed in a centralized architecture. We note that the higher the speed, the greater the number of images processed by the camera decreases. This is due to the fact that the time taken to get out of the camera field decreases as the speed increases. Note that these results are the same for all cameras in the system regardless of the road or the position of the surveillance camera (Figs. 6 and 7).

These curves represent the image processing time for different types of transmission media (Fast Ethernet, WiFi 802.11g, 802.11n) depending on the speed of the mobile. Note that if mobile speed increases, the time used for image transmission decreases. This is due to the fact that fewer images are to be sent as the speed increases. The difference in transmission media is explained by the fact that they do not offer the same transmission rates.

5.2   For a Distributed Architecture

With virtually no processing time, since treatment is done within the embedded systems in CCTV cameras, we have:

- $N_{it} = \frac{P_c}{V_m * T_{ti} * \text{cte}}$
- $D_t = N_{it} * T_{ti} * D_p$
- $T_{pi} = D_t + D_a$

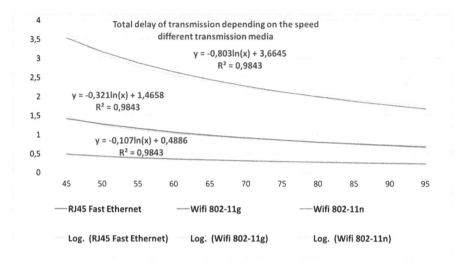

Fig. 7. Total time of transmission

$$Y = -27, 4 \ln(x) + 125, 08$$
$$R^2 = 0, 9843$$

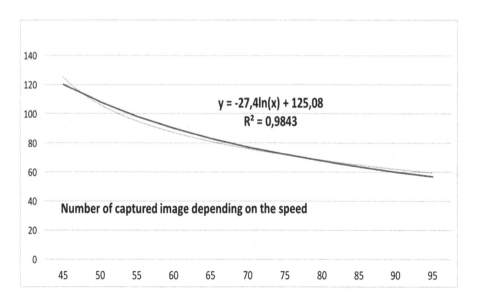

Fig. 8. Number of images processed

The analysis shows the variation in the number of processed image by a camera considering the mobile speed in a distributed type architecture (Figs. 8 and 9). It is noted that the faster the mobile runs, the number of processed images decreases by a logarithmic law. This reflects the fact that the mobile switching time in the camera's field of vision decreases as the speed increases as the time taken $= \dfrac{distance}{speed}$.

$$Y = -0,001 \ln(x) + 0,0163$$
$$R^2 = 0,9843$$

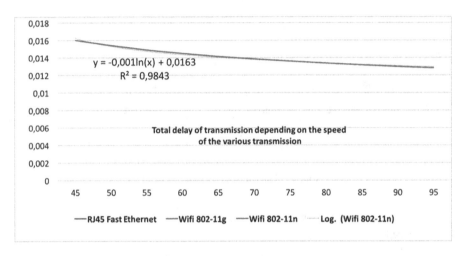

Fig. 9. Total transmission time

We change the processing time of different transmission media according to the speed of the mobile in a distributed architecture. It is noted that the transmission time is low and decreases if the speed of the mobile increases. This is due to the fact that each camera is embedded with a processor and that everything is done at this level until it no longer detects the mobile in the field of view of the latter before passing the relay to the next camera. Although medias do not offer the same transmission rates, it is noted that they all offer the same tendencies (Fig. 10).

The comparative study between distributed and centralized for the different cases studied shows:

- We have more images processed in a distributed architecture when going mobile in a camera field of vision. This reflects the fact that the treatment is much faster and requires less communication between system components through the embedded processing. Therefore, we have a better decision because we have more collected information (metadata) that will allow us to have a better view and understanding of the system.
- In terms of the total time of transmission, we also note that it is much faster for a distributed architecture and is practically the same at the different types of transmission media (RJ-45 Ethernet, Wi-Fi 802.11g and 802.11 not) because for a distributed architecture, processing and following decision makings are made at the embedded processor. Communication between the embedded processor and the monitoring center have no bearing on the process of monitoring and prediction.

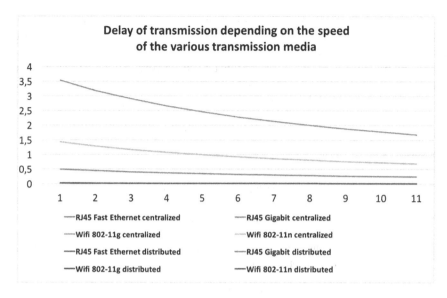

Fig. 10. Comparison between the two models

6   Contribution

The field of prediction is nowadays a major issue in research. It can be applied to several environments: Medicine [16], transport [17], radar [18], collision detection [19], of road or path [8, 12, 20]. But however, the current methods of prediction do not take into account the architecture of the processing system. In most cases, the architecture is fixed and is not the subject to studies for a better system performance. In our case, we did a specific study of the processing system for optimization (communication between devices) to justify our choices and have a guaranteed performance.

According to the results of our research, distributed treatment in video surveillance processing systems offers by far the best performance in processing and data analysis. Data processing time varies from 0.0016 s to a mobile traveling at a speed of 45 km/h in 0012 to a speed of 95 km/h. We note the same transmission 801.11× standard in a distributed processing system (0.0016 s to a speed of 45 km/h and 0.012 s for a speed of 95 km/h) faster than that used in RJ45 giga Ethernet for centralized processing that varies between 0.5 s to a speed of 45 km/h in 0.4 s for a speed of 95 km/h.

7   Conclusion

This experimental and mathematical study of the assessment of the central processing time and distributed in road traffic video surveillance systems shows that the treatment is significantly faster when it is distributed. The information is processed at the same time as monitoring of the mobile. The decision to activate the next camera requires very low latency and makes this type of architecture more appropriate regarding the processing time. The type of architecture does not arise since many see after the experimental data, a distributed type architecture provides better performance in terms of speed of transmission.

We will be called to confirm these results by comparisons with various simulations using an individual centered approach (multi agents based simulations) which are closer to the distributed architecture concepts.

References

1. Gouaillier, V., Fleurant, A.E.: Intelligent video surveillance: promises and challenges. Technological and Commercial Intelligence Report (2009)
2. Krausz, B., Herpers, R.: MetroSurv: detecting events in subway stations. Multimedia Tools Appl. **50**(1), 123–147 (2010)
3. Sicre, R., Nicolas, H.: Human behaviour analysis and event recognition at a point of sale. In: 2010 Fourth Pacific-Rim Symposium on Image and Video Technology (PSIVT), pp. 127–132. IEEE (2010)
4. Karaman, S., Benois-Pineau, J., Mégret, R., Dovgalecs, V., Dartigues, J.F., Gaëstel, Y.: Human daily activities indexing in videos from wearable cameras for monitoring of patients with dementia diseases. In: 2010 20th International Conference on Pattern Recognition (ICPR), pp. 4113–4116. IEEE (2010)
5. Foroughi, H., Aski, B.S., Pourreza, H.: Intelligent video surveillance for monitoring fall detection of elderly in home environments. In: 11th International Conference on Computer and Information Technology, 2008. ICCIT 2008, pp. 219–224. IEEE (2008)
6. Kastrinaki, V., Zervakis, M., Kalaitzakis, K.: A survey of video processing techniques for traffic applications. Image Vision Comput. **21**(4), 359–381 (2003)
7. Nasir, M., Lim, C.P., Nahavandi, S., Creighton, D.: Prediction of pedestrians routes within a built environment in normal conditions. Expert Syst. Appl. **41**(10), 4975–4988 (2014)
8. Yu, B., Lam, W.H.K., Tam, M.L.: Bus arrival time prediction at bus stop with multiple routes. Transp. Res. Part C. Emerg. Technol. **19**(6), 1157–1170 (2011)
9. Chen, L., Lv, M., Ye, Q., Chen, G., Woodward, J.: A system for destination and future route prediction based on trajectory mining. Pervasive Mob. Comput. **6**(6), 657–676 (2010)
10. Chen, L., Lv, M., Chen, G.: A system for destination and future route prediction based on trajectory mining. Pervasive Mob. Comput. **6**(6), 657–676 (2010)
11. Shi, Y., Lichman, S.: Smart cameras: a review. In: Interfaces, Machines And Graphical Environments (IMAGEN) National Information and Communications Technology Australia (NICTA). Australian Technology Park, Bay 15 Locomotive Workshop Eveleigh, NSW 1430, Australia
12. Developing Traffic Signal Control Systems Using the National ITS Architecture, Mitretek Systems 600 Maryland Avenue SW, Suite 755 Washington, DC 20024 TransCore, Inc. 251 Park Avenue South, 14th Floor New York, NY 10010 (See Acknowledgments), Report Date: February 1998
13. Chen, L., Lv, M., Chen, G.: A system for destination and future route prediction based on trajectory mining, College of Computer Science, Zhejiang University, Hangzhou 310027, PR China
14. Wafi, Z.N.K., Ahmad, R.B., Paulraj, M.P.: Wireless cameras network for intelligent traffic surveillance system. In: Proceedings of the International Conference on Man-Machine Systems (ICoMMS), BatuFerringhi, Penang, Malaysia, 11–13 October 2009

15. Brulin, M.: Analyse sémantique d'un trac routier dans un contexte de vidéo-surveillance, THÈSE présentée à L'UNIVERSITÉ BORDEAUX I'ÉCOLE DOCTORALE DE MATHÉMATIQUES ET INFORMATIQUE, Soutenue le, 25 octobre 2012
16. Ohn-Bar, E., Tawari, A., Martin, S., Trivedi, M.M.: On surveillance for safety critical events: in-vehicle video networks for predictive driver assistance systems. Comput. Vis. Image Underst. Laboratory for Intelligent and Safe Automobiles (LISA), University of California, San Diego, CA 92093, USA
17. Wyatt, K.D., Mandrekar, J., Wong-Kisiel, L., Nickels, K., Wirrell, E.: Predictors of recording an event during prolonged inpatient video electroencephalogram monitoring in children. Pediatr. Neurol. **50**, 458–463 (2014). Elsevier Inc.
18. Ohn-Bar, E., Tawari, A., Martin, S., Trivedi, M.M.: On surveillance for safety critical events: in-vehicle video networks for predictive driver assistance systems. Laboratory for Intelligent and Safe Automobiles (LISA), University of California, San Diego, CA 92093, USA
19. Sánchez-Oro, J., Fernández-López, D., Cabido, R., Montemayor, A.S., Pantrigo, J.J.: Radar-based road-traffic monitoring in urban environments, Departamento de Ciencias de la Computación, Universidad Rey Juan Carlos, c/ Tulipán s/n, 28933 Móstoles-Madrid, Spain
20. Castro, J.L., Delgado, M., Medina, J., Ruiz-Lozano, M.D.: An expert fuzzy system for predicting object collisions. Its application for avoiding pedestrian accidents School of Computer Science, University of Granada, Department of Computer Science and Artificial Intelligent, C/Periodista Daniel Saucedo Aranda s/n, E-18071 Granada, Spain
21. Alvarez-Garcia, J.A., Ortega, J.A., Gonzalez-Abril, L., Velasco, F.: Trip destination prediction based on past GPS log using a hidden Markov model, Computer Languages and Systems Dept., University of Seville, 41012 Seville, Spain, Applied Economics I Dept., University of Seville, 41018 Seville, Spain
22. Sodas, T., Le Certen, G., Le Pichon, J.P., Mabo, P.: Approche mbthodologique pour une architecture de monitoring intelligent ,Laboratoire de traitement du signal et de l'image, université de Rennes I, IUT GEII de Rennes, 3, rue du Clos-Courtel, BP 90422, 3.5704 Rennes cedex, France ; 2dkpartement des maladies cardiovasculaires, CHRU de Rennes, 2, rue le Guillou, 35000 Rennes, France
23. Li, Y., Wang, C., You, X., Chen, H., She, W.: Delay and throughput performance of IEEE 802.16 WiMax Mesh Networks. IET Commun. **6**(1), 107 (2012)
24. Jun, J., Peddabachagari, P., Sichitiu, M.: Theoretical maximum throughput of IEEE 802.11 and its applications. In: 2nd IEEE International Symposium on Network Computing and Applications (NCA), Cambridge, MA, USA, pp. 249–256, 18 Apr 2003
25. Alabed, R.A., Mohammed, M.S.: Optimization and improving throughput on WiMAX mobility. Int. J. Eng. Innovative Technol. (IJEIT) **3**(1), 6–8 (2013)
26. Mahasukhon, P., Sharif, H., Hempel, M., Zhou, T., Ma, T.: Distance and throughput measurements in mobile WiMAX test bed. In: The 2010 Military Communication Conference, San Jose, CA, pp. 154–159, October 2010
27. Gumaidah, B.F., Soliman, H.H.: WiMAX network performance improvement through the optimal use of available bandwidth by adaptive selective voice coding. Int. J. Mod. Eng. Sci. **2**(1), 1–16 (2013)
28. El Kafhali, S., El Bouchti, A., Hanini, M., Haqiq, A.: Performance analysis for bandwidth allocation in IEEE 802.16 broadband wireless networks using Bmap queueing. Int. J. Wirel. Mob. Netw. (IJWMN) **4**(1) (2012)
29. Yousaf, F.Z., Daniel, K., Wietfeld, C.: Analysing the throughput and QoS performance of WiMAX link in an urban environment. http://cdn.intechopen.com/pdfs/9477/InTech_Analyzing_the_throughput_and_qos_performance_of_wimax_link_in_an_urban_environment.pdf. Accessed 12 June 2014

30. Lubobyaa, S.C., Dlodlo, M.E., De Jager, G., Zulu, A.: Throughput characteristics of WiMAX video surveillance systems. In: International Conference on Advanced Computing Technologies and Applications (ICACTA-2015) (2015)
31. Velastin, S.A., Remagnino, P.: Intelligent distributed video surveillance systems. The Institution of Electrical Engineers (IEEE) (2005)
32. Detmold, H., van den Hengel, A., Dick, A., Falkner, K., Munro, D.S., Morrison, R.: Middleware for distributed video surveillance. IEEE Distrib. Syst. Online 9(2), 1–11 (2008)
33. Tian, Y., Brown, L., Hampapur, A., Lu, M., Senior, A., Shu, C.: IBM smart surveillance system (S3): event based video surveillance system with an open and extensible framework. Mach. Vis. Appl. 19(5), 315–327 (2008)

Intelligent Mobility and Smart City

Electrical Vehicle Charging Station Deployment Based on Real World Vehicle Trace

Li Yan[1], Haiying Shen[1(✉)], Shengyin Li[2], and Yongxi Huang[2]

[1] University of Virginia, Charlottesville, VA 22904, USA
{ly4ss,hs6ms}@virginia.edu
[2] Clemson University, Clemson, SC 29634, USA
{shengyl,yxhuang}@clemson.edu

Abstract. The fast development of smart-grid technologies and applications calls for new means to meet the transportation and environment requirements of the next trend of mainstream vehicles. Electric vehicle (EV), which has been regarded as an important replacement for present gasoline-based vehicle, is expected to greatly reduce the carbon emissions meanwhile offer acceptable transportation ability. However, most of present market-level electric vehicle heavily rely its capacity-constrained battery which can only support limited driving range. Although there have been many pioneer works focusing on ameliorating the driving experience of EVs through tuning the placement of charging infrastructure, most of them do not consider the heterogeneity of vehicle movement in different scenarios. In this paper, starting from a fine-grained analysis of a real-world vehicle trace, a charging station placement algorithm considering the installation cost, traffic flow and battery capacity, called *EVReal*, is proposed. In comparing its performance with other representative algorithms, *EVReal* outperforms the others in various metrics.

1 Introduction

Electric vehicles (EVs) have been viewed as the potential solution to greenhouse gas emission problem for several decades. EVs are worthy to be considered as a replacement of current gasoline-based vehicles for several reasons (e.g., environment friendliness, fuel economy). However, EVs also have driving range problems (typically 60 to 120 miles on a full charge), long recharge time (takes 30 min to charge up to 80%), and expensive batteries replacement [16]. To make EVs penetrate faster into consumers under the context of current charging infrastructure limitations, researchers have proposed various algorithms to optimize the placement strategy of charging stations, which can be categorized into charging demand based methods and traffic flow based methods.

In the charging demand based methods, vehicles' charging demands are generally analyzed with various models (e.g., queue theory, driver preference, parking positions) [4,5,13–16]. Then the decision is made to maximally fulfill the deduced demands of certain road network. The common problem with these algorithms is that the charging demand deduced by the proposed means cannot

© Springer International Publishing AG 2016
C.-H. Hsu et al. (Eds.): IOV 2016, LNCS 10036, pp. 51–64, 2016.
DOI: 10.1007/978-3-319-51969-2_5

depict the actual charging scenario of the whole road network due to several factors (e.g., timeliness, traffic pattern) [7,12]. Therefore, some algorithms based on fine-grained analysis of traffic flow were proposed. The traffic flow is measured based on EVs' origin-destination pairs (O-D pairs). The traffic flow of a O-D pair is defined as the number of vehicles that travel along the paths included in the O-D pair during a certain period of time [6,12]. In these works, the vehicle parameters (e.g., vehicle density on certain road segment, mobility pattern) are extracted from the movement of vehicles, and the placement of charging stations is designed to maximally capture (i.e., cover) the traffic flows [7,10,12]. In these representative works based on traffic flows, [10,12] provide comprehensive models considering various aspects of traffic flow and road network, but they only validate their works with very small scenarios (50 positions).

To provide a comprehensive EV charging station placement strategy with fine-grained analysis of vehicle mobility, we propose *EVReal*, a charging station placement method based on real world vehicle movement records. Its design is based on the trace analysis of a 28-day vehicle trace in Rome. Then in the model design, the properties and constraints of the vehicles are combined to formulate an optimization problem. Finally, the performance of *EVReal* is evaluated using the trace from various perspectives. In summary, our contributions are threefold:

(1) Our study on a real world trace [3] presents a comprehensive analysis of vehicles' mobility parameters related to the placement of charging stations and their possible influence on the performance of a charging system.
(2) We propose a charging station placement method aiming at maximizing the coverage of vehicle activities under constraints from the trace analysis.
(3) We have conducted extensive trace-driven experiments to validate the performance of *EVReal* from various perspectives.

To our knowledge, this work is the first to formulate a charging station placement optimization problem driven by the observations of vehicles' real-world movement characteristics. Related work is presented in Sect. 2. Section 3 presents the analysis of a vehicle mobility trace. Section 4 presents the detailed design of *EVReal* model. Then Sect. 5 evaluates the performance of *EVReal*. Section 6 concludes this paper with remarks on our future work.

2   Related Work

Charging demand based algorithms. Deploying charging stations based on deduced charging demands has been extensively studied. Bae *et al.* [4] proposed to determine the suitable deployment of charging stations through analyzing the spatial and temporal dynamics of charging demand profiles at potential charging stations using the fluid dynamic model. Zheng *et al.* [16] formulated an optimization problem trying to maximize the number of EVs charged in the charging stations while minimizing the life cycle cost of all the stations. Eisel *et al.* [5] aimed at dealing with customers' range anxiety (i.e., fear of being unable to reach destination due to insufficient charging opportunities on road) through a model that transforms customers' preference in charging positions into planning of station locations. The problems with these works are that the mobility cannot be modeled with independent sources.

Traffic flow based algorithms. To better capture the charging dynamics of vehicles, several traffic flow based methods were proposed. Lam *et al.* [7] formulated the station placement as a vertex cover problem, proved its NP-hardness and proposed four solutions. Sánchez-Martín *et al.* [10] proposed to deploy charging stations at the positions with many parking events and suitable parking time length with the minimum deployment cost. Wang *et al.* [12] determined constraints (e.g., driving range, traffic volume) from EV traffic statistics, and formulated and solved a multi-objective location optimization problem to maximize the coverage of EV traffic. They conducted simulation experiments on a 33-node road network. Although these works have turned their focuses to capturing the vehicles' activities, they either validate their design on small road network (e.g., a road network with 34 intersections) [7,10,12].

EVReal utilizes various vehicle mobility related parameters, which are extracted from a real world vehicle trace, in forming the objective function and corresponding constraints. Therefore, *EVReal* enables the charging system to have higher serving performance.

3   Trace Analysis

In this section, we present our trace analysis on the Rome trace [3]. There have been many works using taxis to analyze traffic flows [3,9,17–19]. We use their insights to support our taxi trace based data analysis. The Rome trace lasts for 30 days from Feb 1, 2014 to Mar 2, 2014. Each taxi reports its location records (timestamp, ID, GPS position) every 15 s. We filtered out positions with precision larger than 20 m, and taxis with few appearances (<500). We extracted intersections, where vehicles make significant movement changes, as landmarks. Finally, the Rome trace has 315 taxis and 4638 landmarks. When a vehicle stays at one landmark for more than 5 min, we call this position *anchor position* that cut the vehicle's trace into several trajectories. Each trajectory is represented as a sequence of landmarks with corresponding arrival timestamps.

3.1   Traffic Flows Deduced from Vehicle Trajectories

When a vehicle follows certain trajectory, it generates traffic flow to the landmarks consisting the trajectory. During the driving process, there may be multiple vehicles driving on the same landmarks. Correspondingly, for each trajectory, we define the number of vehicles driving on the consisting landmarks at the same time as its traffic flow. The traffic flow is crucial because it represents vehicle activity, and is closely related to the possible charging load at the landmark [7,20]. The distribution of traffic flow is not balanced. For illustration, we measured the cumulative distribution function (CDF) of the traffic flows of all trajectories as shown in Fig. 1(a). We see that most of the trajectories (more than 90%) have vehicle flows lower than 15. The largest traffic flow is higher than 80. About 40% of the trajectories have traffic flows lower than 2. The results demonstrate that the vehicles' activities are highly concentrated at certain popular areas (landmarks). Therefore, properly planning charging stations at these landmarks to maximize captured traffic is necessary. Meanwhile, almost half of the trajectories cover areas with low vehicle flows, which means several "unpopular" landmarks also need consideration.

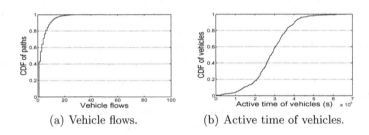

(a) Vehicle flows.   (b) Active time of vehicles.

Fig. 1. Properties related to charging load.

3.2   Vehicle Active Time

The charging ability of the system should be consistent with the number of active vehicles [4,16]. Most previous works only consider transient traffic load. But the temporal dynamics of vehicle activities also need to be considered. We define the active time of a vehicle as the total time it spends in transiting. Then we draw the CDF of the active time of all the vehicles as shown in Fig. 1(b).

Around 50% of the vehicles have total active time between 200,000 s and 400,000 s. But around 20% of vehicles having active time less than 200,000 s and around 15% of vehicles having active time more than 400,000 s. These results demonstrate the fluctuation of the vehicles' active time. Thus, comprehensively collecting the traffic flows is crucial for deploying charging stations.

3.3   Properties of Vehicle Trajectory

In this section, we present the analysis of the properties of trajectories. Range anxiety, which is the EV drivers' concern that they might not reach a planned destination due to a discharged battery, needs consideration in placing the charging stations [5,8,11]. Thus, considering the EV users' habitual travel distance is necessary to increase the charging station accessibility and relieve EV drivers' range anxiety. We define the distance of a travel as the number of landmarks the trajectory covers, and the duration as its time span. In urban scenario, vehicles are likely to drive short trajectory. To confirm this, we measured the CDF of the

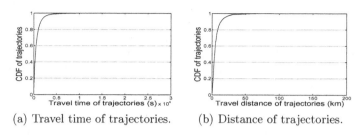

(a) Travel time of trajectories.   (b) Distance of trajectories.

Fig. 2. Properties of trajectories.

distance and the duration of vehicles' travel as shown in Fig. 2(a) and (b). We see that the travel times of 90% of vehicles are less than 5 min, and the travel distances of 90% of vehicles are less than 20 km. These observations inspire us that: when a vehicle needs charging, (1) its distance to the nearest charging station should fit in the distances of majority of travels to avoid range anxiety; (2) its time spent in reaching the nearest charging station should be shorter than most vehicles's travel times.

4   System Design

In this section, we present the details of *EVReal*. In formulating the problem of optimizing deployment of charging stations, *EVReal* utilizes the analysis fruition of Sect. 3 and consider other additional constraints as follows:

- Vehicle flows are highly concentrated within certain ranges (Fig. 1(a)). Therefore, our objective is to maximize the totally captured vehicle flows.
- Vehicles' active time in urban scenario fluctuate (Fig. 1(b)). Correspondingly, we collect the traffic flow of every vehicle's O-D pair as candidates, and use a binary vector to represent whether a traffic flow should be covered.
- Vehicles in urban scenario usually travel short distance and duration (Fig. 2(a) and (b)). We set the amount of energy that can be recharged at each station to be nonnegative. That is, the vehicles will get charged as long as a charging station is available at the position.
- Besides the parameters that directly affect the charging coverage, we also consider the installation cost per station, total budget, battery capacity, etc.

The indices for the parameters and variables are listed in Table 1. The parameters are listed in Table 2. The variables are listed in Table 3. The meaning of the parameters and variables are presented in Sect. 4.1. The formulation of our optimization model is presented in Sect. 4.2.

4.1   System Preliminaries

We view the target road network as an undirected graph $G = (N, A)$, where N and A represent the set of all landmarks, $N = \{i | i = 1, 2, \ldots, n\}$, and the set of edges, $A = \{(i,j)|i,j \in N, i \neq j\}$, respectively. Given two candidate landmarks, i and j, we define d_{ij} as the distance of the shortest path connecting these two landmarks. For each traffic flow, we use r to denote its origin landmark, and s to denote its destination landmark. The collection of the origin landmarks is denoted with R, and the collection of the destination landmarks is denoted with S. We define VR as the driving range, which is the vehicles' maximum driving distance after a full charge. For a subset of landmarks $\hat{N} \subset N$, if a vehicle can reach at least one landmark $j \in \hat{N}$, then $\hat{N}$ is reachable by the vehicle with VR. Therefore, for a road network, if $\hat{N}$ is reachable by any vehicle with VR, the charging stations can capture all vehicle movements on the road network. For convenience, we summarize the notations as in Table 1.

Table 1. Table of notations.

Index	Description	Index	Description
i	Index of candidate sites, $i \in \hat{N} \subset N$	s	A destination landmark in the network, $s \in S \subset N$
r	An origin landmark in the network, $r \in R \subset N$	a	Index of arc set A, $a = (i,j) \in A$

Let f^{rs} be the traffic flow from r to s if there are vehicles following the O-D pair in the records. Ideally, the more traffic flows that the model can capture, the more power load the charging station can offer, and the higher residential power the vehicles can maintain. However, the installation cost of charging station C_i at landmark i, and the total budget m constrains the deployment of charging

Table 2. Table of parameters.

Item	Description	Item	Description	Item	Description
C_i	The installation cost of a charging station, $i \in N$	f^{rs}	Traffic flow from r to s	P^{rs}	A sequence of landmarks on the shortest path from r to s
β	Onboard battery capacity (unified in travel distance), i.e., vehicle range	f^{rs}	Traffic flow from r to s	d_{ij}	Distance between landmark i and landmark j
M	A sufficiently large number denoting restraining effects	δ_i^{rs}	$\delta_i^{rs} = 1$ if node i is in the sequence of nodes P^{rs}, $\delta_i^{rs} = 0$ otherwise; this is an outcome of the deviation paths that are exogenously generated	VR	The maximum distance that an EV can drive after it is fully charged to battery capacity, denoted by β

stations. Thus, to tune the performance of the station deployment with acceptable cost, we further consider parameters: the sequence of landmarks composing the path from r to s, P^{rs}; the distance between landmark i and landmark j, d_{ij}; and the flag denoting whether recharging opportunity should be offered on the path from r to s, δ_i^{rs}. The combination of these parameters formulates the objective of capturing as many traffic flows as possible, but is constrained by the battery capacity, β, which determines VR; the constraint denoting the restraining effect on the length of path, M; and the total budget for deployment, m. For clarity, we summarize the parameters as in Table 2.

We use $X = \{X_i | i = 1, 2, \ldots, n\}$ to represent the decision vector indicating whether a landmark should be installed with a charging station. Due to the constraints, it is possible that not all vehicle flows will be captured. Correspondingly, we use $Y = \{X^{rs} | r \in R, s \in S\}$ to select the vehicle traffic that will be captured by the final strategy. The charging system should maximally keep the remaining driving capacity of vehicles positive whenever the vehicle reaches a landmark installed with charging station. Meanwhile, the power recharged at a charging station should be capped with the maximum battery capacity of the vehicle. Thus, in formulating the constraints, we use $B = \{B_i^{rs} | i = 1, 2, \ldots, n, \ r \in R, s \in S\}$ to denote the remaining driving range of a vehicle when it arrives at landmark i on the path from r to s. Similarly, let $l = \{l_i^{rs} | i = 1, 2, \ldots, n, \ r \in R, s \in S\}$ be the vector denoting the amount of residual power of a vehicle when it arrives at landmark i on the path from r to s. For clarity, the variables that can be manipulated in finalizing the model are summarized in Table 3.

Table 3. Table of variables.

Item	Description	Item	Description
X_i	$X_i = 1$ if a charging station is located at landmark i; $X_i = 0$ otherwise	B_i^{rs}	Remaining range at landmark i on the path of O-D pair $r - s$
Y^{rs}	$Y^{rs} = 1$ if the path between r and s can be completed (taken); $Y^{rs} = 0$ otherwise	l_i^{rs}	Amount of energy recharged at landmark i on the path of O-D pair $r - s$

4.2   Model Formulation

Our goal, which is to maximize the captured traffic flow, is formulated as:

$$\max \sum_{r,s} Y^{rs} f^{rs} \tag{1}$$

Additionally, we consider following constraints. First, the power recharging of an EV can only be accomplished at landmarks equipped with a charging station. Therefore, through combining the parameter δ_i^{rs} (the flag denoting whether recharging opportunity should be offered on the shortest path from r to s) with the variable l_i^{rs} (the amount of energy recharged at landmark i on the path from r to s), we set a constraint corresponding to the EVs' charging behavior. Due to the EVs' mobility, the traffic flow is time-varying and depends on various factors [12]. Thus, we set a constraint to guarantee that the sum of the remaining power (range) and the power recharged at landmarks is no larger than the maximum battery capacity. Besides, the battery consumption should be consistent with the distance between landmarks. As for the budget m, the total cost of the charging system is consistent with the sum of the costs of all charging stations C_i determined by the decision vector X. In summary, the constraints are:

$$B_i^{rs} + l_i^{rs} \leq M(1 - Y^{rs}) + \beta, \; \forall r, s; i \in P^{rs} \tag{2}$$

$$B_i^{rs} + l_i^{rs} - d_{ij} - B_j^{rs} \leq M(1 - Y^{rs}),$$
$$\forall r, s; i, j \in P^{rs}; (i, j) \in A \tag{3}$$

$$-(B_i^{rs} + l_i^{rs} - d_{ij} - B_j^{rs}) \leq M(1 - Y^{rs}),$$
$$\forall r, s; i, j \in P^{rs}; (i, j) \in A \tag{4}$$

$$\sum_{r,s} l_i^{rs} \delta_i^{rs} \leq M X_i, \; \forall i \in \hat{N} \tag{5}$$

$$\sum_i C_i X_i \leq m \tag{6}$$

$$X_i = \{0, 1\}, \forall i \in N \tag{7}$$

$$Y^{rs} = \{0, 1\}, \forall r, s \tag{8}$$

$$B_i^{rs} \geq 0, l_i^{rs} \geq 0, \; \forall r, s; i \in P^{rs} \tag{9}$$

(2) assures that the total onboard electricity each vehicle carries will not exceed the EV battery capacity ($B_i^{rs} + l_i^{rs} \leq \beta$) if the path of that O-D pair is taken to electrify; otherwise no restriction exists when $Y^{rs} = 0$. (3) and (4) work simultaneously to ensure that the energy consumption conservation $B_i^{rs} + l_i^{rs} - d_{ij} - B_j^{rs} = 0$ holds for all links traversed on the path which is taken to deploy adequate stations ($Y^{rs} = 1$). Otherwise, if $Y^{rs} = 0$, then $B_i^{rs} + l_i^{rs} - d_{ij} - B_j^{rs} \leq M$, namely no restraining effects. (5) implies a logic that recharging is only available at node i if there is a charging station. Budget is indicated by (6). (7), (8) and (9) are nonnegativity constraints on remaining power B_i^{rs} and recharged power l_i^{rs}, and binary definition on charging station placement vector X and traffic flow selection vector Y. The problem is a Binary Integer Programming (BIP) problem. We refer to an existing toolbox (e.g. GLPK [2], Cbc [1]) to obtain the integer-feasible solution to the problem.

5   Performance Evaluation

We used the Rome [3] trace for evaluation. The experiments are deployed on a trace-driven vehicular network simulation platform, called CGod. Unless otherwise specified, the experiment setting is the same as in Sect. 3. We first elaborate the charging station placement results in Sect. 5.1. Then we briefly explain the comparison methods and the metrics for illustration in Sect. 5.2. Finally, we present the experimental results and analysis in Sect. 5.3.

5.1 Charging Station Placement

In determining the charging positions, we made assumptions as follows:

- The cost of installing a charging station at any landmark is identical, namely the number of charging stations represents the restriction of budget.
- All the vehicles are homogeneous, having the same vehicle range and fully charged at origins.
- All the drivers are homogeneous. Namely, they will seek charging station when their residual power is below 10% of their battery capacity.

Table 4. Deployment of charging stations under different budget scenarios.

Sites	Deployment of charging stations (Landmark ID)		Sites	Deployment of charging stations (Landmark ID)	
	VR = 50 km	VR = 100 km		VR = 50 km	VR = 100 km
1	3197	2558	7	5, 136, 262, 374, 741, 2957, 3197	-
2	14, 3197	-	8	5, 86, 136, 374, 382, 485, 615, 3197	-
3	14, 136, 3197	-	9	5, 136, 262, 374, 485, 741, 1782, 2980, 3197	-
4	14, 136, 374, 3197	-	10	5, 86, 136, 374, 485, 741, 1097, 1782, 2980, 3197	-
5	86, 136, 374, 382, 3197	-	11	5, 9, 136, 262, 374, 484, 485, 570, 624, 2980, 3060	-
6	136, 262, 374, 741, 2957, 3197	-			

We extract the traffic flows as defined in Sect. 3, and obtained a road network with 2514 landmarks and 27807 edges connecting these landmarks, and EV traffic flows with 16443 O-D pairs. Then we applied the model on the network with the landmarks as the candidate charging sites and the O-D pairs for consideration. Two vehicle ranges are tested for comparison (i.e., VR = 50 km and VR = 100 km). For each range, we first solve the problem with one charging station, and then solve problems by gradually increasing the number of stations until all the travel demand are covered. This is to find the suitable budget for the planning of the charging stations given the road network and traffic flows.

Table 4 presents the detailed deployment of charging stations. Obviously, given limited battery capacity, the more charging stations deployed, the more traffic flows can be captured. Table 5 gives more details on this phenomenon. Moreover, we also observe that vehicle battery capacity (i.e., driving range) would indirectly affect the deployment of charging stations. For example, when budget only allows us to place one charging station, the landmark selected for installing charging station is different for VR = 50 km and VR = 100 km. When the vehicle range is 50 km, all the flows are not captured until 11 stations can be placed at locations as indicated in the table. In contrast, when VR = 100 km, one station located at Landmark 2558 can cover all the traffic flows in the network.

This is mainly because for most urban trips, their lengths are within the vehicle range (100 km). Therefore, we assign VR = 50 km in the following experiments. In Table 5, we can see the total number of traffic flows captured under various deployment of charging stations. As the number of charging stations is increased, we observe a diminishing marginal benefit in terms of coverage of flows.

Table 5. Coverage of flows under different budget scenarios.

Sites	Captured traffic flows		Sites	Captured traffic flows		Sites	Captured traffic flows	
	VR = 50 km	VR = 100 km		VR = 50 km	VR = 100 km		VR = 50 km	VR = 100 km
1	640619	645047	5	644386	-	9	644975	-
2	642058	-	6	644786	-	10	645010	-
3	643048	-	7	644875	-	11	645047	-
4	643830	-	8	644959	-			

5.2 Settings of Performance Comparison

We compared *EVReal* with two representative charging station placement methods. The first one is random placement method (*Random* in short), which randomly chooses landmarks for deployment. The second one is a traffic density constrained, drivers' interest based method which considers both quantitative and qualitative attributes of the target road network [5] (*MaxInterest*). In *MaxInterest*, the landmarks with the highest average vehicle densities and long vehicle staying time are treated as candidate charging places. The metrics are:

- *Average charging station power load*: Power load distribution on charging stations. It is calculated by averaging the total power that vehicles recharged in different hours during a day.
- *Average vehicle residual power*: The vehicles' average residual power under different hours during a day. It illustrates the methods' ability in keeping the vehicles' operability on road network.
- *Average number of necessary charges*: The average number of charges for keeping each vehicle operable per day under different number of charging stations. We define a necessary charge is needed when a vehicle's residual power is lower than 10%. It illustrates the methods' ability in capturing vehicles' traffic flows.
- *Average travel time to the nearest charging stations*: The average travel time to the nearest charging stations when a necessary charge is needed. It is used to measure the methods' performance in properly distributing the charging stations considering the reachability of vehicles.

5.3 Experimental Results

We conducted two kinds of experiments. In one experiment, given that the number of total charging stations is 11, we measured the average power load of charging stations and the average residual power of vehicles under different hours during a day. In the other experiment, we varied the total number of charging stations from 1 to 11 and measured the average number of charges and the average travel time to the nearest charging station a vehicle needs per day.

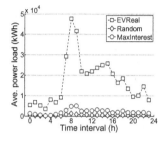

Fig. 3. Average station power load.

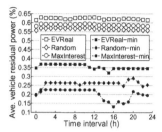

Fig. 4. Average vehicle residual power.

Average Charging Station Power Load. Figure 3 shows the measured average charging station power loads. We see the results follow: *MaxInterest* >*EVReal*>*Random*. The power load of *EVReal* is higher than the others at all times. Note that the results are obtained with 11 landmarks installed with charging stations. This means the determined positions for placing charging infrastructure of *EVReal* can serve more vehicles than others with comparative power load pressure.

MaxInterest has the second highest power load. This is because it focuses on satisfying the charging need of most vehicles by placing charging stations at vehicles' most visited places. During rush hours, these charging stations can fulfill the need of most vehicles. But during normal hours (e.g., 14:00 ∼ 16:00), *MaxInterest*'s power load is much lower than the one of *EVReal*. To illustrate the difference of the methods in fulfilling vehicles' charging needs, we further measure the vehicles' residual power in Fig. 4. *Random* always achieves the lowest power load on landmarks. This is because vehicles have highly biased preference on visiting landmarks. Randomly placing charging infrastructure on landmarks can hardly meet the charing requirement of most vehicles.

Average Vehicle Residual Power. Figure 4 shows the average vehicles' residual power in different hours during a day. We see that the results follow: *EVReal*>*MaxInterest*>*Random*. We also measured the minimum vehicle's residential power, which follows: *EVReal-min*>*Random-min*>*MaxInterest-min*.

EVReal has the highest vehicle residual power. This is because the charging stations determined in *EVReal* can timely fulfill the charging need of vehicles. The residual power of vehicles can be kept at relatively stable level within different hours. Besides, there are two obvious drops at around 8:00 and 16:00, which correspond to the peaks in Fig. 3. This means that the rush hours with active vehicle movements can affect the vehicle residual power. *MaxInterest* has the second highest vehicle residual power. This is because *MaxInterest* aims to place charging stations at landmarks that can maximize the charging need of most vehicles. *Random* has the lowest vehicle residual power. The reason is that most vehicles cannot be charged timely. Furthermore, we measured the average number of charges that vehicles can have under different number of charging stations, as shown in Fig. 5. *EVReal* can still maintain the vehicles' residual power at around 35% under the worst case. *Random* achieves the second highest minimum vehicle's residual power. *MaxInterest* results in the lowest minimum metric. This is because *MaxInterest* concentrates on the areas with dense vehicle movements, so some vehicles in non-dense areas cannot be sufficiently charged.

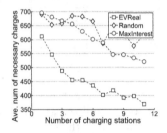

Fig. 5. Average number of charges.

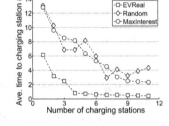

Fig. 6. Average time to charging station.

Average Number of Necessary Charges. Figure 5 shows the average number of the vehicles' necessary charges under various number of charging stations. We see the results follow: *Random*>*MaxInterest*>*EVReal*.

EVReal has much lower number of necessary charges, and the gap increases along with the increasing of the number of charging stations. This is because *EVReal* aims to cover most of the traffic flows. As for *MaxInterest* and *Random*, their performance is comparative with *EVReal* only when the total number of charging stations is small. The reason is similar to that explained in vehicles' residual power.

Average Travel Time to Nearest Charging Stations. Figure 6 shows the average travel time to the nearest charging station under various number of charging stations. We see the results follow: *MaxInterest*≈*Random*>*EVReal*.

Vehicles in *EVReal* always have much shorter travel distances to the nearest charging stations. This is because *EVReal* aims to maximize the covered vehicle flows in balanced manner. Note that when the number of charging stations is larger than 4, the improvement of the metric becomes smaller than before. This is because when VR = 50 km, *EVReal* can use 5 charging stations to fulfill the charging needs. In contrast, *MaxInterest* results in locating the charging stations at popular places (e.g., downtown area). Therefore, vehicles need to travel longer distances to these positions. *Random* cannot guarantee reasonable placement of charging stations, leading to bad reachability in charging.

6 Conclusion

Electric vehicle is expected to fulfill the blueprint of zero pollution meanwhile offering acceptable transportation ability. However, most current market-level EVs have limited driving range. Multiple pioneer works focusing on tuning the placement of charging stations have been proposed. They fail to support the continuous movement of the EVs due to lack of vehicle mobility analysis. In this paper, we establish *EVReal*, which considers various factors which are critical for the planning of charging stations based on a real-world trace. Driven by our trace analysis, we determined the parameters that need consideration, and formulated an optimization model composed by these parameters. Compared with other representative methods, *EVReal* outperforms in distributing power load, vehicle residual power, the number of charges needed and travel time to the nearest charging station. In the future, we will explore more in the effect of traffic events (e.g., jam, accident) in placing charging stations.

Acknowledgements. This research was supported in part by U.S. NSF grants NSF-1404981, IIS-1354123, CNS-1254006, and Microsoft Research Faculty Fellowship 8300751.

References

1. Coin-or branch and cut. https://projects.coin-or.org/Cbc. Accessed 6 Jun 2015
2. Gnu linear programming kit. http://www.gnu.org/software/glpk/glpk.html. Accessed 6 Jun 2016
3. Amici, R., Bonola, M., Bracciale, L., Loreti, P., Rabuffi, A., Bianchi, G.: Performance assessment of an epidemic protocol in VANET using real traces. In: Proceedings of MoWNeT (2014)
4. Bae, S., Kwasinski, A.: Spatial and temporal model of electric vehicle charging demand. TSG
5. Eisel, M., Schmidt, J., Kolbe, L.: Finding suitable locations for charging stations. In: Proceedings of IEVC (2014)
6. Haberman, R.: Mathematical models: mechanical vibrations, population dynamics, and traffic flow
7. Lam, A., Leung, Y.W., Chu, X.: Electric vehicle charging station placement: formulation, complexity, and solutions. TSG
8. Nilsson, M.: Electric vehicles: the phenomenon of range anxiety. ELVIRE
9. Piórkowski, M., Sarafijanovic-Djukic, N., Grossglauser, M.: A parsimonious model of mobile partitioned networks with clustering. In: Proceedings of COMSNETS (2009)
10. Sanchez-Martin, P., Sanchez, G., Morales-Espana, G.: Direct load control decision model for aggregated EV charging points. TPS
11. Tuttle, D., Baldick, R.: The evolution of plug-in electric vehicle-grid interactions. TSG (2012)
12. Wang, G., Xu, Z., Wen, F., Wong, K.P.: Traffic-constrained multiobjective planning of electric-vehicle charging stations. TPD
13. Wang, S., Fan, C., Hsu, C.H., Sun, Q., Yang, F.: A vertical handoff method via self-selection decision tree for internet of vehicles. IEEE Syst. J. **10**(3) (2016)

14. Wang, S., Lei, T., Zhang, L., Hsu, C.H., Yang, F.: Offloading mobile data traffic for qos-aware service provision in vehicular cyber-physical systems. Future Gener. Comput. Syst. **61**, 118–127 (2016)
15. Wang, X., Yuen, C., Hassan, N.U., An, N., Wu, W.: Electric vehicle charging station placement for urban public bus systems. IEEE TITS **PP**(99) (2016)
16. Zheng, Y., Dong, Z.Y., Xu, Y., Meng, K., Zhao, J.H., Qiu, J.: Electric vehicle battery charging/swap stations in distribution systems: comparison study and optimal planning. TPS
17. Zheng, Y., Liu, Y., Yuan, J., Xie, X.: Urban computing with taxicabs. In: Proceedings of UbiComp (2011)
18. Zhu, H., Chang, S., Li, M., Naik, K., Shen, S.: Exploiting temporal dependency for opportunistic forwarding in urban vehicular networks. In: Proceedings of INFOCOM (2011)
19. Zhu, Y., Wu, Y., Li, B.: Trajectory improves data delivery in urban vehicular networks. TPDS (2014)
20. Zi-fa, L., Wei, Z., Xing, J., Ke, L.: Optimal planning of charging station for electric vehicle based on particle swarm optimization. In: Proceedings of ISGT Asia (2012)

Anticipatory Control of Vehicle Swarms with Virtual Supervision

Andrzej M.J. Skulimowski[1,2(✉)]

[1] Decision Science Laboratory, Chair of Automatic Control and Biomedical
Engineering, AGH University of Science and Technology,
30 Mickiewicza Ave., 30-059 Kraków, Poland
ams@agh.edu.pl

[2] Progress and Business Foundation, 12B J. Lea Street, 30-048 Kraków, Poland

Abstract. This paper presents an application of anticipatory network theory to
model the behavior of a swarm of autonomous vehicles that share a common
goal. In addition, each vehicle optimizes its individual performance criterion that
is subordinated to the group goal. The internal swarm organization resembles a
hierarchical control system where the top level is distinguished only by the
hierarchy of goals, instead of a fixed assignment of powers or permissions. The
arising variable hierarchy depends on the type of momentary performance of the
swarm units: those performing activities leading directly to reaching the
superordinated goal have the right-of-way and priority access to shared
resources. Two principal problems need to be solved in this context. The first
one is to recognize temporal hierarchies by swarm vehicles. This is accomplished by ensuring appropriate communication between vehicles via a local
network. The second problem is to define behavior strategies that yield the best
attainment of the common goal while individual indicators are nondominated.
Solving both problems ensures a balance between cooperative (reaching a
shared goal) and self-interested (individual goals) behavior. Finding a com-
promise strategy is equivalent to solving a certain anticipatory network. This
model can be applied to supervising mining vehicle cooperation, where efficient
communication and coordination of individual actions play central roles.

Keywords: Vehicle swarms · Anticipatory networks · Discrete-event control ·
Dynamic multicriteria optimization · Internet of vehicles

1 Introduction

The rapid development of autonomous vehicles, specifically autonomous cars, results
in the need to create new decision algorithms capable of employing near-human
decision-making principles. Among the latter, anticipation is a crucial principle in
traffic management of interacting vehicles driven by autonomous decision makers,
human or artificial. According to this principle, in an anticipatory traffic coordination
problem, each of the decision makers is responsible for exactly one vehicle and knows
the parameters of decision problems (constraints, criteria) which are being solved by
other decision makers when driving their vehicles as well as their decision algorithms.
Given the external circumstances, this knowledge makes it possible to simulate the

© Springer International Publishing AG 2016
C.-H. Hsu et al. (Eds.): IOV 2016, LNCS 10036, pp. 65–81, 2016.
DOI: 10.1007/978-3-319-51969-2_6

future behavior of other vehicles. Together with the knowledge of technical parameters, such as mass, maximum velocity, minimum turning radius, current speed and position, the decision makers are able to calculate the distribution of potential next moves and undertake an appropriate action. A system's knowledge of another vehicle's dynamics, which pre-determines its future states, fulfills the definition of an *anticipatory system* in the sense of Rosen [9]. He termed a system anticipatory if it contains a model of itself and of its environment suitable for generating forecasts and using them to plan future behavior.

In vehicle swarm applications, the environment of an anticipatory system usually contains other such systems. Consequently, any anticipatory decision process should take into account models of these systems. Anticipatory systems capable of modelling anticipation in other systems are termed *superanticipatory* [13]. *Anticipatory networks* [12] constitute a relevant subclass of superanticipatory systems especially well-suited to modelling interaction phenomena among anticipatory systems.

This paper presents an application of the anticipatory network theory in modelling the behavior of a swarm of standardized unmanned autonomous vehicles that share a common goal. A brief introduction to the theory of anticipatory networks is presented in Sect. 2. In the same section, we will also define timed anticipatory networks that model sequences of decisions made at different moments by each vehicle. The anticipatory problem statement and a solution proposal are provided in Sect. 3. We assume that beyond the common goal, each vehicle acts according to its own particular goals, which are subordinated to the principal group goal. Although this decision problem resembles a hierarchical optimal control system, the top level is not assigned to a permanent supervisor with fixed powers, permissions or competences. Instead, it is represented only by the hierarchy of temporary goals. What follows, in such systems there arises a time-varying hierarchy of system units that depend on their momentary functions. Specifically, vehicles performing activities leading directly to the superordinated goal have the right-of-way and priority access to common resources.

The first fundamental problem in such systems is to identify the above-mentioned momentary hierarchy by all vehicles in the swarm. This can be accomplished by ensuring efficient digital communication between vehicles. The second problem consists in defining swarm behavior strategies that result in a near-best fulfilment of the common goal and in reaching nondominated values by each vehicle's performance indicator. Solving both problems should yield a balance between the cooperative (shared goal) and self-interested (attempts to reach individual goals) behavior strategies of the swarm units. When formulated as a multicriteria optimization problem, its solution can be found by solving a certain timed anticipatory network. This model can be applied to supervising vehicle cooperation, where the efficient communication and coordination of individual activities play central roles. An illustrative example is provided in Sect. 5.

2 Anticipatory Networks as Models of Autonomous Vehicle Swarms

Anticipatory system modelling has evolved over time to accommodate an increasing number of complex real-life situations. Anticipation plays an important role in controlling transport networks [6] and computing traffic equilibria as well as in coordinating multiple mobile robots [2, 3, 7] and managing trust in vehicular networks [5], and clusters [17]. The research on anticipation is also driven by accelerating efforts to construct autonomous cars [4] for regular road traffic. A concise survey of autonomous driving, including the anticipation-related issues, is given in [1].

A further development in anticipatory system theory led to the introduction of *anticipatory networks* (AN), which generalize anticipatory models of consequences in multicriteria optimization [12, 13]. The main assumption of this theory concerns the way decision makers take into account anticipated outcomes of future decision problems linked by the causal relations with the current problem. This causality implies that the decisions made previously can influence the algorithms and decision scope of causally linked decision makers. Thus arises a network of linked decision problems, a digraph where causal relations are defined as vertices between some of the time-ordered nodes which represent decision problems. This digraph is supplemented by one or more relations of anticipatory feedback, which point out future problems whose anticipated outputs are taken into account when choosing a decision by a decision maker that precedes the feedback source in the causal order. The causal dependences of the future decisions on the solution to the current problem are used by the decision makers to influence the outcomes of future problems. They select their decisions in such a manner so that future choices should satisfy some additional preference requirements implied by anticipatory feedbacks.

Anticipatory networks can be used as an auxiliary preference structure [12] to solve the following general class of optimization problems with a vector criterion F:

$$(F : U \to E) \to min(\theta), \tag{1}$$

where E is a vector space with a partial order $\leq_\theta$ defined by a convex cone θ, i.e. iff

$$x \leq_\theta y \Leftrightarrow y - x \in \theta \quad \text{for each } x, y \in E$$

The problem (1) models a variety of simultaneous tasks and goals to be performed by autonomous vehicles. The solution to (1) is the set of nondominated decisions

$$\Pi(U, F, \theta) := \{u \in U : [\forall v \in U : F(v) \leq_\theta F(u) \Rightarrow v = u]\} \tag{2}$$

Anticipatory networks which contain only decision problems based on optimizing certain scalar or vector functions are termed *optimizer networks* [12]. As we assumed that all vehicles form a team that performs a common task, throughout this paper we will build solely vehicle swarm models with optimizers meant as cooperative optimizing units. Constructive algorithms for computing solutions to multicriteria decision making problems taking into account the above anticipatory preference information feedback have been presented in [12]. They may be applied if we know that:

- All agents who are modelled in an AN are rational, i.e. their decisions comply with the order in the criteria space and other prior preference structures.
- An agent can assess the desirability or usefulness of outcomes of those future decision problems that causally depend on the problem being solved.
- The causal dependence is described as relations binding the decisions in the current problem with constraints and/or preference structures of future problems. Relations affecting constraints are usually defined as multifunctions.
- Desirability assessments are transformed into decision rules for the current decision problem. The rules affect outcomes of future problems so that they can comply with the assessments. The set of rules so derived forms an additional preference structure for the decision problem under consideration.
- Future decision makers can use the same anticipatory principles to make their decisions and this must be taken into account at all decision planning stages.

Before formulating a formal definition of an anticipatory network, we will define the anticipatory feedback relation [12] which plays a central role in the AN theory:

Definition 1. Suppose that A is a causal network consisting of optimizers and – possibly - other units, and that an optimizer V_i in A precedes another optimizer, V_j, in the causal order r. The *anticipatory feedback* between V_j and V_i is the information on the solicited outputs from V_j, where the latter is a subset of all anticipated decisions that can be made at V_j when it is used to influence the decision choice at V_i so that a solicited decision can be made at V_j. This influence relation will be denoted by $f_{j,i}$. ∎

By Definition 1, the existence of an anticipatory information feedback between two anticipatory network units V_j and V_i means that the following three conditions are satisfied:

- The decisions made at V_i can causally influence the decisions made at V_j.
- The decision maker at V_i is capable of anticipating the decisions to be made at V_j and their consequences.
- The anticipation results are taken into account when selecting the decision at V_i.

Definition 2. An *anticipatory network* is a directed multigraph comprising at least one causal and at least one *anticipatory feedback* relation, and at least one *initial node*. ∎

The parameters of nodes and causal relations in an AN result from forecasts and scenarios that are updated every time a decision in the network is made. The anticipated outcomes of future decision problems serve as a source of preference information to solving the current problem at an initial node cf. [12, 13].

In the original formulation of the Anticipatory Decision Problem [12], all linked problems in an anticipatory network were used merely as a source of auxiliary preference information to solve a multicriteria optimization problem at the initial node.

In a vehicle swarm, each active node performing the common task may contribute to reaching the common goal. Furthermore, in anticipatory networks the decision-making agents do not act simultaneously and there is no direct impact except the causal influence on future agents. Anticipatory feedback and other information flows intervene via assumptions and rules included in the decision-making algorithms. In addition, anticipatory networks are usually asynchronous, i.e. only the order of future events is relevant, not the absolute time when they will happen.

To cope with vehicle swarms efficiently and to comply with the above rationality assumption, by the solution to the system of problems modelled in an anticipatory network, we will mean a collection of solutions to all decision problems represented in the network such that the common goal is performed in an optimal way, and the values of each set of individual unit criteria are nondominated.

Moreover, we will define the discrete solution time interval T and *timed antici-patory networks* $A(t)$, TAN, where for a fixed optimization problem to be solved and for all $t \in T$ the anticipatory multigraph varies in time. In a TAN, any unit's decision is a sequence of simple decisions made by the same evolving agent at subsequent moments of time. The decisions made by future agents at moment t become known to their predecessors at time $t + 1$ and may be used for supervisory learning of decision rules, supplementing the anticipatory feedback information.

The following principles, derived from real-life interpretations of a timed AN will serve to model the evolution and compute the optimal solutions of structured TANs:

- A discrete time interval $T = [t_0, t_f]$ is finite and plays the role of evolution period.
- (*Non-trivial progress*) At least one decision, namely at an initial node, is made and at least one causal impact is executed at each time step t.
- For every $t \in T$ the causal subgraph of $A(t)$ is embedded in a given structure graph $S(A)$ that is characteristic for this TAN; $S(A)$ is a finite digraph with no cycles.
- Non-isolated nodes with no predecessors are termed *initial nodes*.
- The functions of TAN units are characterized by their positions in the structure graph, i.e. different physical units and decision makers may be substituted for the same specific node in the structure graph during the network evolution.
- All units are initially homogeneous and anonymous; this may change for $t > t_0$.
- (*Network stationarity principle*) If a unit $V_i(t)$ remains in the network at time $t + 1$ then its native decision scope U_i and performance criteria F_i remain unchanged.
- Some units may be deleted and some new ones may be admitted to the network as time changes from t to $t + 1$.
- The decision maker responsible for the decision at a unit $V_i(t)$ can remain in the network at time $t + 1$ as the decision maker at a new unit $V_j(t + 1)$.

Referring to the solution concept presented above, the solution of a timed AN is a combination of solutions for $t \in T$. Without a loss of generality, this paper will con-sider additive combinations only. There are two main solution principles:

(P1)   a temporal combination of momentary criteria values is calculated for the initial node for all $t \in T$, irrespectively whether different V_i play the role of $V_0(t)$,

(P2)   a temporal combination of momentary criteria values is calculated for the same physical unit, for all or only for some selected units.

The next section provides further details motivated by vehicle-swarm applications.

3   Anticipatory Control of a Vehicle Swarm with Virtual Supervision

We will consider a swarm of unmanned autonomous *vehicles* $\Xi: = \{V_1, \ldots, V_n\}$ that share a common goal. The vehicles may be either heterogeneous or identical, or they may be grouped into classes consisting of similar units. The vehicles should perform a given task jointly. This task is first defined by human supervisors (not included permanently into the executive system) then expressed in quantitative terms that are commensurate with the output from the vehicle's sensors or combinations of them. These effectuate a permanent monitoring of the environment, of the vehicle itself, and the activity of other vehicles. For example, a common task of mining vehicles can be presented as the maximization of the cumulative probability of eliminating all sources of threats in a possibly largest area within a given period of time, usually a standard cyclic operational period of the swarm.

Vehicles are equipped with world models composed of a complex knowledge base and an update procedure based on the monitoring results. Therefore, the world models of individual vehicles may temporarily differ. These are also initially endowed with a set of activity rules that is inherited from the experience of former vehicle generations and conforms to the technical specifications of vehicle components. For example, if a vehicle is equipped with a drill then the rules specify the maximum temperature of the drill during drilling and the value of resisting force that should cause the system to stop drilling.

The autonomous control is performed at the following three levels:

- The main task performance is executed by an internal upper-level decision-making algorithm, which is specific for each type of vehicle. This algorithm processes the task description, merges it with sensor information, activity rules, world model, former task execution record and transforms it into an operational plan composed of activities. At this level, the information about the progress of task performance by other vehicles is exchanged between the vehicular peers.
- Middle-level control circuits are responsible for updating the knowledge base and the activity rules; anticipatory learning principles (cf. [16]) can be used here along with other machine learning approaches. This level translates the activities received from the upper level into technical instructions and forwards them to the executive (lower) control level. It is also capable of modifying the lower-level algorithms based on the updates in the world model. Middle-level algorithms contain procedures that optimize the accrued energy consumption, select shortest paths, avoid potential dangerous sites on the way etc.
- The lower-level algorithms control the movement and the technical integrity of the vehicle using the input provided by upper-level control procedures and measurements from sensors and actuators.

A scheme of information processing in an individual vehicle is shown in Fig. 1.

As mentioned above, all vehicles share a common task. The quality and completeness of its performance is described by a criterion G that maps all feasible

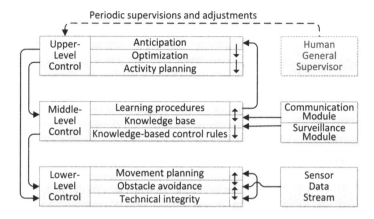

Fig. 1. A scheme of the internal vehicle decision and data flow architecture

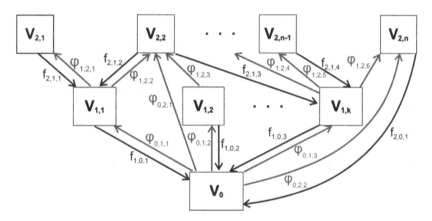

Fig. 2. The layered structure of a general anticipatory network modelling the mutual relations between a vehicle swarm

activities into the criteria space IR^N. A vehicle V_i selects its activity from the set $U_i(t)$ taking into account an individual criterion F_i and commands received from its coordinating units in the anticipatory network. The above control scheme is shown in Fig. 2.

In Fig. 2 V_0 is the initial element in the network that corresponds to the coordinating vehicle, $V_{i,p}$, $p = 1, ..., k$, are coordinated, $V_{2,q}$, $q = 1, ..., n$, are monitored vehicles. $\varphi_{i,j,x}$ denote causal influence relations between the elements of i-th and j-th layers, $f_{j,i,y}$ are anticipatory feedbacks between the units in j-th and i-th layers.

In the static problem formulation, the vehicles depicted as nodes in Fig. 2 solve a series of optimization problems with the following criteria and constraints:

$$[\text{Vehicle } V_0] \quad (G : U_0 \to I\!R^N) \to opt, (F_0 : U_0 \to I\!R^M) \to opt \tag{3a}$$

$$\left[V_{1,i} \right] \quad (G : U_{1,i} \to I\!R^N) \to opt, (F_{1,i} : \varphi_{0,1,i}(u_o) \cap U_{1,i} \to I\!R^M) \to opt, i = 1, \ldots, k \tag{3b}$$

$$\left[V_{2,j} \right] \quad (F_{2,j} : \varphi_{0,2,q(j)}(u_o) \cap \varphi_{1,2,r_1(j)}(u_o) \cap \ldots \cap \varphi_{1,2,r_p(j)}(u_o) \cap U_{2,j} \to I\!R^M) \to opt, \\ j = 1, \ldots, n \tag{3c}$$

with the anticipatory feedbacks f defined as the requirements imposed on $u_{1,i}$ and $u_{2,j}$:

$$f_{1,0,i} : u_{1,i} \in G^{-1}(g), \text{ for } i \in [1 : k] \text{ such that } \varphi_{0,1,i} \text{ is defined,} \tag{4a}$$

$$f_{2,0,j} : u_{2,j} \in W_{2,0,j}, \text{ for } j \in [1 : n] \text{ such that } \varphi_{0,2,j} \text{ is defined,} \tag{4b}$$

$$f_{2,1,j} : u_{2,j} \in W_{2,1,j}, \text{ for } j \in [1 : n] \text{ such that } \varphi_{1,2,j} \text{ is defined,} \tag{4c}$$

where g is an aspiration level for G – a desired or a satisfactory value of this criterion, while $W_{2,0,j}$ and $W_{2,1,j}$ are sets of potential actions of the vehicle $V_{2,j}$ such as the communication between the V_0, resp. $V_{1,i}$, remains established after the next action of $V_{2,j}$, as anticipated from the perspective of V_0, resp. $V_{1,i}$. The value of g has been derived within the exploration planning activity of V_0 as optimal for the present time. The above problem statement makes it possible to apply Algorithms 1 and 2 from [12].

4 Discrete-Event System (DES) Control of Anticipatory Networks

The network topology in timed networks is variable and the dynamics of role-vehicle substitution in $A(t)$ is driven by discrete-event dynamics of each vehicle's status and goals. An agent-oriented formulation of the supervisory multicriteria optimal control problem has been proposed in [10], cf. also [2] for heterogeneous mobile robot control applications. For the modelling purposes of the vehicle swarm control and supervision we will use the following class of DES:

$$V = (Q, \sigma, \delta, Q_0, H, Q_f) \tag{5}$$

where:

- Q is the set of all feasible states of event-driven vehicle and/or its components,
- σ is the set of all admissible operations (controls σ_1, spontaneous or random transitions σ_2, $\sigma = \sigma_1 \cup \sigma_2$) over the states from Q,
- $\delta : \sigma \times Q \supset Q_\sigma \to Q$ is the transition function defining the results of operations; it is defined as a set of rules for (v, q), $v \in \sigma$, $q \in Q$, from the set Q_σ,
- $Q_0 \subset Q$, $Q_0 \neq \phi$ is the set of initial states of event-driven model components,
- $H : \sigma \times Q \to I\!R^s \cup \{\infty\}$ is the transition (multicriteria) cost function; its values are infinite if a transition is infeasible,

- $Q_f \subset Q$, $Q_f \cap Q_o = \phi$, is the set of reference (or final) states of event-driven model components corresponding to alerts or points of reporting the modelling results.

Moreover, it is assumed that the system (5) is coupled with another discrete-event system S without an own cost function, termed *supervisor,* with the following notation:

$$S = (\Theta, \Lambda, \rho, \Theta_0, \Theta_f),\tag{6}$$

where

- Θ is the set of all feasible states of the supervisor
- Λ is the set of all admissible operations over the supervisor's states $\theta \in \Theta$,
- $\rho: \Lambda \times \Theta \supset \Theta_\Lambda \to \Theta$ is the transition function that defines the results of operations from Λ over states; ρ is defined as a set of rules for (λ, θ) from the subset $\Theta_\Lambda \subset \Lambda \times \Theta$,
- $\Theta_0 \subset \Theta$, $\Theta_0 \neq \phi$ is the set of feasible initial states of the supervisor,
- $\Theta_f \subset \Theta$, $\Theta_f \cap \Theta_0 \neq \phi$, is the set of final states of the supervisor; when reached, the system stops.

Events in a discrete event system (5) are defined as causally connected pairs of states $e: = (q_1, q_2)$, i.e. such that $q_2 = \delta(v, q_1)$ for certain $v \in \sigma$.

Supervisor defines *control patterns*, i.e. multivalued functions $\gamma: \Theta \to 2^\sigma$ that specify admissible transitions of the controlled system's status. In a DES there may be more subordinated systems (5) for one supervisor (6). However, the communication restrictions in control of the vehicle swarm Ξ require that the supervisor issues one control pattern at one time for all vehicles. This problem can be resolved by designing an appropriate complex internal structure of subordinated units and of the supervisor [14].

A feasible control approach under the above-mentioned communication restrictions is to relate supervisor's transitions governed by Λ to the states of V_i, with a feedback function

$$\xi : Q \to \Lambda \tag{7}$$

such that for each admissible supervisor event (τ_1, τ_2) and feedback-dependent control pattern $\gamma: \Lambda(\Theta, \xi(Q)) \to 2^\sigma$ there exists $q \in Q$ with the property

$$\gamma(\Lambda(\tau_1, \xi(q)) = \gamma(\tau_2).\tag{8}$$

In a vehicle swarm $\Xi = \{V_1, ..., V_n\}$ discrete-event control is a separate control level that governs the *status* of each i-th vehicle rather than its movement and other physical activities from the set U_i. The structure of the discrete-event control system overlaps partly with the anticipatory network, where the coordinating unit V_0 will play the supervisor role. Each unit V_m in an anticipatory network A is characterized by its status in the network. The status may admit values from a discrete set Q. A transition from q_i to q_j may be either random, allowed by the supervisor V_0, or forced by V_0.

The above presented class of controlled discrete systems is sufficient to analyse vehicle swarms and teams. General rules binding an anticipatory network A and a discrete-event system governing the status of units of A are given below:

- Each unit V_i in the network is fully characterized by its position in the network A and by its status $q \in Q_i$.
- Supervisor defines control patterns and forces the status change of all or only of some of units in the network A; the latter evolves accordingly.
- Some events may occur randomly at any time and result in a status change.
- Upon a status change of a unit, the supervisor applies the appropriate rule to change this unit's position in the anticipatory network A.
- Only one unit at a time can change its status to supervisor,
- If in Ξ there are two or more, say $s > 1$, supervisors at one time, they must cooperate when coordinating the same unit(s), i.e. for any $1 \leq i < j \leq s$, the values of the joint goal function (G_i, G_j) resulting from their activity must be nondominated. G_i is the goal function of the i-th supervisor, for $i = 1, \ldots, s$.

To analyse the case of vehicle swarms, we will admit several additional assumptions:

- The network $A(t)$ is layered: unit characteristics are fully determined by pointing out the layer in $A(t)$, where it is situated; all units in a layer are anonymous.
- Some units need not be assigned to any layer; if so, they are isolated units.
- Units in the 0-th layer in $A(t)$ play the role of supervisors in the DES (5)–(6); any unit moved to this layer automatically becomes a supervisor, and vice versa.
- If an initial network $A(t_0)$ contains no active supervisor then for formal reasons it will be assumed that there is a trivial supervisor with one state θ and $\gamma(\theta) = \sigma$.
- In a network with only a trivial supervisor, any unit may become one spontaneously if one of the pre-defined rules is satisfied, depending on uncontrolled event occurrence.

The network evolution rules derived from the above assumptions can be formulated as follows:

$$q_i(t+1) \in \delta(q_i(t), \gamma(\tau_i(t))), i = 1, \ldots, n, t = t_0, \ldots, t_f \tag{9}$$

$$\tau_i(t) = \lambda(\tau_i(t-1), \xi(q(t-1))) \tag{10}$$

$$V_{i(t+1)j(t+1)}(t+1) = V_{i(t)j(t)}(t) \tag{11}$$

$$i(t+1) = a(i(t), j(t), q_i(t+1)) \text{ and } j(t+1) = b(i(t), j(t), q_i(t+1)) \tag{12}$$

where t_f is the final time of the control period, $q(t) := (q_1(t), \ldots, q_{n-1}(t))$, the functions $a(t)$ and $b(t)$ define the layer and the subsequent number of a given vehicle in this layer, respectively. Moreover, it is assumed that the causal influence functions φ_{ij} depend only on the function of vehicles in the swarm and not on their identity. This means that the layers i_1 and i_2 and subsequent numbers of the starting and target units in $A(t)$ in their layers determine $\varphi_{i1,i2,j}$ uniquely. This reduces the network evolution rules to the specification of a new layer for each vehicle while the anticipatory feedbacks are adjusted to the needs of current task. They are calculated at the lower control level, where the current exploration needs are analyzed to optimize G. To sum up, the operation of a vehicle swarm proceeds as follows:

- A General (human) Supervisor defines the goal G, the operation area, rules and constraints, and assigns the vehicles to the swarm Ξ.
- Discrete event system D-S governs the roles of each vehicle in the swarm.
- Anticipatory network A organizes Ξ in a goal-oriented productive structure.
- The change of the role in D-S is synchronized with changing the position in A.
- The conjunction of the supervisor's role in the discrete event system D-S and the top-level node in A ensures the feasibility of the goal attainment by the swarm.
- The swarm operation may be terminated after the goal G is reached, after a maximum admissible operation time, or when all vehicles have a disabled status.

An example of an anticipatory network processed by vehicle's upper-level decision algorithm is shown in Fig. 3. The symbols D, H and P in small circles aside the network units denote the current status of these units governed by the DES (5)–(6) with $Q = \{A, D, E, H, P\}$. The general subdivision of the timed network structure into layers does not change, but the roles of $V_{i,j}$ are played by different vehicles at different moments of time. The status of the units without these symbols is defined by default by

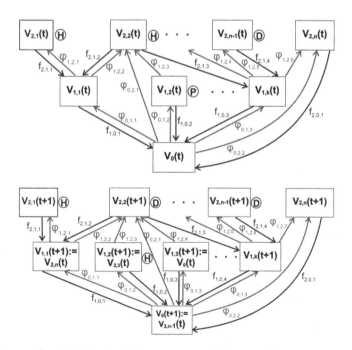

Fig. 3. An example of the timed anticipatory network evolution from t (top) to $t + 1$ (bottom)

their position in the network: the layer 1 units, i.e. $V_{1,i}$, $i = 1, ..., k$, have the status A, the layer 2 units, i.e. $V_{2,j}$, $j = 1, ..., n$, have the status E. The units of layer 0 are supervisors with internal status dynamics. A real-life application of the above anticipatory network is presented in the next section.

5   An Illustrative Example: A Swarm of Mining Vehicles

Let us consider a small swarm of 9 identical robust vehicles exploring a salt mine and looking for threats such as water leaks, which would jeopardize the entire mine. Upon locating a leakage, several vehicles must cooperate to stop it. The optimal number of cooperating vehicles and the time necessary to achieve the goal depend on the physical properties of the leakage. This may vary from case to case, with the minimum number 2 and maximum 4. The swarm patrols a system of interconnected mine corridors. The main performance index G is the percentage of threats discovered and neutralized out of a history-based estimated number of all leaks and other threats that may appear in the explored part of the mine during the operation time. G is to be maximized for each

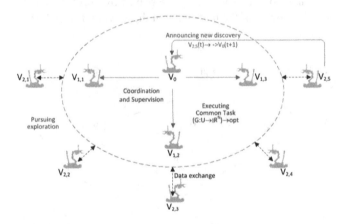

Fig. 4. An example of an anticipatory control scheme of multiple autonomous mining vehicles

operation period separately. With the network evolution laws defined at Level 2 in Box 1, the simulated appearance of threats in a simple 2-corridor mine within a 24-hour period, and an initial linear configuration of vehicles starting their operation with a 10–20 m distance from each other, the simulated time of performing the mitigation activities was satisfactory to reach the desired mitigation probability level. This situation is shown in Fig. 4 above.

The roles in the swarm and positions of other vehicles in the anticipatory network are rearranged according to the discrete event system dynamics. The set of states Q of the vehicle swarm is presented in Table 1.

Each vehicle V_i can change its status according to the discrete event system's graph depicted in Fig. 5 below. We have admitted there the following notation:

Table 1. States of the vehicles V_i and their interpretation

Notation	State name	Description of the vehicle's status
E	Exploring	Explores the environment according to its own plan
M	assisting team Members	Assists the Coordinator in performing its goal G
P	discovery Probable	Sends information about a potential discovery
H	discovery Highly probable	High probability of discovery acknowledged by S
D	Discovery confirmed	Exploration resulted in a Discovery
W	Waiting after discovery	A graded state indicating the position in the wait list
C	Coordination	Coordinating the exploration, optimization of G
F	subtask Fulfilled	End of operation due to finishing the main task
R	Recovery or Repair needed	Loss of communication or damage, needs recovery

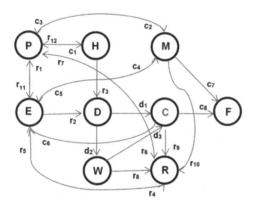

Fig. 5. The discrete event transition scheme for the system states from Table 1. Each unit may remain in the current state and self-loops are not shown for the sake of clarity

- $c_1, ..., c_8$ are controllable operations over the states of V_i,
- d_1, d_2, d_3 are controllable operations that depend on states of other vehicles,
- $r_1, ..., r_{12}$ are random or spontaneous transitions between states.

Schemes similar to Fig. 5 govern status transitions of all vehicles in the swarm except the current supervisor. The function δ in (5) is directly defined by the topology of the state transition network shown in Fig. 5. The internal transition structure of the supervisor depends on the number of vehicles in the swarm and should be minimal.

The control laws shown in Fig. 5 allow any vehicle that discovers a source of threat or another object to become the supervisor and assign tasks to other team members. After fulfilling this task, the supervisor becomes a regular team member and resumes exploration. This control principle will be termed *virtual supervision*. Thus the optimization of G is performed at two levels: one attributed to the supervisor as the initial node in the anticipatory network and one as a temporary supervisor.

The supervisor's states $\tau(t) \in \Theta$ determine the control to be used, i.e. the control pattern γ defined by (8) is forcing the controlled transitions of each vehicle's states Q. The transitions have the following structure: for each V_i there is a sequence of *elementary* states $\tau_i(t_0), \ldots, \tau_i(t_f)$. Compound states $(\tau_1(t), \ldots, \tau_{n(t)}(t))$ correspond to the entire timed anticipatory network $A(t)$ containing $n(t)$ vehicles. The V_i's status change implies its simultaneous position change in the anticipatory network $A(t)$ according to Eqs. (11)–(12). Therefore a change of topology of $A(t)$ when passing from t to $t + 1$ corresponds to the transition λ among states of S determined by a feedback function ξ (7) so that the change of the status of V_i conforms to its new role in the network $A(t + 1)$. The optimization of G is performed at three levels shown in Box 1, cf. also multilevel control scheme depicted in Fig. 1.

Box 1. Three optimization levels of a supervised timed anticipatory network $A(t)$

Level 1. The supervisor optimizes the structure of the network by simulating different team compositions; it takes into account the physical situation of V_i and the time needed to come to the task execution site, the number of vehicles with the waiting status W and the option of a new team forming with one or more waiting vehicles becoming other supervisors. The optimization yields the indices of vehicles to become current team members, $k_1(t),\ldots,k_{m(t)}(t)$, the expected optimal value of $G(t)$, the logical function $L(t)$ defined for all vehicles with status W; $L(t)(V_i) = 1$ iff V_i is selected to form its team parallel to the current supervisor; otherwise $L(t)(V_i)=0$.

Level 2. In any vehicle network $A(t)$ the status M implies that $i(t+1) = 1$, the status D, E, P, W or H implies $i(t + 1) = 2$; for any supervisor $i(t + 1) = 0$. The value of $j(t + 1)$ is assigned on the first-come-first-assigned basis for the team members. It is re-assigned monotonically from 1 to $n(t) - m(t) - n_s(t)$ for all other vehicles within the communication range. If the status of V_i is R then this vehicle is regarded as not contained in $A(t + 1)$, so no index assignment is necessary. The causal influence functions φ_i depend on the physical situation after assignment: they are defined jointly with the controls c_2 and c_4. The physical situation of a vehicle V_i determines its capacity to use actuators and sensors and affects the overall performance of this unit. V_i is not controlled remotely by the supervisor but optimizes G together with F_i within its scope of autonomy.

Level 3. S defines a minimum acceptable value g_i of G to be reached by each vehicle; a requirement to reach g_i defines anticipatory feedback condition to be fulfilled. S occasionally sends signals that help V_i to reach or surpass g_i; these result from the anticipatory optimal problem solving and decisions made by S in $A(t)$.

At the second level of optimization shown in Box 1 an optimal topology of $A(t)$ is determined simultaneously with solving the simulated next-step network $A(t + 1)$ with the anticipatory decision algorithms from [12] applied to the supervisor's criterion $G(t)$. In this example, the topology of $A(t + 1)$ is determined by the explicitly defined values of the functions a and b (12) that indicate a new layer and the position in it for each V_i. In turn, the optimal topology of $A(t + 1)$ determines the corresponding status transitions of vehicles to be performed by the supervisor.

The above control principles have first been tested with simulation experiments. Vehicles that can perform the above operations are based on a hybrid caterpillar-wheel platform with stabilizers and manipulators. A team of robust vehicles capable of installing autonomous decision software will be deployed first for research purposes. Different vehicle configuration strategies will be tested in mine circumstances to confirm the efficiency of the above approach.

6   Discussion and Conclusions

Anticipation can be regarded a substitute for efficient cellular communication in an environment where the latter is barely reachable or cannot be ensured at all. If a vehicle swarm is coordinated within a WLAN or a cellular network, these can be severely overloaded [15] that may cause a communication fallout. Interference of different access networks in a mine, e.g. leaky-cable-based and WLAN, may cause additional problems [3]. Anticipatory algorithms can serve as an emergency solution for the case of temporal communication failure. Simulation experiments of swarm operation in a mine with random communication fallouts have shown an advantage of virtual anticipatory supervision compared to permanent communication. In general, the organization of a vehicle swarm into an anticipatory network may bring considerable advantages compared to a general anticipation meant as a relation between two systems. First, the current supervisor can assign an optimal number of other units to perform the principal goal of the overall system. Second, after the assignment the vehicles can act in a flexible way, fulfil their own goals and may be re-assigned as soon as the previous task has been fulfilled. The advantage in terms of the principal criterion G shows when compared to anticipation based on self-organization of cooperating vehicle teams. In the latter situation – upon a discovery – the exploration is pursued by the discoverer and by some of the surrounding units that spontaneously join the discoverer based on an anticipatory assumption that they are expected to do so.

Along with finding optimal coordination strategies for vehicle swarms, the approach presented in this paper can be used in a similar way to establish efficient collaboration of heterogeneous teams consisting of vehicles or mobile robots and humans. Timed anticipatory networks can also be applied to improve general passenger transport management by optimizing the timetables according to anticipated demand [7].

We conclude that previous autonomous vehicle decision models did not fully satisfy the requirements defined for mobile standardized units acting in swarms. In some situations these systems have to make autonomous decisions that outperform the capabilities of their hypothetical human supervisor, who could be constrained by harsh mine conditions. Ideally, such vehicles should demonstrate creative decision-making abilities in sense of Skulimowski [11]. They should be able to identify the features of the scene, then convert some of them into optimization criteria or monitored variables and update their values continuously. This will ensure a flexibility of individual units and an ability to perform efficiently in unplanned situations. According to the freewill principle of the 3rd kind [11], the vehicles will be endowed with some kind of freedom allowing them to formulate problems and make decisions, restricted by well-specified security measures and constraints. The network of interconnected external decision-making vehicles can serve as a model of an external environment extending to the predictable future. Environmental factors and agents can either be collaborating units (humans or other vehicles) with decision-making principles assumed to be known, or they can model disturbances, caused by natural processes, or by non-cooperative units, e.g. a vehicle with damaged decision software. The external processes can also be identified by statistical filtering, prediction and other uncertainty-handling methods.

New methodologies of modelling the consequences of decisions made by autonomous vehicles, based on anticipatory networks and other cognitive models will play a significant role in implementing human decision-making features in driving an individual vehicle as well as in coordinating group or swarm behavior. It is expected that the threat mitigation algorithms confirmed by experiments in mine environments can also be applied to the design of surveillance strategies in other industries and in cities. The anticipatory decision-making models can also be used to simulate long-term autonomous vehicles and VANET development strategies taking into account their contribution to future software trends. The latter may be helpful in deriving recommendations for vehicle design teams concerning the features of swarm-optimized vehicles.

Acknowledgement. The background results on anticipatory networks have been obtained during the research project "Scenarios and Development Trends of Selected Information Society Technologies until 2025", No. WND-POIG.01.01.01-00-021/09, financed by the ERDF within the Innovative Economy Operational Program 2006–2013.

References

1. Berger, C., Rumpe, B.: Autonomous driving-5 years after the urban challenge: the anticipatory vehicle as a cyber-physical system. In: Proceedings of the 10th Workshop on Automotive Software Engineering (ASE 2012), Braunschweig, September 2012, pp. 789–798 (2012)
2. Dai, X., Jiang, L., Zhao, Y.: Cooperative exploration based on supervisory control of multi-robot systems. Appl. Intell. **45**, 18–29 (2016)
3. Fan, C., Hsu, C.H., Sun, Q., Yang, F.: A vertical handoff method via self-selection decision tree for internet of vehicles. IEEE Syst. J. **10**(3), 1183–1193 (2016)
4. Hoogendoorn, S., Ossen, S., Schreuder, M.: Empirics of multianticipative car-following behavior. transportation research record. J Transp. Res. Board **1965**, 112–120 (2006)
5. Huang, D., Hong, X., Gerla, M.: Situation-aware trust architecture for vehicular networks. Commun. Mag. IEEE **48**(11), 128–135 (2010)

6. Huang, W., Viti, F., Tampère, C.M.J.: Repeated anticipatory network traffic control using iterative optimization accounting for model bias correction. Transp. Res. **C67**, 243–265 (2016)
7. Jiang, Z., Hsu, C.H., Zhang, D., Zou, X.: Evaluating rail transit timetable using big passengers' data. J. Comput. Syst. Sci. **82**(1, Part B), 144–155 (2016)
8. Kanamori, R., Takahashi, J., Ito, T.: Evaluation of anticipatory stigmergy strategies for traffic management. In: 2012 IEEE Vehicular Networking Conference, Seoul, pp. 33–39 (2012)
9. Rosen, R.: Anticipatory Systems - Philosophical. Mathematical and Methodological Foundations. Pergamon Press, London (1985). 2nd edn. Springer (2012)
10. Skulimowski, A.M.J.: Optimal control of a class of asynchronous discrete-event systems. In: Automatic Control in the Service of Mankind. Proceedings of the 11th IFAC World Congress, Tallinn (Estonia), 1990, vol.3, pp. 489–495. Pergamon Press, London (1991)
11. Skulimowski, A.M.J.: Freedom of choice and creativity in multicriteria decision making. In: Theeramunkong, T., Kunifuji, S., Sornlertlamvanich, V., Nattee, C. (eds.) KICSS 2010. LNCS (LNAI), vol. 6746, pp. 190–203. Springer, Heidelberg (2011). doi:10.1007/978-3-642-24788-0_18
12. Skulimowski, A.M.J.: Anticipatory network models of multicriteria decision-making processes. Int. J. Syst. Sci. **45**(1), 39–59 (2014). doi:10.1080/00207721.2012.670308
13. Skulimowski, A.M.J.: The art of anticipatory decision making. In: Kunifuji, S., Papadopoulos, G.A., Skulimowski, A.M.J., Kacprzyk, J. (eds.). AISC, vol. 416, pp. 17–35. Springer, Heidelberg (2016). doi:10.1007/978-3-319-27478-2_2
14. Skulimowski, A.M.J.: Selected methods, applications, and challenges of multicriteria optimization. In: Committee for Automation and Robotics of PAS, vol.19. AGH Publishers, Kraków (2016)
15. Wang, S., Lei, T., Zhang, L., Hsu, C.H., Yang, F.: Offloading mobile data traffic for QoS-aware service provision in vehicular cyber-physical systems. Future Gener. Comput. Syst. **61**, 118–127 (2016)
16. Witkowski, M.: An action-selection calculus. Adapt. Behav. **15**(1), 73–97 (2007)
17. Yang, S., Li, J., Liu, Z., Wang, S.: Managing trust for intelligence vehicles: a cluster consensus approach. In: Hsu, C.-H., Xia, F., Liu, X., Wang, S. (eds) IOV 2015. LNCS, vol. 9502, pp. 210–220. Springer, Heidelberg (2015). doi:10.1007/978-3-319-27293-1_19

Building iCaution and Traffic Game in Smart Cities

Tang-Hsien Chang[⊠], Li-Kai Yang, and Bor-Chia Hsieh

Traffic and Transportation, Department of Civil Engineering,
National Taiwan University, Taipei 10617, Republic of China
thchang@ntu.edu.tw

Abstract. This paper concerns about constructing intelligent transportation systems (ITS) of a smart city, particularly its warning and cooperative traffic management subsystem. This paper firstly addresses current available short-range communication and long-range technologies (4G) for the services. Secondly, under prevailing roadside traffic management and control systems, an innovative iCaution device is proposed along roadsides, which functioned to deliver local traffic messages, directly broadcasting to nearby/coming mobile phones. Thirdly, by means of the iCaution device and its stores to compose a game story with respect to local traffic or travel, which is for the fun of travelers, and traffic management and control are presented.

Keywords: Smart city · Internet of things · ITS · Near field information · MANET · Real-time information · V2I · Traffic message · Traffic game

1 Introduction

Building a smart city has triggered many essential infrastructure projects around the world. The projects include smart home, smart market, smart health care, smart security system, smart sightseeing & leisure zones, smart water & power provision, and intelligent transportation systems (ITS). All these projects rely heavily on a seamless communication system which plays an important role in a smart city.

This paper firstly will address current available short-range communication and cooperative to long-range technologies (4G) for the services. Secondly, under prevailing roadside traffic management and control devices, an iCaution device equipped along roadsides will be proposed. The device functions to deliver local traffic messages, particularly those related to emergency events, broadcasted directly to nearby/coming mobile phones. Thirdly, by means of iCaution device and local stores to compose a game story with respect to local traffic or travel situation, which is for the fun of travelers and for traffic management and control will be presented.

In summary, the architecture of iCaution and traffic game system as service for travelers/road users will be depicted. Some feasible cases will be demonstrated.

© Springer International Publishing AG 2016
C.-H. Hsu et al. (Eds.): IOV 2016, LNCS 10036, pp. 82–90, 2016.
DOI: 10.1007/978-3-319-51969-2_7

2   Communication Technology

To successfully implement a smart city, selecting a proper communication technology that is inexpensive and commonly shared/owned is essential. Although 3G and 4G mobile systems are in service, they are insufficient for the demands required in a smart city, particularly for the applications related to internet of things (IOT) and intelligent Transportation Systems (ITS) like V2I/V2V. We especially concern that 3G/4G still cannot *directly* link between/among handsets, car onboard devices, roadside units as well as indoor facilities. This leads to the need for an ad hoc network to fulfill the gap, particularly for social networking. A Near Field Informatics (N-Fi) system is presented to compensate for the communication gap. To accomplish the N-Fi system, a VIP net is introduced herein. The letters V, I, and P denote Vehicles, Infrastructure, and Person/People, respectively. "Infrastructure" could be roadside units (such as traffic signal controllers (TSC), changeable message signs (CMS), toll gates, bus stops, convenience shops, schools, and public building facilities, (see Fig. 1) [1–3].

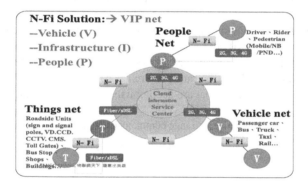

Fig. 1. The concept of VIP net

Considering direct linkage with the ad hoc networking from application standpoint, the most difficult situation is providing services for moving objects (cars and/or people). Obviously, it should be implemented through wireless techniques with quick access/connect characteristics, should be easy to carry or install, and have common protocols and be inexpensive. Considering the system to concurrently support static objects and moving objects, MONET conversion to VANET is studied, where VANET is built for communication among vehicles and roadside units and drives informatics that satisfy travelers' demands (information on demand, IOD).

In this domain, Japan's VICS (Vehicle Information and Communication System) [4] successfully applies beacon technology (2.4 GHz microwave signals for expressways and infrared for local streets) and NHK FM subcarrier signals for traffic information transmission. The USA's VII (Vehicle Infrastructure Integration) [5, 6] proposes a frequency of 5.9 GHz applying the IEEE 802.11p protocol for communication among vehicles (V2V) and infrastructure (V2I). Europe's SAFESPOT [7, 8] also includes development for V2V and V2I. However, these propositions represent a barrier to international marketing due to the lack of portability, not sharing common frameworks, and not being easily affordable (e.g. without any additional charges to users).

Some short-range technologies where IEEE 802.11.x, IEEE 802.15.x, and RFID are used the most currently, and are applied in Near Field Informatics (N-Fi) services and may have potential if they are applied to ad hoc networking.

IEEE 802.11x is widely used for electronic devices such as WiFi devices (IEEE 802.11a,b,g,n). Almost all personal handsets are equipped with WiFi. Many cities in the world offer free service in public sites such as airports, public transportation stations, and social activity squares. Then, one can easily access the Internet or other network to obtain information or perform their business online. However, it is difficult to obtain WiFi service when one is moving above 20~30 km per hour (kph). The IEEE 802.15.x protocol generally built-in personal handsets is Bluetooth (IEEE 802.15.1), and now most auxiliary positioning devices are accomplished by Bluetooth, like i-beacon. Another IEEE 802.15.x is Zigbee (IEEE 802.15.4). Bluetooth has a 1~2 Mbps transfer rate, but Zigbee has only 250 Kbps. Nevertheless, Zigbee enables to push messages available for high speed moving carriers due to that authentication process is unnecessary. Sub1Giga (Sub1G) is also developed for low rate transmission, like LoRa (433, 866, 915 MHz), for IOT. Passive RFID is also currently popular for very short-range conditions, approximately 10 cm or less, such as for contactless tickets or door-keys. Extending passive RFID's reader power allows detection of the tags mounted on high speed vehicles, which the detection range can reach 10~15 m. Active two-way RFID is utilized for ranges of 10–100 m that are accomplished using Zigbee (see Table 1).

Table 1. Short range comm. tech and attributes

	Bluetooth	ZigBee/ Sub1G (LoRa)	Wi-Fi	RFID
Moving constraint	<5 kph	50~100 kph	<30 kph	30~80 kph
Service range	10~100 m	10~1000 m	10~100 m	<10 m
Connection speed	5~10 s	<1 s	1~10 s	<1 s
Bandwith	~1 Mbps	250 Kbps	>1 Mbps	–
Transmission	Two ways	Two ways	Two ways	One way
Handset	Build-in	Extra	Build-in	Extra (eTag-like)

Synthetically, due to handset build-in, WiFi and Bluetooth is the most potential technologies for ad hoc social networking and large message packets delivery. Therefore, a tightly (and perhaps even loosely) coupled network using Zigbee, WiFi, and/or Bluetooth has its potential selected in N-Fi.

3   Near-Field Informatics

N-Fi is the acronym for the Near Field Informatics domain that utilizes the combined chips of Zigbee/WiFi/Bluetooth as the ad hoc basis for VIP link, particularly for social networking. They all operate at 2.4 GHz. Figure 2 illustrates the N-Fi topology for the proposed implementation. It connects four layers including Vehicles (Occupants) and/or Driver/Travelers, Roadside Units (RSU), Cloud Operational Center, and Web Users. The structure supports and is consistent with the VANET framework.

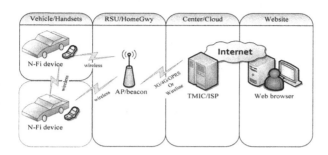

Fig. 2. N-Fi simplified topology

Basically equipped with a N-Fi module (using Zigbee, WiFi and/or Bluetooth) in vehicles' onboard units or mounted to handsets (mobile phones), the Zigbee mode drives short messages and the WiFi/Bluetooth modes drive transferring messages, file or picture, depending on what field of applications would be. In the example application case of ITS, the equipped RSU receives all nearby OBUs and/or Handsets' identification (ID) and then sends its own SSID and information related to a vehicle's passing time and local speed to the operational center. The operational center stores and processes all the messages (data). The center may issue predicted traffic information through XML to web pages and OBUs via RSU. In N-Fi, the applied protocol is guided by and follows the NTCIP (National Transportation Communication for ITS Protocol) [9]. Due to the different networks and their different maximum transmission units (MTU), all packets will be regrouped before transmitting. To avoid errors occurring when regrouping, a formatting protocol for transmitting packets is applied.

The scenarios described above activate between/among mobile phones or similar devices that are equipped with N-Fi APP.

4   iCaution System Architecture

The iCaution's system architecture is depicted in Fig. 3, where,

1. N-Fi's roadside unit (RSU) and mobile APP: By WiFi/Bluetooth AP transmission, road users get traffic information (including traffic sign, signal, marking, guidance, etc.), emergency messages and location-based services through mobile APP from RSU (Fig. 4(a)); by 4G, road users get overall status, prediction trends and statistics from Cloud (Fig. 4(b)). Shown in Fig. 4(a), WiFi/Bluetooth AP act as message-code broadcasters, but in Fig. 4(b), they act as beacons, all with MAC/SSID identifier. The latter messages are pushed by 4G to mobiles. However, this can work alone without connecting without Cloud linking.

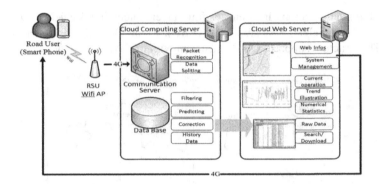

Fig. 3. System architecture

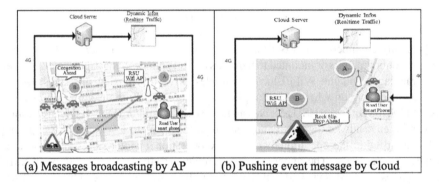

| (a) Messages broadcasting by AP | (b) Pushing event message by Cloud |

Fig. 4. Message transmission

2. Cloud computing server: On account of the collected traffic raw data (Mac code) from the WiFi/Bluetooth equipped in RSU, the cloud server executes numerical analysis and trend prediction, and provides the results to the web server.
3. Cloud web server: Present overall status, prediction trends, statistics, etc. This also works for registered members. They can access and get other services.

In fact, the iCaution system not only transmits traffic message but also delivers general living messages, like food, store, coupons etc.

5   Traffic Game

The following aims at developing a game related to traffic on the base of transportation/ traffic devices, events, as well as surroundings. The system is linking to ITS applications successive in 'Smart Phone System', 'Internet of Things', and Telematics. The implementation is a pioneer work in the world, which not only improves traffic management but also creates new business opportunities.

Wireless communication technology has been upgraded and/or improved for three and/or four generations. Due to the popularity of smart phones, information exchangeability and flows are speedy up at any time and any site. However, commercialized contents are too monotonic for moving objects (vehicles and persons) to support traveler demands, particularly hard to attract the youth. In addition, that online games in web attracts young people to stay in house all the time and causes many healthy problems. Therefore, this stimulates an innovative thinking to link games with traffic.

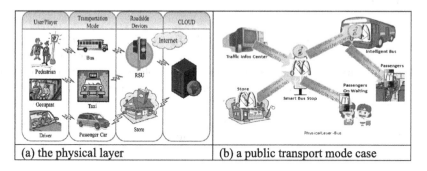

| (a) the physical layer | (b) a public transport mode case |

Fig. 5. Operational units

In the past, traffic management and transportation service provides a monotonic scope. The service does not follow current trend of ICT which attracts young people in styles. Herein, through a game activity may attract them to change their behavior of modal choice, route selection, etc. In addition, developing traffic games can break out business barrier of traffic and online games. Meanwhile, with VIP-net, the traffic game is an innovative domain of activity. The objective is to improve industries extensive, business spirited, and make ITS more active/alive.

1. Operational Units (Fig. 5)
   (1) Cloud operation center (OPC): OPC handles all activities with respect to handsets and RSUs or stores/pos connection, game mission assignment, game flow control, competition strategy, relative traffic control logic, business operation, player's account management.
   (2) Onboard unit (OBU): OBUs on buses/transits or taxicabs act as positioning or offering certificates for players, message transferring or broadcasting, merchant DM delivering, etc.
   (3) Roadside Unit (RSU): RSUs such as bus stops, CCTV, CMS, traffic signal controllers and sign plates with N-Fi module can act as positioning or offering certificates for players, message transferring or broadcasting, merchant DM delivering, etc.
   (4) Store: All stores in the alliance (franchise) can be equipped with a laptop with operating package software linking to OPC, and providing services for players. They also act as positioning or offering certificates for players, message transferring or broad-casting, merchant delivering and exchanging etc.
   (5) Player: Players should download traffic game APP, register an account, e-money, coupons…

2. Stories

   A traffic game can be edited like a monopoly game, a story conjunct to history, novel or fiction in reality of sites, to fit different grades of age, gender, or local custom... etc. A story has its purpose and function, some for traffic management (route guidance), some for local economics (e-commence), some for human health (outdoor sports) and so forth.

3. Rules example

   A game has its designed deal rule or bargain, for examples: Reward points or eco-money to travelers (1) by green levels of service (like road pricing), or the number of encountering traffic signal or equipped message pole/beacon in a route, each pole can be set by different points, different time slot; (2) if taking a certain route certain bus, or being in a play, a scenario; (3) Traffic signal timing can be on a voucher (rewarded by his/her local contribution) or eco-money to actuate, even extend a fighting scheme, particularly in a sightseeing/tourism county/zone.

4. Cases

   (1) BRT signal priority: A traffic game can be built in the logic of BRT signal priority (TSP) system. Passengers can use specific BRT APP to vote traffic signal timings and earn a voucher if avoid a certain red light in his/her trip. This way can attract people to use public transportation modes.

   (2) Route guidance in a game: Advanced Driver Information Systems are developed since the emergence of smart phones. People need a better path planning results and a shorter computing time. In the past, most of path planning systems and their related theories' development based on shortest path and shortest travel time and take these factors as a target. But in some cases like scenic areas, people may not regard these as the most important factors. We put a scenario

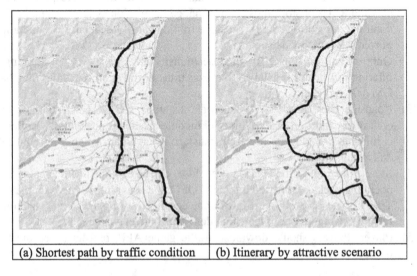

| (a) Shortest path by traffic condition | (b) Itinerary by attractive scenario |

Fig. 6. Travel paths comparison between traffic parameter and scenic parameter

game story with e-commerce parameters practicing by A*algorithm to generate out different outputs of itinerary. (Fig. 6).

(3) Traffic Control with a game: Assumed that to replace loop detectors/radar detectors by mobile phone detectors for vehicle detection, traffic signal timing and split will be computed on human-based logic. In addition, if approaching mobile phones can send their eco-money or points or gentle/age for requesting green phase and timing, the system will become very active, almost over-whelming traditional logic. Therefore, the factors in traffic management will be considered not only of stop, delay, pollution, but also such as consumers' inter-esting items or game intents. This could be considered as "The 5th generation of transportation technology". Transportation circumstance/field turns become mixed use, multi-function roles.

6   Conclusion

This paper describes how to build iCaution and traffic game in transportation fields. The important condition is about communication technology compatibility with popularly owned devices, particularly compatible with communication protocols already built-in to mobile phones. Obviously, WiFi and Bluetooth are definitely feasible for this purpose.

The iCaution is used for performing emergent transmission of traffic messages directly from RSU to nearby approaching mobile phones. In fact, this technical platform can work with other business in together. This study finally proposes traffic game considered in this platform to alter traditional logic be active. Some cases about traffic games such as BRT, route guidance and traffic control are depicted.

Acknowledgement. This paper is digested from the report of Traffic Game Research Project sponsored by the Ministry of Science and Technology (MOST), Taiwan (MOST 103-2221-E-002-145-MY3.)

References

1. Chang, T.H.: The Revolution of ITS—Introduction to PVT-net with N-Fi Technology, an IOT/ Telematics System. In: International Symposium on ITS Research, National Taiwan University, Taipei, Taiwan, June 2011
2. Chang, T.H., Yang, L.K. Tsai, J.J.: A Telematic builder for V2V and V2I via N-Fi system. In: 19th World Congress on ITS, Vienna, Austria, 22–26 October 2012
3. Chang, T.H.: Near field informatics with a PVT-net building up seamless life. In: 14th International Conference on Computing in Civil and Building Engineering, Moscow, 27–29 June 2012
4. How VICS Works: VICS Web Site. http://www.vics.or.jp/english/vics/index.html
5. VII Architecture and Functional Requirements, ITS Joint Program Office, US Department of Transportation, 20 July 2005
6. From VII to IntelliDrive. http://www.its.dot.gov/press/2010/vii2intelli-drive.htm

7. Brignolo, R.: Co-operative Road Safety - The SAFESPOT Integrated Project, Vienna, 12 May 2006
8. SAFESPOT - Co-operative systems for road safety 'smart vehicles on smart roads'. (n.d.). www.safespot-eu.org/. Accessed June 2008
9. AASHTO, ITE, NEMA. The NTCIP Guide. NTCIP 9001 v.03.02, October 2002

An Avoiding Obstacles Method of Multi-rotor UAVs

Shouzhi Xu[1], Yuan Cheng[1], Huan Zhou[1(✉)],
Chungming Huang[2], and Zhiyong Huang[1]

[1] College of Computer and Information Technology,
China Three Gorges University, Yichang, China
zhouhuan117@gmail.com
[2] Computer Science and Information Engineering,
National Cheng Kung University, Tainan, Taiwan

Abstract. As UAVs (Unmanned Aerial Vehicle) being widely used in remote sensing of agriculture resources and many other areas, the security of UAVs flying at a low altitude is getting more and more serious. This paper studies on the problem of obstacle avoidance while the UAV cruises at low altitude for agriculture sensing. Two kinds of obstacles are taken into account. A rapid obstacle-avoidance algorithm with adding a compensation waypoint is proposed for the avoidance of static obstacles; and a real-time method with dynamic information of navigation status and flying control sequence is proposed for tackling dynamic obstacles. Based on the sharing obstacle avoidance information, UAVs optimize their flight paths dynamically. Simulation results show that UAVs can avoid both static and dynamic kinds of obstacles quickly and their heading angles have a good convergence effect after flying over obstacles which can save much more energy for UAVs.

Keywords: UAV · Obstacle avoidance problem · Compensation waypoint

1 Introduction

UAV (Unmanned Aerial Vehicle) has attracted more and more attention from researchers in wide areas. The flight of UAVs can be controlled either autonomously by onboard computers or by the remote controller of a pilot on the ground or in a moving vehicle [1]. In the past, UAV technology is mainly used for military, but the technology is increasingly used in civil applications now, such as remote sensing of agriculture resources, agriculture producing work and many other fields [2]. For example, Joao Valente has analyzed the weed coverage rate of maize field using UAV carried with near infrared multispectral camera [3].

When UAVs are cruising in the same airspace, the overlap of time and space will happen in flight path of an UAV with the complexity of the task and the increasing number of UAVs. It brings interference or even collisions in the airspace, especially in the field of massive flight operation for precision agriculture [4]. Cruising in the limited area may encounter two types of obstacles: One is fixed facilities or static obstacles such as buildings in the airspace; the other one is the dynamic obstacles of moving UVAs. Actually, several methods have been proposed to avoid obstacles for UAVs. A method of avoiding obstacles

© Springer International Publishing AG 2016
C.-H. Hsu et al. (Eds.): IOV 2016, LNCS 10036, pp. 91–103, 2016.
DOI: 10.1007/978-3-319-51969-2_8

was based on Dubins path [5]. When UAVs are flying at different altitudes, the selection of Dubins paths is very complicated, and the requested condition is also very strict. Combined with height information of the terrain, a genetic algorithm was proposed to avoid the threat of terrain factors (such as mountains) in [6], and an algorithm based on the shortest path was proposed to avoid the known obstacles in [7]. However, these mentioned methods do not take into account the special circumstances of other UAVs in the same area. It is very important to control the UAVs formation to make flight stable [8]. Although the UAVs cooperative flight has been well studied, the application of the flight obstacle avoidance problem is still lack of investigation [9]. An UAV obstacle avoidance method is proposed with potential filed under dynamic environment [10], but the method needed much more calculation on the Khatib's potential function. Path planning for obstacle avoidance boils is converted down to gamma (flight path angle) tracking and vehicle velocity tracking problems in [11], which needed the high real-time performance of tracking algorithm. It is not practical to apply these algorithms on UAV with limited computing resource. According to the specific application background, avoiding obstacles has become an urgent problem to be studied when UVAs cruise in the limited space across which there are crops planting area and signal towers. Compared to other kind of UAVs, UAVs with multiple rotors have wider applications and can adapt to various flight tasks in precision agriculture [12]. Therefore, in this paper, we focus on investigating the obstacle avoidance problem based on the multi-rotorcraft UAV.

The remainder of the paper is organized as follow: a model is designed to avoid static obstacles firstly. Then a real-time method with dynamic information of navigation status and flying control sequence is proposed for tackling dynamic obstacles. Simulation test for both static obstacles and dynamic obstacles is analyzed subsequently.

2   Obstacles Avoidance Algorithms

During the cruising, UAVs need to do online path planning continually to adapt to the current environment because of obstacles in the indefinite field. For the prevention of crash among UAVs, the non-cooperative visual sensor can be used, because UAVs use their own measurement values without any means of communication [13]. The visual sensor is suitable to monitor the obstacle that occurs abruptly and avoid accidents owing to the slight weight, the small volume and the non-cooperative mode.

2.1   Flight Path Planning for Static Obstacles Avoidance

UAV is considered as a dot with some weight in this paper. When UAVs detect a certain size of static obstacles ahead by visual sensor, they will change attitude to avoid the collisions according to the safe circle or the obstacle circle in Fig. 1. As shown in Fig. 1(a), the center of a circle is the current location of a UAV, and R_s is the radius of the circle. UAVs can fly without limit in this area. The obstacle circle in Fig. 1(b) shows that the obstacle is considered as the circle solid with the radius of R_o and the circular area with the width of ΔR ($\Delta R = R_s - R_o$), which is considered as a buffer of the obstacle circle. If the UAV does not adjust to enter the buffer zone timely, the alarm index of avoiding collisions should be improved, and adjustments of the attitude and the flight path should be carried out rapidly. If obstacles exist in the trajectory of the UAV, the path planner will modify the flight route in [14].

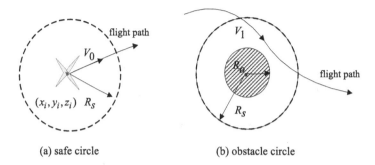

(a) safe circle   (b) obstacle circle

Fig. 1. Safe circle and obstacle circle of UAV

According to constraints of the available flying, the reference path can be generated to avoid obstacles.

In the specific design of obstacle avoidance, a flyable path can be acquired based on the attitude point of UAV or the point for the flight path. The path planner will program the flight route quickly by adding compensational points.

As shown in Fig. 2, UAV flies from A to B. The shade of the circle is obstacle, S_1 is the original path. Obstacle will be detected in the process. Then an algorithm is designed as follows with the fly-time and driving security being taken into account.

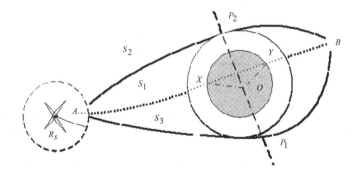

Fig. 2. Compensational points for obstacles avoidance

Step 1: Calculate the locations of points X and Y in Fig. 2. These two intersections are generated while the original path was stretched across the obstacle circle;

Step 2: X and Y are in straight line and the perpendicular bisector of the straight line is made at the same time. The perpendicular bisector, which is shown as the imaginary line in Fig. 3, passes the center and intersects the obstacle circle at P_1 and P_2, which are named safe compensation points;

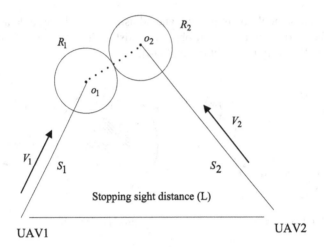

Fig. 3. Model for collision avoidance in the dynamic environment

Step 3: The lengths of A-P_1-B and A-P_2-B are calculated respectively and defined as S(A-P_1-B) and S(A-P_2-B);

Step 4: If the value of S(A-P_1-B) is less than S(A-P_2-B), then choose P_1 as the compensation point. Otherwise, choose P_2.

Providing that the converged point between AB and P_1P_2 are chosen as the origin of coordinates, the direction of A to B are regarded as X-axis, and the direction of P_1 to P_2 as Y-axis. Then related coordinate points are A($-x_1$,0), O(0,0), B(x_2,0), P_1(0, $y_0 - R_s$), P_2(0,$y_0 + R_s$). The equations are set up as follows

$$\begin{cases} t_1 = (\sqrt{x_1^2 + (y_0 + R_s)^2} + \sqrt{x_2^2 + (y_0 + R_s)^2})/V_0 \\ t_2 = (\sqrt{x_1^2 + (y_0 - R_s)^2} + \sqrt{x_2^2 + (y_0 - R_s)^2})/V_0 \end{cases} \quad (1)$$

The front arithmetic forecasts that S_2 and S_3 are the safe and optimal routes passing P_2 and P_1 respectively. Then t_1 and t_2 are compared to choose which compensation waypoint is the best one.

After UAV flies over the obstacle, the location of the obstacle is recorded. As a result, the obstacle locations in the flying fields for troop of UAVs are acquired. Then other UAVs can avoid the obstacle automatically.

2.2   Flight Path Planning for Dynamic Obstacles Avoidance

In contrast to the static obstacle, this part mainly describes how to avoid the dynamic obstacles, namely, the other flying UAVs in mission of the precision agriculture. The entire conditions of multiple UAVs and the collision of every two UAVs in local conditions must be taken into account. Figure 3 shows the geometric shape of collision avoidance. UAV_1 is in the distance of L to UAV_2 with the different direction. These UAVs are flying at different rates with V_1 and V_2. The radius of the safe circle is R_1 and another is R_2. If the closest distance between the two UAVs is less than the sum of R_1 and R_2, then the path will be dangerous and measures must be taken swiftly to avoid the obstacle. On the contrary, the flight path is safe.

As for UAV_i, the feature of platform can be described with the kinematic model consists of continuous time-dots [15], which can be expressed as:

$$\begin{cases} X_i = V_i \cos \phi \\ Y_i = V_i \sin \phi \\ \phi = \omega_i \cdot \eta_{max} \end{cases} \tag{2}$$

where the coordinate (X_i, Y_i) is UAV's location in the search plane, ϕ is the yaw angle, V_i is the rate, η_{max} is the maximum turn rate, and ω_i is the change rate of the angular velocity. Furthermore, the status of UAV_i can be described as:

$$T_i(k) = \left[X_i(k), Y_i(k), \phi_i(k)\right]^T (k = 0, 1, 2, \ldots) \tag{3}$$

$$S_i(k) = \left[V_i(k), \omega_i(k)\right]^T (k = 0, 1, 2, \ldots) \tag{4}$$

Equation 3 describes the condition of the UAV at time k. The condition includes the location state and the yaw angle state. Equation 4 describes the track-control input of the UAV, including the adjustment of direction and rate. In order to ensure UAV safety, information and distributed cooperation must be shared with each other in real time.

Before the coordination optimization with control and state sequences, UAVs need to take a rough estimate in order to generate a reference path. According to the location of UAV at time k, the distance to the target point of UAV_i is $D(k)$, which is expressed as follows:

$$D(k) = \sqrt{(x_g(k) - x_s(k))^2 + (y_g(k) - y_s(k))^2} \tag{5}$$

$(x_g(k), y_g(k))$ is the coordinates of the target point, $(x_s(k), y_s(k))$ is the coordinates of the current point. We use $S_D(k)$ to denote the sum distance for which multiple UAVs fly to the target point, which can expressed as:

$$S_D(k) = \sum_{i=1}^{n} D_i(k) \tag{6}$$

According to the distance from a starting point to a target point, an expense of time can be evaluated.

$$T_i(k) = T_0 + D_i(k)/V_i(k) \tag{7}$$

$$S_T(k) = \max\{T_i(k)\} \ (i = 1, 2, \dots, n). \tag{8}$$

Equation 7 describes the total flight time from the starting point to a target point of UAV$_i$. T_0 is the flight time from the starting point to the current point. Then under the current decision, the flight time of multiple UAVs, which is named as $S_T(k)$ can be estimated using Eq. 8.

$$C(k) = \alpha * S_D(k) + \beta * S_T(k) \tag{9}$$

In conclusion, $C(k)$ in Eq. 9 is the comprehensive evaluation index which directs UAVs to generate optimized trajectories. Here, α and β are the corresponding weighted coefficients.

The algorithm for collision avoidance between the two dynamic UAVs is illustrated as follows:

Step 1: The current status is acquired. The UAV gets and calculates the status parameters with the information of sensors;

Step 2: The future status are predicted. Based on the current condition $T_i(k)$ and the control parameters, UAV can predict the location in the period of Δt time, and get the predicted information within the scale time of $[k, k + t-1]$;

Step 3: The information is shared. The front UAV will broadcast information to others that are predicted using their own platforms. At the same time, the control center receives the condition and predicts information rapidly, then gives an analysis;

Step 4: Path planner optimizes the results continuously according to the following processes. The obstacle-avoidance problem needs to be decided and optimized continuously [16]. Based on the fundamental mind of optimizing and getting results continuously, the state sequences and path control sequences which belong to the UAV$_i$ are as follows:

$$P_i \cong [T_i(k)^T, T_i(k + 1)^T, \cdots, T_i(k + t - 1)^T]^T \tag{10}$$

$$Q_i \cong [S_i(k)^T, S_i(k + 1)^T, \cdots, S_i(k + t - 1)^T]^T \tag{11}$$

At the same time, the common particle swarm algorithm [17] is used to generateflight paths of multiple UAVs. The method of finding flight path can expand the navigation covering area of UAV and improve efficiency of working. UAVs keep uniform speed and turning under the condition of a small curvature. As any UAVs should save energy in the limited time, it is an efficient way to make less off-course from the original route as far as possible. For a minimum cost of a track adjustment, the yaw angle rate $\Delta\phi$ was introduced. ϕ_k is the yaw angle at time point k shown as

$$\begin{cases} \phi_k = \dfrac{y_i(k + 1) - y_i(k)}{x_i(k + 1) - x_i(k)} \\ \phi_{k+1} = \dfrac{y_i(k + 2) - y_i(k + 1)}{x_i(k + 2) - x_i(k + 1)} \end{cases} \tag{12}$$

Then the yaw angle at time point $k + 1$ can be deduced as ϕ_{k+1}. There would be the change of the yaw angle rate which is defined as $\Delta\phi_i(k + 1)$, as it is $\Delta\phi_i(k + 1) = \phi_{k+1} - \phi_k$;

Step 1: After getting status information, UAVs take the aforementioned method to solve the problem of local optimization control independently. It is searching for input sequence Q_i of control optimization;

Step 2: Information sharing is the key step. One UAV sends its input sequence Q_i to the other subsystems and receives control inputs from other UAVs at the same time;

Step 3: The forecast information is updated constantly;

Step 4: If the relative distance between two UAVs satisfies $R_i + R_j \leq d_{i-j}$. So,

$$R_i + R_j \leq \sqrt{(y_i(k + n) - y_j(k + n))^2 + (x_i(k + n) - x_j(k + n))^2},$$ where n is any real

number, and $\Delta\phi_i(k + 1)$ become small as time is increasing, then calculation is terminated, turn to Step 5: Otherwise, it turns to Step 1 that can solve the local optimization problem;

Step 5: The optimal tracking control input sequence is adopted to calculate the current target path and update the sequence P_i according to the current value of P_i;

Step 6: For $k = k+1$, return to the Step 2.

Shared information of UAVs depends on the stable and rapid network communication [18]. If a crisis happened in the situation such as communication interrupt, the pause time is inserted because it is the simplest coordination strategy. Namely one drone continues flying along the path planning, the other is hovering in situ. The two UAVs can be restored to move on until no path conflict exists.

3   Simulation and Analysis

In order to verify the effectiveness of the control model and algorithm with control strategy, extensive simulation experiments are carried out in the section. The process of cruise operation is based on the avoidance of static obstacles and dynamic obstacles. Simulation experimental platform is MATLAB 2012b under the Windows 7 operating system.

3.1   Static Obstacle Simulation Test

Assuming the experimental scenario is specified in the 5 km * 5 km area, which is shown in Fig. 4. The flight speed of UAV is controlled in the range of 0 to 20 m/s, and the initial flight speed is set to 20 m/s. The dotted line represents the flight track.

In this experiment, the UAV flys to the experiment point $(0, 0)$ in the two-dimensional coordinates, there is an obstacle with coordinate $(300, 400)$ with danger radius of 40 m on the planned route. UAVs need to bypass static obstacle objects by adding track compensation point fast. As a compensation point (x_0, y_0) is on the perpendicular bisector, the location coordinate meets $(x_0 - 300)^2 + (y_0 - 400)^2 = 40^2$.

In order to avoid static obstacles, the flight path is determined by calculating the distance of the UAV from point $(0, 0)$ to the compensation point. The UAV can avoid the obstacle by adding the compensation point and using the ant colony algorithm which

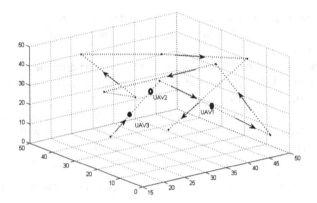

Fig. 4. Three-dimensional space operation of UAV

has been considered as complex algorithm in [19]. The response curve of the yaw angle can be analyzed, as shown in Fig. 5. The unmarked curve is a barrier to the sudden detection of obstacles in the absence of human navigation, and the UAV platform makes a yaw response quickly by adding the compensation waypoint. The curve of the marked line is a complex calculation method. However, its response to the detection of obstacles is slow, and the degree of yaw response with adding compensation is greater than the complex algorithm. It is known that long response time and the greater degree of adverse yaw will make more harmful to the UAV platform.

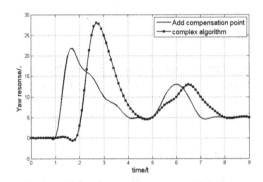

Fig. 5. The response curve of yaw after detecting obstacles

If there are many UAVs in this area for which an example is shown in Fig. 6, UAV_1 can communicate with other UAVs through the network. Then UAV2, UAV3 and other related UAVs get the static obstacle location coordinates. It can help other UAVs to reduce the calculation process of obstacles. Figure 6 shows the location of the three drones along fixed paths.

Figure 7 shows experiments structure which multiple UAVs avoid the static obstacles along a fixed path. There is the initial relative position at a particular time and the corresponding distance between each other, such as UAV_1 and UAV_2, UAV_2 and UAV_3, UAV_1

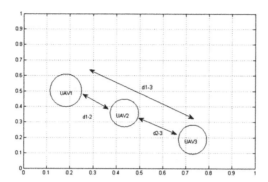

Fig. 6. Position of the three aircraft in fixed route

and UAV_3 is 600 m. The relative distance of UAV_1 and UVA_2 is defined as d_{1-2}, UAV_2 and UAV_3 defined as d_{2-3}. In the time series $(t_1, t_2, \cdots, t_n)$, d_{1-2} with the time of collection is $((t_1, d_1), (t_2, d_2), \cdots, (t_n, d_n))$, d_{2-3} with corresponding time is $((t_1, d_1^*), (t_2, d_2^*), \cdots, (t_n, d_n^*))$, d_{1-3} is $((t_1, d_1 + d_1^*), (t_2, d_2 + d_2^*), \cdots, (t_n, d_n + d_n^*))$ accordingly.

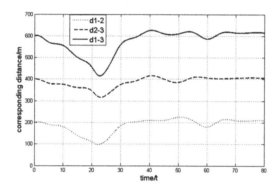

Fig. 7. The curve of the relative distance between multiple UAVs

Time of experiment is set up as 10 s. As shown in Fig. 7, UAV_1 finds there is a static obstacle ahead through distance sensor. The relative distance between three drones begins to decrease, and reaches the minimum time about 21 s. UAVs begin to speed up after flying over the obstacles, the separation between each other expands gradually. The relative position between the three drones tends to be stable as time goes by, these status conform to the fleet of the overall flow characteristics in [20].

3.2 Dynamic Obstacle Simulation Test

This test is set to avoid dynamic obstacles, which need to control mutual restrictions of the dynamic obstacles. In a short period of time, there is a demand for a collision between UAV and others to facilitate the rapid verification of results. The initial position of the multi UAV is shown in Fig. 8, the relative distance between these three UAVs are 500 m, 400 m and 300 m.

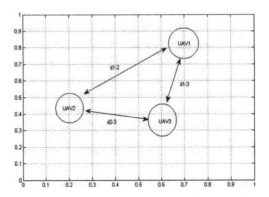

Fig. 8. Sketch maps of three UAVs along the dynamic path

The safe radius of multiple UAVs which was defined for avoidance dynamic obstacles is 30 m, the interval time of the discrete sample is 0.2 s, the interval time of the multiple UAVs are 1 s, the period time is $T = 20$ s, so the prediction step is $n = T/\Delta t$. In the process of local optimization, the general Particle Swarm Optimizer algorithm is used to improve speed of solving [21]. The location of UAVs at time k and optimal path which have been traversed can be record, the distance between each other which named the adaptive value. According to the distance and location of UAVs, the new state solution can appear under the action of each other. It is assumed that the UAV_1 flown in accordance with the prior generation path, the flight paths of UAV_2 and UAV_1in conflicts. If UAV_1 and UAV_2 do not adjust to the trajectory, there will come to a collision.

In this setting, UAV_1 does not need to change the heading angle, and UAV_2 is adjusted to the yaw angle relative to UAV_1. The three UAVs could communicate with each other. Above all, the simulation assumes that there is no delay in the communication link, and every UAV can receive the information of the other UAV in real time. It is necessary to refer that the selection of geographic coordinate system is flexible and the scale range of the course angle is associated with various missions in precision agriculture [22].

The simulation results are shown in Figs. 9 and 10. The heading angle of multiple UAVs and the relative distance of them are described as follows. The corresponding distances between each other are 600 m, 550 m and 500 m. The initial heading angles are 50°, 0°, and 100° because of many tasks need large angle change in precision agriculture. The whole process of simulation is set to 30 s. It is tested to avoid obstacles in short time. The dotted line in Fig. 10 represents the heading angle of UAV_3, and the solid line represents the heading angle of UAV_2. The line parallels with time axis shows the drone security radius are d_{1-2}, d_{2-3} and d_{1-3} respectively. The distance between each other is larger than the safe radius of UAVs. The relative distances between multiple UAVs are gradually smaller when the heading angle tends to the same. The relative distances between UAVs are gradually enlarged when the course angle deviates. It ensures that no collision between these UAVs

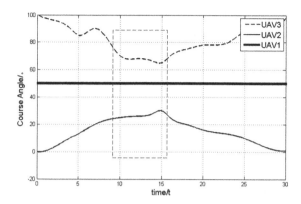

Fig. 9. The variation curve of the heading angle

during the 10 s and 15 s. At the same time, the cross angles with UAV_2 and UAV_3 are stable. Meanwhile, the consumption of energy is the minimum during the whole process of path planning.

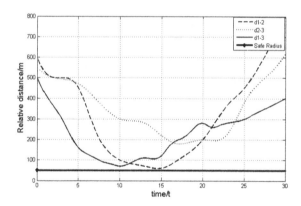

Fig. 10. Relative positions of multiple UAVs along the dynamic path

4   Conclusion

This paper has investigated the obstacle avoidance problem while multiple UAVs are flying for agriculture sensing in a limited space. For the static obstacles, a rapid obstacle-avoidance algorithm with adding a compensation waypoint is proposed. The proposed method has a fast response in detecting obstacle because of light computational load about control center. For the dynamic obstacles, a real-time method with dynamic information of navigation status and flying control sequence is proposed. Based on the sharing obstacle-avoidance information, UAVs optimize their flight paths dynamically. Extensive simulation results show that the proposed methods have a good effect on the avoidance of these two types of obstacles. The proposed method can help to solve obstacle-avoidance problems in UAVs' flying work at a low altitude in precision agriculture.

Acknowledgement. This research was supported in part by Natural Science Foundation of China (61174177 and 41172298), National Technology R&D Program (2013AA10230207) and BRCAST-KFKT2014001.

References

1. Liu, W., Zheng, Z., Cai, K.: Adaptive path planning for unmanned aerial vehicles based on bi-level programming and variable planning time interval. Chin. J. Aeronaut. **26**(3), 646–666 (2013)
2. Gómez-Candón, D., Virlet, N., Costes, E., et al.: UAV thermal imagery contribution to high throughput field phenotyping of apple tree hybrid population and characterization of genotypic response to water stress. In: Plant Biology Europe FESPB/EPSO Congress, p. 2014 (2014)
3. Valente, J., Del Cerro, J., Barrientos, A., et al.: Aerial coverage optimization in precision agriculture management: A musical harmony inspired approach. Comput. Electron. Agric. **99**, 153–159 (2013)
4. Gallagher, K., Lawrence, P.: Unmanned systems and managing from above: the practical implications of UAVs for research applications addressing urban sustainability. In: Gatrell, J.D., Jensen, R.R., Patterson, M.W., Hoalst-Pullen, N. (eds.). GE, vol. 14, pp. 217–232. Springer, Heidelberg (2016). doi:10.1007/978-3-319-26218-5_14
5. Fossen, T., Pettersen, K.Y., Galeazzi, R.: Line-of-sight path following for Dubins paths with adaptive sideslip compensation of drift forces. IEEE Trans. Control Syst. Technol. **23**(2), 820–827 (2015)
6. Peng, Z., Li, B., Chen, X., et al.: Online route planning for UAV based on model predictive control and particle swarm optimization algorithm. In: Proceedings of the 10th World Congress on Intelligent Control and Automation (WCICA), pp. 397–401 (2012)
7. Wang, Y., Han, S., Deng, B.: UAV route planning based on the shortest path. Surveying Mapp. **36**(3), 125–128 (2013)
8. Deng, W., Wang, X., Wang, Y.: Controller design of UAVs formation keep and change. Comput. Simul. **28**(10), 73–77 (2011)
9. Xiang, M., Li, J.Y., Liu, B.: Framework of autonomous cooperative control for multi-UAV team. Electron. Opt. Control **22**(3), 1–6 (2015)
10. Budiyanto, A., Cahyadi, A., Adji, T.B., et al.: UAV obstacle avoidance using potential field under dynamic environment. In: 2015 International Conference on Control, Electronics, Renewable Energy and Communications (ICCEREC), pp. 187–192. IEEE (2015)
11. Arya, S.R., Ashokkumar, C.R., Arya, H.: Gamma and velocity tracking for UAV obstacle avoidance in pitch plane. In: 2016 Indian Control Conference (ICC), pp. 362–368. IEEE (2016)
12. Gao, Q., Yue, F., Hu, D.: Research of stability augmentation hybrid controller for quadrotor UAV. In: Proceedings of the Control and Decision Conference (2014 CCDC), pp. 5224–5229 (2014)
13. Choi, H., Kim, Y., Hwang, I.: Reactive collision avoidance of unmanned aerial vehicles using a single vision sensor. J. Guid. Control Dyn. **36**(4), 1234–1240 (2013)
14. Xargay, E., Dobrokhodov, V., Kaminer, I., et al.: Time-critical cooperative control of multiple autonomous vehicles. IEEE Control Syst. Mag. **32**(5), 49 (2012)
15. Jin, Y., Liao, Y., Minai, A., et al.: Balancing search and target response in cooperative unmanned aerial vehicle (UAV) teams. IEEE Trans. Syst. Man Cybern. B Cybern. **36**(3), 571–587 (2006)

16. Wen, N., Zhao, L., Su, X., et al.: UAV online path planning algorithm in a low altitude dangerous environment. IEEE/CAA J. Automatica Sin. **2**(2), 173–185 (2015)
17. Alejo, D., Cobano, J.A., Heredia, G., et al.: Particle swarm optimization for collision-free 4D trajectory planning in unmanned aerial vehicles. In: Unmanned Aircraft Systems (ICUAS), pp. 298–307 (2013)
18. Peng, H., Huo, M., Liu, Z., et al.: Challenges and technologies for networked multiple UAVs cooperative control. In: IEEE International Conference on Electrical and Control Engineering (ICECE), pp. 3860–3863 (2011)
19. Chen, Y., Su, F., Shen, L.C.: Improved ant colony algorithm base on PRM for UAV route planning. J. Syst. Simul. **21**(6), 1658–1666 (2009)
20. Fan, Q.J., Yang, Z., Fang, T.: Research status of coordinated formation flight control for multi-UAVs. Acta Aeronaut. Astronaut. Sin. **30**, 683–691 (2009)
21. Kennedy, J.: Particle swarm optimization. In: Sammut, C., Webb, G.I. (eds.) Encyclopedia of Machine Learning, pp. 760–766. Springer, Heidelberg (2011)
22. Román, M.O., Gatebe, C.K., Schaaf, C.B., et al.: Variability in surface BRDF at different spatial scales (30 m–500 m) over a mixed agricultural landscape as retrieved from airborne and satellite spectral measurements. Remote Sens. Environ. **115**(9), 2184–2203 (2011)

Protocols, Modeling and Simulations

VTCP: A Clustering Protocol Based on Traffic Flow States for Vehicular Networks

Shi Yan[1(✉)], Lu Changkai[1], Huang Xiaohong[1], Lu Meilian[1],
Qiao Liqiang[1], and Chen Shanzhi[2]

[1] State Key Laboratory of Networking and Switching Technology,
Beijing University of Posts and Telecommunications, Beijing, China
shiyan@bupt.edu.cn
[2] State Key Laboratory of Wireless Mobile Communications,
China Academy of Telecommunications Technology, Beijing, China

Abstract. Clustering is one of the challenging technologies in vehicular networks to decrease data congestion and enhance network scalability. It is believed that the clustering approach most adaptive to the mobility features of the vehicles will achieve best stability performance. In this paper, VTCP (Traffic-based Clustering Protocol for VANETs), a clustering protocol based on traffic flow states, is proposed. It defines different cluster formation and maintenance operations, as well as dynamic transmission range for different traffic flow states. Simulation results show its performance advantages in cluster stability.

Keywords: VTCP · Clustering · Traffic flow state · Vehicular networks

1 Introduction

Vehicular networks, as the important supporting technology for ITS (Intelligent Transportation System), attract more and more research interests in recent years. V2X communications can be provided based on vehicular networks to improve driving security, information services and traffic efficiency [1–3].

Vehicular networks face great challenges due to the special features in mobility, such as high mobility, road layout constrained, frequent topology changes and uneven distribution of vehicles. Clustering is one of the key technologies in vehicular networks to decrease data congestion and enhance network scalability [4–6]. The nodes geographically in proximity are organized into a cluster, in which a cluster head is selected the representative. The cluster head receives data packets from its cluster members and then relays the packets outside (and vice versa) [7].

Cluster stability is the critical performance evaluation metric which depending on the design of the criteria for cluster head selection, cluster formation and cluster

This work is partially funded by the National Science Foundation Projects (Grant No. 61300183 and 61271185) and the National Science Fund for Distinguished Young Scholars (Grant No. 61425012) in China.

C.-H. Hsu et al. (Eds.): IOV 2016, LNCS 10036, pp. 107–119, 2016.
DOI: 10.1007/978-3-319-51969-2_9

maintenance operations. Existing research proposed different clustering solutions for vehicular networks.

In existing research works, many clustering algorithms have been proposed. According to the hops between cluster members and their cluster head nodes, the clustering protocols can be classified into 1-hop formation/1-hop maintenance clustering, 1-hop formation/multi-hop maintenance clustering, as well as multi-hop formation/multi-hop maintenance clustering. Depending on the criteria for head determination, the clustering protocols can be classified into CDS (Connected Dominating Set) clustering based on static graph model, node feature based clustering, micro-mobility based clustering, mobility prediction based clustering and application based clustering.

As we know, the traffic flow states affect the networking parameters directly [8]. Latest progress about three-phase traffic theory [9, 10] in modern traffic engineering divided the traffic states into three phases: free flow, synchronized flow and wide moving jam flow. In our previous work, [11], quantitative analysis of mobility metrics based on three-phase traffic theory were conducted. The mobility metrics about mobility patterns and connectivity performance based on different granularities (e.g., individual nodes, groups and networks) show considerable different regulations under different traffic flow states. Therefore, in this paper, VTCP (Traffic-based Clustering Protocol for VANETs) is proposed, fully taking into account the different traffic flow states. The cluster formation and maintenance strategies in VTCP are designed based on the traffic flow states and state transitions, thus is expected to facilitate adaptive capability under different traffic states.

The rest of this paper is organized as follows. Analysis on features of different traffic flow states and the inspirations we get about clustering operations are presented in Sect. 2. Section 3 introduces the proposed VTCP protocol. Section 4 introduces the simulation environments and quantitative results with necessary discussions. Finally, Sect. 5 concludes this paper.

2 Analysis on Traffic Flow States for Clustering in Vehicular Networks

In order to enable VTCP with the capability to be adaptive to different traffic status, it is primarily important to identify the different traffic flow states and the state transitions, and then different cluster formation and maintenance operations can be designed accordingly. Therefore, in this paper, five states of a vehicle are defined: F (Free Flow), S (Synchronization Flow), J (Jam Flow), $FtoSJ$ (Free Flow transferring to Synchronization Flow or Jam Flow) and $SJtoF$ (Synchronization Flow or Jam Flow transferring to Free Flow). In this section, the mobility features of different states and the inspirations we get about clustering operations in different states are discussed.

2.1 *F* State

In *F* state, the stability in mobility relies greatly on the vehicles' velocity, especially desired velocity. The features in mobility include: no obvious group mobility, short link durations, low node density and serious network partitions.

Accordingly, relative desired velocity between vehicles should be considered in cluster head determination. M_f defines the main cluster head determination criteria for *F* state:

$$M_f = \log \frac{\left\| \overrightarrow{N_i} \right\|}{\sum\limits_{j \in \overrightarrow{N_i}} \Delta v_{i,j,t}} \tag{1}$$

where $\Delta v_{i,j,t} = v_{i,t}^{desired} - v_{j,t}^{desired}$ is the relative desired velocity between i and j, $\left\| \overrightarrow{N_i} \right\|$ is the number of nodes in the neighboring node set with same direction of vehicle i. If there exist the nodes with same M_f value, the node with lower node ID is selected as the cluster head. That is, the tuple defining cluster head determination for *F* state is (M_f, ID).

Cluster maintenance in *F* state should pay more attention to avoid large cluster radius to cope with serious network partitions.

2.2 *S* State

The Mobility of nodes in *S* state depends greatly on the gap distance between vehicles. *S* state presents more obvious group mobility and higher node density than *F* state. Therefore, in cluster head selection, the group relationship between a node and its neighboring nodes should be considered. M_s defines the main cluster head determination criteria for *S* state:

$$M_s = w_1 * \left\| \overrightarrow{N_i} \right\| + w_2 * M_f \tag{2}$$

Where w_1 and w_2 are the weight factor, $w_1 + w_2 = 1$ and $w_1 > w_2$. If there exist the nodes with same M_s value, the node with larger D_{df} value, which is the distance of a node to the downstream front of the synchronization flow, will be selected as the cluster head. The tuple defining cluster head determination for *S* state is (M_s, D_{df}, ID).

For cluster maintenance, the cluster heads approaching to the downstream front of the synchronization flow, i.e., those with small D_{df} value, should transfer the cluster head task to other head nodes in advance.

2.3 *J* State

J state presents most obvious group mobility, highest node density, largest link duration but serious contention in wireless channels. The stability in mobility relies mainly on the distance between current location and the downstream front of the jam flow.

In *J* state, the nodes with large degree and long distance from the downstream front of the jam flow could be selected as cluster heads. M_j defines the main cluster head selection criteria for *J* state:

$$M_j = \left\| \overrightarrow{N_i} \right\| \tag{3}$$

Similar to that in *S* state, for nodes with same M_j value, the node with larger D_{df} value will be selected as the cluster head. The tuple defining cluster head determination for *J* state is (M_j, D_{df}, ID).

Because of the very large node density, cluster maintenance for *J* state should pay more attention to the cluster radius in cluster merging operation, and the node transmission range could be decreased to reduce interference.

2.4 *FtoSJ* State

Vehicles in *FtoSJ* state are experiencing state transferring from a metastable state (free flow) to a stable state (synchronization flow or jam flow). As shown in Fig. 1, the vehicle in *FtoSJ* state is moving out of a parse topology area and into a dense topology area. And the vehicle decelerates because of the upstream front of the synchronization or jam flow.

Fig. 1. Traffic flow state *FtoSJ*

Because the traffic state changes greatly for the vehicles in *FtoSJ* state, cluster formation operation should be delayed to when the vehicles go into *S* state, to avoid unnecessary overheads for clustering and maintenance.

Because the vehicles are heading to a dense topology area, it is easy to occur cluster head collision and contention. Therefore, the cluster maintenance operation should be delayed a period of time. After the vehicles go into *S* state, M_s could be calculated again according to Eq. (2) and select an appropriate cluster head to join in.

2.5 *SJtoF* State

As shown in Fig. 2, the vehicles in *SJtoF* state are in bursting accelerating state. Therefore, these nodes may lose considerable amount of neighbors and wireless links.

For the nodes losing connection to cluster head, it is evident that they are at or leaving the downstream front of the synchronization flow or jam flow. They can select a downstream cluster to join in if possible, or temporarily set themselves as cluster head.

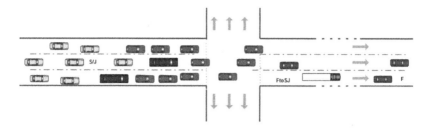

Fig. 2. Traffic flow state *SJtoF*

For the cluster head losing most of its cluster members, it could transfer the head task to its upstream node and set itself as non-clustered node. When it moves into *F* state, the joining a new cluster or cluster formation operation could be conducted.

3 The Proposed VTCP Protocol

Because the motivation of VTCP comes from the features of different traffic states and corresponding illuminations about clustering and cluster maintenance operations, this section introduces the traffic detection method firstly. In order to reduce clustering overhead while improve cluster stability, VTCP defines dynamic transmission range for different traffic flow states, as discussed in Sect. 3.2. The VTCP clustering strategy is introduced in detail in Sect. 3.3.

3.1 Traffic State Detection

The traffic state of a vehicle can be decided based on its velocity, desired velocity, neighboring node number and surrounding vehicle density. Defining n_{syn_min} as the minimum threshold of node number in free flow, it can be calculated as:

$$n_{syn\_min} = R * \rho_{syn\_min} \tag{4}$$

where ρ_{syn_min} is the minimum vehicle density in free flow.

The network density, k_i, can be calculated as:

$$k_i = \frac{\sum\limits_{m,n \in \overrightarrow{N_i}} X_{m,n}}{\frac{1}{2} * \left\|\overrightarrow{N_i}\right\| * \left(\left\|\overrightarrow{N_i}\right\| - 1\right)} \tag{5}$$

where $X_{m,n} = \begin{cases} 1, if & D_{m,n} \leq R \\ 0, if & D_{m,n} > R \end{cases}$, $D_{m,n}$ is the distance between vehicle m and n.

The detection of the traffic state of vehicle i can be completed following two steps.

Step 1: Detecting basic traffic flow state (i.e., *F*, *J* and *S*). Vehicle i decides its traffic flow state periodically according to the following Eq. (6):

$$Tr_i = \begin{cases} F, & if \quad v_{c,i} > V_{syn\_max} \quad or \quad \left\|\overrightarrow{N_i}\right\| < n_{syn\_min} \\ S, & if \quad V_{jam\_max} < v_{c,i} < V_{syn\_max} \quad and \quad \left\|\overrightarrow{N_i}\right\| > n_{syn\_min} \\ J, & if \quad v_{c,i} < V_{jam\_max} \quad and \quad \left\|\overrightarrow{N_i}\right\| > n_{syn\_min} \, and \quad k_i > K_{jam\_min} \end{cases} \quad (6)$$

where $v_{c,i}$ is the current velocity of vehicle i, V_{syn_max} is the maximum velocity of synchronization flow, V_{jam_max} is the maximum velocity of jam flow, K_{jam_min} is the minimum network density of jam flow.

Step 2: Detecting possible traffic flow transition state. Vehicle i detects the list of neighbors with the same direction. It resets its state according to the following rules based on the state of its preceding vehicles.

(1) The state will be set as *FtoSJ* if Traffic_State of i is F and Traffic_State of i's preceding vehicles are *S/J*;
(2) The state will be set as *SJtoF* if Traffic_State of i is *S/J* and Traffic_State of i's preceding vehicles are F.

3.2   Dynamic Transmission Range

As discussed in [11], the various traffic flows present different impacts on network connectivity. In order to reduce clustering overhead while improve cluster stability, VTCP defines dynamic transmission range for different traffic flow states.

Vehicles at free flow traffic state may located in a sparse network with serious network partition, in which exist very small cluster, even isolated cluster heads. VTCP enlarge the node's transmission range for such a scenario. However, too large transmission range may extend into the synchronization flow or jam flow. Therefore, VTCP defines dynamic transmission range for free flow as $(R_{free\_min}, R_{free\_max})$. For a vehicle i, if $\left\|\overrightarrow{N_i}\right\| < n_{syn\_min}/2$, the transmission range is enlarged according to Eq. (7):

$$R_n = \begin{cases} R_{c,i} * (2 - S_i), & if \quad R_{c,i} * (2 - S_i) < R_{free\_max} \\ R_{free\_max}, & else \end{cases} \quad (7)$$

where S_i is the saturation rate of vehicles in the same direction of vehicle i, which can be defined as:

$$S_i = \left\|\overrightarrow{N_i}\right\|/C, \; in \; which \; C = \frac{R_{free\_max}}{L+S} * N_L \quad (8)$$

where L is the average vehicle length, S is the jam distance and N_L is the number of lanes.

If $\left\| \overrightarrow{N_i} \right\| > n_{syn\_min}$, the transmission range is shrunk according to Eq. (9):

$$R_n = \begin{cases} R_{c,i} * (1 - S_i), & if \quad R_{c,i} * (1 - S_i) > R_{free\_min} \\ R_{free\_min}, & else \end{cases} \qquad (9)$$

For vehicles in synchronization flow, the transmission range is set as R_{free_min}.

For vehicles in jam flow at high node density, the transmission range should be shrunk to reduce collision. VTCP defines the transmission range as $(R_{jam\_min}, R_{free\_min})$. It is initially set as R_{free_min}. The vehicles check the number of its neighboring nodes with same direction. If $\left\| \overrightarrow{N_i} \right\|$ is larger than a threshold N_j, the vehicle should adjust its transmission range according to Eq. (10) until its neighboring nodes with same direction become less than N_j or the minimum transmission range is achieved.

$$R_n = \begin{cases} R_{c,i} * (1 - k_i), & if \quad R_{c,i} * (1 - k_i) > R_{jam\_min} \\ R_{jam\_min}, & else \end{cases} \qquad (10)$$

3.3   VTCP Clustering Strategy

VTCP follows 1-hop clustering and 2-hop maintenance principle, that is, the cluster head is chosen from the 1-hop neighbors while the maintenance operations are conducted within 2-hop distance. VTCP defines five cluster states for the nodes: *Cluster_Head, Cluster_Gateway, Cluster_Member, Head_Contention* and *Head_Alone*.

3.3.1   Cluster Formation

Firstly, all the nodes are initialized as *Head_Alone* state. Initially, all the nodes periodically broadcast CF_HELLO message, carrying node ID, location, moving direction, traffic state, cluster state, expecting velocity and mobility metric for clustering. When a vehicle receives the CF_HELLO messages from the neighbors in same direction, it can calculate its mobility metrics for clustering according to its traffic state. Then, this metric for clustering is filled in the CF_HELLO message for second round broadcasting. After the second round broadcasting, each vehicle compares its metric value with its neighbors to determine whether it behaves as a cluster head. The procedure for cluster head determination could be described as the following Algorithm 1:

Algorithm 1. Cluster_Head_Determination

---

i.degree: the degree of vehicle i
i.neighbor_list_d: the list of neighbors that has same direction with vehicle i
i.traffic_state: traffic states of vehicle i
i.cluster_state: cluster states of vehicle i
i.M: metric of vehicle i for cluster head selection
i.metric_turples: metric turples of vehicle i for cluster head determination

     i.cluster_state = Head_Alone;
    switch(i.traffic_state)
    case F:

$$i.M \text{ as } i.M = M_f = \log \frac{\left\|\vec{N_i}\right\|}{\sum_{j \in N_i} \Delta v_{i,j,t}}$$

       i.metric_tuples = (M_f , ID)

       break;

    case S:

       cacluate i.M as i.M = $M_s = w_1 * \left\|\vec{N_i}\right\| + w_2 * M_f$

       i.metric_tuples = (M_s , D_{df} , ID)

       break;

    case J:

       calculate i.M as i.M = $M_j = \left\|\vec{N_i}\right\|$

       i.metric_tuples =(M_j , D_{df} , ID)

       break;

    case FtoSJ:
    case JStoF:

       i.cluster_state = Head_Alone;

       break;

    if(i.metic_tuples win all the vehicles in i.neighbor_list_d)

       i.cluster_state = Cluster_Head

    if(i.cluster_states == Cluster_Head)

       BroadCast(i ,i.cluster_state, i.traffic_state, i.M)

In the above procedure of cluster head determination, if the vehicle has best metric for clustering, it will set its cluster state (*i.cluster_state*) as *Cluster_Head* and broadcast cluster head invitation message to its neighbors. Otherwise, the vehicle will wait for cluster head invitation from other nodes. When the vehicle receives cluster head invitation, it will join that cluster and set its cluster state as *Cluster_Member*. If a vehicle receives multiple cluster head invitations, it will select one cluster to join in and set its cluster state as Cluster_Gateway.

3.3.2   Cluster Maintenance

In order for efficient cluster maintenance, VTCP defines priority for the different flow states: they are *SJtoF*, *F*, *FtoSJ*, *S/J* from lowest to highest priority, according to the stability of the traffic flow. VTCP implements cluster maintenance within 2-hop distance. In order for high cluster stability, if a node choose to join in a cluster head at 2-hop distance, the traffic state priority of the selected cluster head must be higher than that of this node.

In cluster maintenance, the vehicles continuously check their cluster state and conduct the following maintenance operations accordingly:

(1) Cluster state update for non-clustered nodes: as shown in Fig. 3.

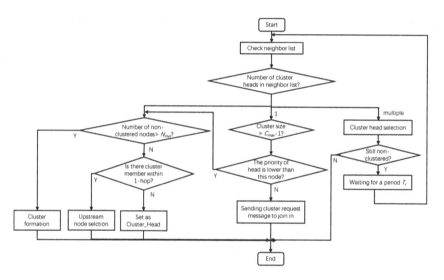

Fig. 3. Cluster state update for non-clustered nodes

(2) Upstream node selection: when a node determines to join in a cluster head at 2-hop distance, it should select upstream node to forward cluster request message. The upstream nodes are selected according to their traffic state priority, and according to the distance for the same priority.

(3) Cluster member maintenance: if a 1-hop cluster member does not receive hello message from cluster head for a predefined duration, it will set as HEAD_ALONE state. If a 2-hop cluster member can receive hello message directly, it will change to 1-hop member and delete the upstream node.

(4) Cluster head selection: the cluster head with full size of members (i.e., the cluster member reaches C_{max}) and with lower traffic state priority are ignored. The nodes in *F* or *SJtoF* state select the cluster head moving at the most proximate velocity. The nodes in *S*, *J* or *FtoSJ* state select the nearest cluster head.

(5) Cluster head task transferring: a cluster head at *S* or *J* state will transfer the head task to its member with best cluster metric (as discussed in Sect. 2) when the

portion of succeeding members is more than a threshold, μ. If a cluster head is at *SJtoF* state, it implies this node has moved across the downstream front of the traffic flow. Therefore, it should transfer cluster head task to its members in *S* or *J* state.

(6) Cluster head contention: when two cluster heads moving at the same direction encounter, the cluster head contention operation should be performed. The one with higher traffic state priority wins the contention and remains as the cluster head.

4 Simulation and Results

The simulation is conducted in VanetMobiSim and NS2 integrated simulation environment. VanetMobiSim is used to generate traffic scenario and NS2 is the network simulation software used to implement the clustering algorithms. The simulation parameters are listed in Table 1.

Table 1. Simulation parameters

Parameter	Value	Parameter	Value
Network size	5 km * 3 km	V_{jam_max}	20 km/h
Simulation time	2500 s	K_{jam_min}	0.8
Traffic light	5	C_{max}	200
Mobility model	IDM_LC	R_{free_min}	300 m
$v^{desired}$	120 km/h	R_{free_max}	1000 m
ρ_{syn_min}	25 veh/(km·lane)	R_{jam_min}	200 m
V_{syn_max}	50 km/h	μ	0.8

The following metrics are used to evaluate the stability performance of the clustering algorithms [12, 13]:

- Mean cluster head lifetime: Also known as cluster lifetime, this refers to the average time duration of all the nodes acting as cluster heads during the entire simulation. This is an important metric for cluster stability.
- Mean re-affiliation times: The mean times of a node (cluster head or member) leaving one cluster and joining another. A lower value reduces bandwidth consumption during message exchanges for member updates.
- Mean cluster residence time: It is defined as the average affiliation time of an ordinary node to a particular cluster.
- Number of clusters: The total number of clusters formed in the network during simulation time. This is a metric for the scalability of the clustering approaches.

The proposed VTCP clustering method and other classical approaches (HCC [14], MOBIC [15] and MobDHop [16]) are implemented in simulation. In order to improve the comparability, these benchmark algorithms are modified: the strategy dealing with opposite direction vehicles are added into them to avoid joining a cluster moving in the opposite direction; cluster contention operation are added for HCC. In the following sections, the revised approaches are called HCC-V, MOBIC-V and MobDHop-V.

Figure 4 illustrates the performance results of the proposed VTCP, HCC-V, MOBIC-V and MobDHop-V with varying number of nodes in simulation.

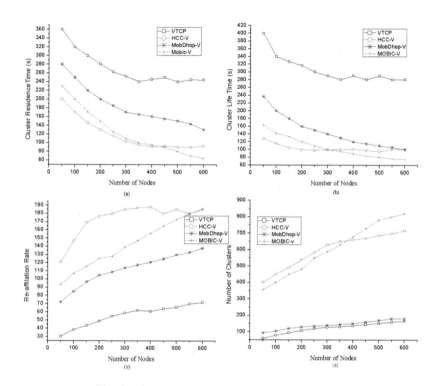

Fig. 4. Simulation results on clustering performance

Figure 4(a) shows the cluster residence time of different clustering approaches. Generally, with the increasing number of nodes, cluster residence time decreases. This is because the vehicles experience more frequent traffic state transitions when the number of nodes increases, and thus it becomes more difficult for the vehicles to maintain connectivity to cluster head, especially at the downstream front of the synchronization flow and jam flow. It can be seen from Fig. 4(a) that the clustering strategies based on mobility features (i.e., MOBIC-V, MobDHop-V and VTCP) show performance advantages in cluster residence time. VTCP shows more obvious performance advantages at high node density than other mobility based clustering approaches. This benefits from the cluster head selection considering the features of different traffic states and timely cluster head transferring.

In terms of cluster life time, as shown in Fig. 4(b), it decreases with the increasing number of nodes. For a low node density, there exist many isolated nodes acting as cluster heads, thus long cluster head life time could be achieved due to those isolated cluster heads. When the number of nodes increases, cluster life time decreases because of more cluster head contentions. Especially at the downstream front of synchronization flow and jam flow, the vehicles accelerate sharply into low density area, and thus suffer decreasing cluster head life time. VTCP outperforms the other approaches because of its dynamic transmission range, 2-hop cluster maintenance and in advance cluster transferring at the downstream front.

In Fig. 4(c), VTCP shows obvious advantage in re-affiliation times than the other cluster approaches. The first reason is because the dynamic transmission range, which ensure long time connectivity to cluster head even though at a low node density. VTCP also benefits from its cluster head selection in cluster maintenance considering the traffic state priorities of both the cluster head node and the joining node, thus avoiding the vehicles at S and J state joining a cluster head at $SJtoF$ state and decreasing re-affiliation times accordingly. From the perspective of cluster radius, multi-hop cluster maintenance increases the re-affiliation times due to the increasing probability of a node losing connectivity to its cluster head at multi-hop distance. Therefore, VTCP defines cluster maintenance with maximum radius of 2-hop, in which 1-hop cluster head is preferred than 2-hop cluster head, and only 2-hop cluster head with higher traffic state priority will be selected.

As shown in Fig. 4(d), the number of clusters increases with the increasing number of nodes. Obviously, the number of clusters of 2-hop clustering (VTCP and MobDHop-V) is much less than that of 1-hop clustering (MOBIC-V and HCC-V). VTCP employs dynamic transmission range which can decrease cluster number at a low density scenario and improve cluster stability at a high density scenario.

5   Conclusions

In this paper, VTCP, a clustering protocol based on traffic states is proposed for vehicular networks. It is motivated by our observations about the impacts of different traffic flows on networking parameters. The analysis on mobility features, clustering metrics and clustering strategies of these traffic flow states are given firstly. The traffic flow state detection method is designed. And the dynamic transmission range strategy is introduced to reduce clustering overhead while improve cluster stability. The cluster formation and maintenance operations of VTCP are presented in detail. The simulation results in VanetMobiSim and NS-2 integrated environment show that VTCP outperformed other classical clustering approaches in terms of cluster stability.

References

1. Al-Sultan, S., Al-Doori, M.M., Al-Bayatti, A.H., Zedan, H.A.: A comprehensive survey on vehicular Ad Hoc network. J. Netw. Comput. Appl. **37**(1), 380–392 (2014)
2. Karagiannis, G., Altintas, O., Ekici, E., Heijenk, G., Jarupan, B., Lin, K., Weil, T.: Vehicular networking: a survey and tutorial on requirements, architectures, challenges, standards and solutions. IEEE Commun. Surv. Tutorials **13**(4), 584–616 (2011)

3. Wang, S., Fan, C., Hsu, C.H., et al.: A vertical handoff method via self-selection decision tree for internet of vehicles. IEEE Syst. J. **10**(3), 1183–1192 (2016)
4. Su, H., Zhang, X.: Clustering-based multichannel MAC protocols for QoS provisionings over vehicular ad hoc networks. IEEE Trans. Veh. Technol. **56**(6), 3309–3323 (2007)
5. Konstantopoulos, C., Gavalas, D., Pantziou, G.: Clustering in mobile ad hoc networks through neighborhood stability-based mobility prediction. Comput. Netw. **52**(9), 1797–1824 (2008)
6. Bali, R.S., Kumar, N., Rodrigues, J.J.P.C.: Clustering in vehicular Ad Hoc networks: taxonomy, challenges and solutions. Veh. Commun. **1**(3), 134–152 (2014)
7. Hossain, E., Chow, G., Leung, V.C.M., et al.: Vehicular telematics over heterogeneous wireless networks: a survey. Comput. Commun. **33**(7), 775–793 (2010)
8. Nagel, R.: The effect of vehicular distance distributions and mobility on VANET communications. IEEE Intell. Veh. Symp. **23**(3), 1190–1194 (2010)
9. Kerner, B.S.: Introduction to Modern Traffic Flow Theory and Control: The Long Road To Three-Phase Traffic Theory. Springer, Heidelberg (2009)
10. Kerner, B.S.: Three-phase traffic theory and highway capacity. Phys. A: Stat. Mech. Appl. **333**, 379–440 (2004)
11. Shi, Y., Lu, C.K., Qiao, L.Q., Chen, S.Z.: Exploring mobility metrics quantitatively for vehicular networks based on three-phase traffic theory. In: IEEE International Conference on Connected Vehicles and Expo. 2015 (ICCVE 2015), October 2015
12. Shi, Y., Xu, X., Lu, C.K., Chen, S.Z.: Distributed and weighted clustering based on d-hop dominating set for vehicular networks. KSII Trans. Internet Inf. Syst. **10**(4), 1661–1678 (2016)
13. Rituparna, G., Stefano, B.: Mitigating the impact of node mobility on ad hoc clustering. Wirel. Commun. Mob. Comput. **8**(3), 295–308 (2008)
14. Parekh, A.K.: Selecting routers in ad-hoc wireless networks. In: IEEE International Telecommunications Symposium, pp. 420–424 (1994)
15. Basu, P., Khan, N., Little, T.D.C.: A mobility based metric for clustering in mobile ad hoc networks. In: IEEE International Conference on Distributed Computing Systems Workshop, pp. 413–418 (2001)
16. Er, I.I., Seah, W.K.G.: Mobility-based d-hop clustering algorithm for mobile ad hoc networks. In: IEEE Wireless Communications and Networking Conference (WCNC 2004), pp. 2359–2364 (2004)

A Cluster–on–Demand Algorithm with Load Balancing for VANET

Yun Zheng[1,2], Yi Wu[1,2], Zhexin Xu[1,2(✉)], and Xiao Lin[1,2]

[1] Key Laboratory of OptoElectronic Science
and Technology for Medicine of Ministry of Education,
Fujian Normal University, Fuzhou 350007, People's Republic of China
`fsd_zhengyun@sina.com`, {`wuyi,xuzhexin,linxiao`}`@fjnu.edu.cn`
[2] Fujian Provincial Key Laboratory of Photonics Technology,
Fujian Normal University, Fuzhou 350007, People's Republic of China

Abstract. Cluster–on–Demand VANET clustering algorithm (CDVC) along with load balancing for urban is proposed. Urban vehicles are characterized by unpredictable moving direction. These challenges are solved by CDVC, which is composed of three main procedures; that is, initial clustering, cluster merging, and cluster head selection. In initial clustering, vehicles are clustered determines the boundary of each cluster. In cluster merging, Self–Organizing Maps (SOMs) is used for re–clustering by the similarity of nodes, which guarantees the stability of clusters. It leads to achieve load balancing. In cluster head selection, the information of location and mobility are combined to select a more stable cluster head. The performance of CDVC is evaluated and compared with the Lowest ID (LID) and Mobility based on clustering (MOBIC). Finally, the simulation results reveal that CDVC is superior to LID and MOBIC in terms of cluster head duration, clusters number, and load balancing.

Keywords: Vehicular ad hoc networks · Clustering · Cluster–on–demand · IEEE 802.11p · Load balancing · Urban environment

1 Introduction

Clustering is defined as a process to group all of the mobile nodes into clusters [1]. The main purpose for a VANET clustering algorithm is to maintain cluster stability, avoid frequent re–clustering operations.

The aim of this paper is focus on the urban environment of VANET. The characteristics of urban environment are described as follows: 1. there are more different type of roads and vehicles, 2. a large number of data is needed to transfer, 3. network topology varies frequently, 4. an outburst of accident phenomenon is difficult to predict. These characteristics determine the some problems, such as data collision, data loss, high end–to–end delay, unstable network.

Recently, Seyhan Ucar et al. [1] proposed VANET safety message dissemination by multi–hop cluster architecture, which achieved high data packet delivery ratio and low delay. It does not consider the load balancing. Jerry John Kponyo et al. [2] proposed

© Springer International Publishing AG 2016
C.-H. Hsu et al. (Eds.): IOV 2016, LNCS 10036, pp. 120–127, 2016.
DOI: 10.1007/978-3-319-51969-2_10

cluster–on–demand Minimum Spanning Tree (MST) prim algorithm in that it gave the finite method to determine the number of clusters and cluster member. However, the analysis of stability was not provided. For this reason, in 2013, Jung-Hyok Kwon et al. [3] proposed neighbor stability–based VANET clustering for urban vehicular environments, which guarantees the reliable delivery of data by keeping network stable. However, it neglected the load balancing, affected the data delivery in time. The Lowest ID–based (LID) clustering scheme is proposed in [4] neglected the mobility of nodes, which is simple but has to frequently re–select CHs. More recently, mobility based for clustering (MOBIC) is proposed in [5]. Unfortunately, the performance of MOBIC is impacted by the fixed clustering period. The clustering algorithms mentioned above haven't been analyzed the completeness and contradictory of packet delivery rate, end–to–end delay, and stability. Besides, the recent clustering algorithms have neglected the spatial boundary in ad hoc network, see [6].

In this paper, CDVC is proposed to solve the above mentioned problems. To degrade the end–to–end delay of nodes, we presented a cluster–on–demand algorithm, which clusters the communication message according to the demand. It decreased the time cost by different kind of messages. It does not need to wait for accessing to the channel, the shortened the message queuing time competition, and the reduced the transmission delay of message data. Furthermore, to improve the network stability in the same communication demand categories, we proposed the SOM clustering algorithm, which clusters the nodes due to the communication radius and the relative location of nodes. Each sub–clusters limit the sorted number N_s and the cluster structure N_u. In order to achieve load balancing, message should be delivered equally to CHs in sub–clusters. As a result, it benefits for network more stable. In addition, we present the initial clustering algorithm to determine spatial boundary mentioned above, see [6].

The rest of the paper is organized as follows: Sect. 2 describes clustering system model. Section 3 delineates the proposed clustering algorithms. The comparison of the proposed clustering algorithm to the LID and MOBIC is given in Sect. 4. Finally, this paper concludes with a brief summary in Sect. 5.

2   Clustering System Model for Vanet

2.1   Urban Scenario for Cluster–Based VANET

Assume that vehicles move with different moving velocities and directions in urban traffic environment. Various kinds of roads cause the frequent topological variability so that clustering plays an important role as a controlling scheme. Figure 1 shows the cluster–based vehicular system architecture, where CMs communicate with their designed CH. Also, it assumes that clusters have been formed from adjacent vehicles in specific regions. Note that CHs are network coordinators. Both CHs and CMs prefer to communicate with base stations once required resource exists in neither inter–cluster nor adjacent clusters.

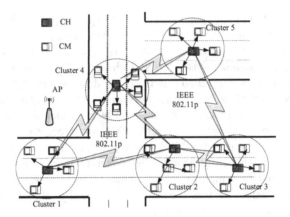

Fig. 1. System architecture for cluster–based vehicle scenario

2.2 Assumptions

Clustering hypotheses are made as follows:

- In physical layer and MAC layer, we use GPSR protocols [1] and IEEE 802.11p [7] respectively in that IEEE 802.11p provides data rate ranging from 3 to 27 Mbps.
- The vehicles can use GPS to retrieve vehicle information includes nodes ID, velocity, destination, and vehicles communication demand. Vehicles are equipped with high–speed computing hardware.
- Initially, all nodes equipped with multiple onboard equipments to support various forms of communication [2].

2.3 Status of Vehicles in Clustering

In VANET clustering, there are four possible statuses for each vehicle. That is,

- Cluster Head (CH) is which the vehicles are responsible for the coordination tasks of intra–cluster and inter–cluster such as transmitting the data.
- Isolated Cluster Head (Iso–CH) cannot connect to any existing cluster.
- Cluster Member (CM) is which the vehicles belong to a constructed cluster.
- INITIAL (IN) is the starting status of each vehicle.

3   Clustering Algorithms Operations

To improve the network stability, we should keep the cluster stability, which needs to degrade the occurrence of CH bottleneck. This leads to cause the number of CMs as little as possible. On the contrary, in order to reduce the end–to–end delay between the nodes data delivery and decrease the route cost, the number of clusters need to be reduced. For fixed network, the reduction of the number of CMs definitely implies the increase of the number of clusters. Therefore, CDVC is designed to provide load balancing of VANET in urban traffic environment, which clustered the trade–off between stability and end–to–end delay, and limited the cluster number under certain conditions. The number of differences between CMs should be as closed as possible.

In the sub–clusters, CDVC consists of three procedures, such as initial clustering, cluster merging by using SOM, and cluster head selection.

3.1 Initial Clustering

The initial clustering aims to determine spatial boundary with one–hop limitation and to guarantee high packet delivery ratio. All vehicles are regarded as Iso–CHs initially. They access the channel by Distributed Coordination Function (DCF). If nodes don't receive clustering message, they become Pseudo Iso–CHs (PICHs). Surrounding nodes, which are in the communication radius, try to join PICHs cluster. After PICH sends a clustering message, each receivers, which is willing to join in the cluster, will feedback a join application messages within the limit of $T_1 = 10$ ms. PICH will decide to accept or neglect the nodes according to N_u. If it accepts the nodes, the CMs number accumulates. If the response message from any nodes does not receives, PICH needs to resend clustering message following $t_1 = 0.1$ ms cycle until the end of T_1. Once the time exceed T_1, PICH neglects any join application message and a cluster is generated if some nodes have joined. When the nodes receive clustering message from the existing PICH, they send join message to PICH if they want. The nodes wait for the respond message from PICH within $T_2 = 10$ ms to become CMs. Otherwise, they resend join application message following $t_2 = 0.1$ ms cycle until the end of T_2. Once exceed T_2, the nodes which haven't been accepted, retain Iso–CHs. After a cluster creates, cluster head selection will be invoked. It is of interest to note that the cluster merging dont execute until the actual CH is selected.

3.2 Cluster Merging by SOM

In clustering networks, re–clustering operation may cause change of CHs and topological variability. To form stable and load balancing cluster, the maximum number of clusters is limited during the cluster merging. Here, the traditional SOM is applied to classify nodes because its performance is already good enough [8]. The process controls N_s to keep the network stability and load balancing. During cluster merging, if the sum of CMs is less than the upper limit of cluster size, these clusters integrate to a larger cluster. Otherwise, let N_c denotes the number of clusters before cluster merging in a region, N_s denotes the sorted number, and N_u denotes the upper limit of cluster size. Ns can be calculated by $N_s = \dfrac{N_c}{N_u}$. Then, N_s clusters will be generated after cluster merging is executed.

It follows from [1] that the maximum hop is set to be 2 in order to guarantee clustering stability. The cluster merging procedure using SOM. CHs share their cluster information when they are within the communication range of each other. If CHs receive the cluster merging message, each of CHs invokes the SOM algorithm, and broadcasts the sorted results and the ID of re–selected CHs to their own CMs. Besides, CHs will send cluster merging message if they haven't receive any clustering message from other CHs during clustering merging.

3.3 Cluster Head Selection

The authors in [1–3] proposed an algorithm for creating stable clusters. In this algorithm, clustering metric combining location with mobility of vehicles is utilized for cluster head selection.

4   Performance Evaluation

4.1   Simulation Scenarios

The simulations are performed by using SUMO and MATLAB. The total simulation time appears to be 800 s. The clustering process starts at the 151st sec when all the vehicles have entered the road. All the performance metrics are evaluated for the next 250 s. In VANET, vehicles are considered to be the nodes. For simplicity, communication demand consists of voice traffic, streaming (Video), and data traffic (BE and BK) according to QoS category classes [7, 9, 10]. Different communication demand resulted in different waiting time [11], the same communication demand considers to be clustered in a cluster, thereby degrading the waiting access time. Since the different communication demand message can used for parallel processing, which improves the transmission time effectively. Each type of message with maximum number of CMs is different due to the average delay, see [7, 10]. Thus, it can be seen that communication demand consideration relation between the number of clusters and the number of the members in the clusters is the same as load balancing.

During our simulation, we select the voice traffic as a example. Nu in each cluster is set to be 30 according to the relation between the end–to–end delay and the nodes numbers [7]. Other simulation parameters are listed in Table 1.

Table 1. Simulation parameters for VANET

Simulation time	800 s
Maximum velocity	30/40/50/60 m/s
Max-hop	2
Scenario scale	2 km * 3 km
HELLO-PACKET size	129 bytes
DATA-PACKET size	1024 bytes
Max number of cluster members	30

4.2 Simulation Results and Performance Analysis

Assuming N and R represent the number of vehicles within distance in a region and the communication radius respectively. When the value of N is less than N_u, the communication radius R can be shorten properly in order to keep cluster more stable. Once $N > Nu$, N_s will change due to the different size of cluster. Hence, the impact should be considered of R and the number of the vehicles N.

Figure 2 shows the average cluster head duration of the CDVC under different communication radiuses change from 50 to 700 m when node number fixes to be 600 per kilometer. The average cluster head duration decreases as the communication radius increases. The reason is that larger communication radius possesses more one-hop neighbors. Mobility similarity and correlation of CMs decline when they are far apart. In this case, clusters become unstable. However, cluster head duration of CDVC is longer and decreases more slowly due to more stable clusters. So, it can be speculated that there requires fewer reclustering operations and less routing cost in CDVC than other two mechanisms in cluster merging and cluster head selection process.

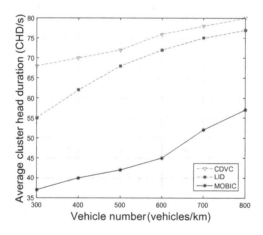

Fig. 2. Average cluster head duration versus vehicle number

Figure 3 shows the average number of clusters using CDVC while the vehicle number increases from 300 to 800 per kilometer. R mentioned earlier is given to 250 m. As vehicles increase, the number of clusters also increases because N_u is fixed to be 30 during simulation. One observes that the average number of clusters in CDVC slightly increases when compared to LID and MOBIC. The reason is that the number of clusters in CDVC is controlled by the optimal modification of N_s and the limitation of N_u. Obviously, more clusters will cause larger end–to–end delay. Hence, the performance of end–to–end delay by using CDVC will be better than other two mechanisms.

Figure 4 shows the distribution of cluster members at different simulation time using box diagram. Except a few points, CM number in each cluster using the CDVC fluctuates in a smaller range compared to LID and MOBIC. With the action of N_s and the limitation

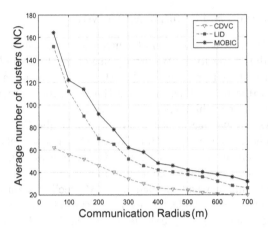

Fig. 3. Average number of clusters versus communication radius

of N_u in SOM, clusters become more stable. Meanwhile, CM number in each cluster become more balanced and more concentrated than others.

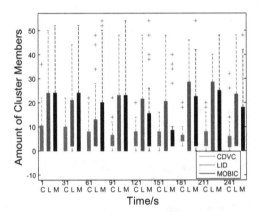

Fig. 4. Amount of cluster member's distribution during the simulation

5 Conclusion

A cluster–on–demand clustering algorithm in urban scenarios is presented. Clustering based on communication demand degrades the end–to–end delay of nodes. Under the sub–clusters, the proposed algorithm consists of three critical procedures, such as initial clustering, cluster merging, and cluster head selection. In this case, the initial clustering achieved by limiting the clustering communication range within one–hop. Cluster merging by using SOM and cluster head selection control cluster structure and cluster number through the limited maximum two– hop range and N_s. So, data packet delivery ratio increases and the end–to–end delay decreases. These procedures trade off load balancing and stability. Finally, the simulation results show that the proposed algorithm is superior to LID and MOBIC.

Acknowledgements. The authors would like to thank Dr. Hsin–Chiu Chang for his help in the comments and preparation of this paper. This research was financially supported by the National Natural Science Foundation of China (No. 61571128), the Research Fund for the Doctoral Program of Higher Education of China (No. 20133503120 003), the Natural Science Foundation of Fujian Province (No. 2013J01224), the Key Projects of Science and Technology Plan for Industry of the Science and Technology Department of Fujian Province (No. 2014H0019), and it also was financially supported by the Program for Changjiang Scholars and Innovative Research Team in University (Grant No. IRT 15R10), the Education Department of Fujian Province Science and Technology Project (JB13005).

References

1. Ucar, S., Ergen, S.C., Ozkasap, O.: Multihop-cluster-based IEEE 802.11p and LTE hybrid architecture for VANET safety message dissemination. IEEE Trans. Veh. Technol. **65**, 2621–2636 (2015)
2. Kponyo, J.J., Kuang, Y., Zhang, E., Domenic, K.: Vanet cluster-on-demand minimum spanning tree (MST) prim clustering algorithm. In: International Conference on Computational Problem-Solving, pp. 101–104 (2013)
3. Kwon, J.H., Chang, H.S., Shon, T., Jung, J.J., Kim, E.J.: Neighbor stability-based vanet clustering for urban vehicular environments. J. Supercomput. **72**, 1–16 (2015)
4. Lin, C.R., Gerla, M.: Adaptive clustering for mobile wireless networks. IEEE J. Sel. Areas Commun. **15**, 1265–1275 (1997)
5. Basu, P., Khan, N., Little, T.D.C.: A mobility based metric for clustering in mobile ad hoc networks. In: International Conference on Distributed Computing Systems Workshop, pp. 413–418 (2001)
6. Wong, W.S.: Transmission sequence design and allocation for wide-area ad hoc networks. IEEE Trans. Veh. Technol. **63**, 869–878 (2014)
7. Chatzimisios, P., Boucouvalas, A.C., Vitsas, V.: Performance analysis of the IEEE 802.11 MAC protocol for wireless LANs. Int. J. Commun. Syst. **18**, 545–569 (2005)
8. Kohonen, T.: Self Organizing Map. Springer, Berlin (2001)
9. Ghayet, E., Tabbane, N., Labiod, H., Tabbane, S.: A fuzzy multi-metric QoS-balancing gateway selection algorithm in a clustered VANET to LTE advanced hybrid cellular network. IEEE Trans. Veh. Technol. **64**, 804–817 (2015)
10. Hafeez, K.A., Zhao, L., Mark, J.W., Shen, X., Niu, Z.: Distributed multichannel and mobility-aware cluster-based MAC protocol for vehicular ad hoc networks. IEEE Trans. Veh. Technol. **62**, 3886–3902 (2013)
11. Wang, S., Fan, C., Hsu, C.H., Sun, Q.: A vertical handoff method via self-selection decision tree for internet of vehicles. IEEE Syst. J. **99**, 1–10 (2014)

Real Time Classification of American Sign Language for Finger Spelling Purpose

Amit Kumar[✉], Mansour Assaf, and Utkal Mehta

School of Engineering and Physics, The University of the South Pacific,
Laucala Campus, Suva, Fiji Islands
{amit.a.kumar,mansour.assaf,utkal.mehta}@usp.ac.fj

Abstract. Real time communication with use of sign languages is addressed. Sign language used in this study is performed in uniform lighting conditions. The system looks at image processing of the hand gestures followed by some feature extraction techniques to verify the gesture. Different classification techniques and logics are applied to classify the images and results are compared experimentally. Conditional classification is also used in the research to test for accuracy and is compared with previous results.

Keywords: Communication · Sign language · Image processing · Feature extraction · Classification

1 Introduction

Computer vision is enabling a computer or a machine to perceive objects based on its processing speed. Human vision differs from computer vision since computer vision works with frames. At 60 frames per second (fps) the perception is much smoother [1]. Computer vision can be used to detect and recognize objects of interests. Hand gestures which are a mode of communication for hearing impaired can be recognized using computer vision by applying image processing and pattern recognition techniques.

In this paper we look at the image processing techniques and feature extraction of gestures. The ASL is fourth frequently used language in The United States of America. Human eyes can only see objects in presence of adequate lighting. Presence of uniform light will keep the objects needing recognition unique. Palmistry [2] shows that there are six types of palms regardless of the skin color. ASL characters in finger spelling differ from one another, and to contrast between these characters, a number of features need to be identified that makes each gesture unique. Image processing with uniform light distribution and scattered lighting on the scene has different output.

Different approaches are available for classification. Euclidean distance is the simplest approach and Paansare et al. [4], achieved a minimum of 85% recognition accuracy for 26 different classes. A database of image needs to be established first before classification process.

Gestures with altering background require background segmentation prior to feature extraction process. This is done so that only the features of the gestures are extracted.

© Springer International Publishing AG 2016
C.-H. Hsu et al. (Eds.): IOV 2016, LNCS 10036, pp. 128–137, 2016.
DOI: 10.1007/978-3-319-51969-2_11

Kulkarni and Lokhande [5] proposed the method for static gestures where the background was kept constant. The region of interest is the gesture, and since the background remains constant there is not much need to track hands and do foreground subtraction. Skin color detection is very sensitive to lighting conditions [6] thus it is better to work with a color space which is intensity normalized [7].

The paper is structured as follows. Section 2 discusses the basics of image processing and image acquisition for the implemented system. In Sect. 3, the feature extraction of the gestures is introduced. Classification method is shown in Sect. 4. Results from real-time experimentation are discussed in Sect. 5. The conclusion and future recommendation and the proposed work is given in Sect. 6.

2   Image Acquisition and Processing

In computer vision approach it is necessary to interface a visual device for the machine and acquire videos or frames of videos from the 3D surroundings. A web cam is used in acquiring image. Cameras sensitivity to light is determined by its ISO speed and a camera has ability to function at different ISO speeds. High ISO can give a noisy image by amplifying the image together with the noise present thus involving more image processing and filtering. For a real time system it is preferable to work in an environment with adequate lighting so that the web cam can acquire images fast enough for processing. Extremely high luminance can cause occlusion problems and presence of multiple shadows and noises. Hand gesture is dynamic movement of static hand postures [3] and in order to acquire image from the video input to the machine, it is a good practice to track the hand before taking snapshots or acquiring the frames from the real time video. The tracking and detection of hand is excluded from the algorithm since the system is designed where the gestures are performed in a confined space with a static background. Video resolution of 640×480 was set for the webcam interfaced with the machine before grabbing images from the video. Since 640×480 resolution image have 4 times more data for processing compared to 320×240, the images acquired were scaled down to 320×240. The features of the gesture were envisioned to be extracted from the edge representation of the image. The scale used to convert any image with 4:3 aspect ratio to 320×240 resolutions is given in Eq. 1. The scale was multiplied element wise to the matrix representation of size of the image.

$$\sqrt{\frac{320 \times 240}{sum\ of\ pixels\ per\ column \times sum\ of\ pixels\ per\ row}} \tag{1}$$

The step to feature extraction is image processing. The images are processed to give a binary image. The color space for input image will be different depending on the video input settings. Some color spaces used in acquiring images are YCbCr, RGB, YPbPr which is scaled version of YUV color space [8, 9]. HSV color space is used mostly for skin detection purposes. Figure 1 shows a gesture, representing the character 4 in the ASL gesture for finger spelling, is converted from RGB to HSV. The gesture was performed on a reflective white background. It can be clearly noticed that the skin color part is contrasted as green and blue from the background. However the edges of thumb is not noticeable thus losing its feature to some extent.

Fig. 1. Converted from RGB to HSV (Color figure online)

The acquired images are converted to binary images for extracting features. Figure 2 shows the major processes involved in image conversion. The result of the conversion is shown in Fig. 3 where the gesture representing the number 1 in ASL finger spelling is used.

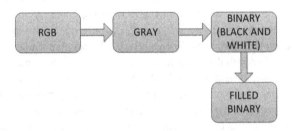

Fig. 2. Image conversion process

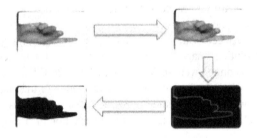

Fig. 3. Image processing of a gesture

There are some image processing techniques used to achieve the desired binary image. Light and illumination are factors that affect the results. One of the approach is to adjust the brightness and contrast or and correct the illumination.

An image can be represented as a two dimensional function [10], $(x,y) \rightarrow f(x,y)$. The intensity of an image is proportional to the light energy input to the device capturing image and its resolution. The image can be regarded as function of light with two parameters which are the luminance of the light on the scene and the reflective index of the objects in the scene.

$$f(x, y) = i(x, y)r(x, Y) \tag{2}$$

Where i is the illumination from the light source and ranging from 0 to infinity and r is the reflective index of the object limited from 0 to 1. A value of zero indicates total absorption whereas values of 1 indicates total reflection. The brightness and contrast of snapshots is adjusted in the processing stage so the output after edge detection has less noise and more relevant data. The contrast was manually adjusted in photo viewer and then the values were tested for image in Matlab. The brightness of an object determines the presence of light in the image whereas contrast is the difference between objects and regions [11]. In constant lighting environment, brightness does not need to be altered much. To minimize noises and to smoothen the objects in the scene, illumination correction methods are applied. Figure 4 shows the results of illumination correction on the static background which is used. The image becomes smoother with uniform illumination.

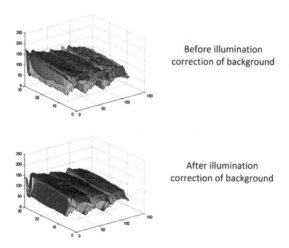

Fig. 4. Uniform illumination of background

Figure 5 illustrates the gesture performed on a white reflective background with its surface plot before and after distribution of light on the scene. Illumination correction helps in removing the noise caused by highly reflective regions.

To distinguish between the background and the object in background, background segmentation technique is utilized in which the background is removed from the entire image. Since the background is the same at all times, tracking and foreground segmentation is not given much priority in the system. The system is designed with a fixed video input which is projected on a static white background where the gestures are performed and tested. The light acting on the background plane has uniform intensity and varies very little. Any scattering of light on scene is normalized and distributed in the image processing step.

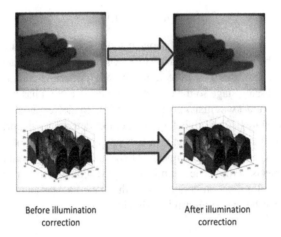

Before illumination   After illumination
correction   correction

Fig. 5. Illumination correction of gesture in background

3   Feature Extraction

Feature extraction relies mostly on the success of the image processing. In feature extraction, unique features which distinguish one gesture from the other is mined. These features are represented as feature vectors. Two common geometric features used are the area and perimeter of the segmented image. Integral image is used by [12] in which sum of rectangular area in the image is used to get the area. For feature extraction, three processed images were used for simplicity. First image is the boundary or edge representation of the gesture, second image is the filled area of the edge representation of first image. Two edge detection techniques, the 'canny' edge detection and 'Laplacian of Gauss' edge techniques were multiplied together to get the third image which had much finer boundary but was more discontinuous. Sum of pixels in filled edge image gives the area whereas the total pixel of the edge image gives the perimeter. The relationship between the perimeter of a circle and area of a circle was used to find the value of r, which was termed as apothem of the gesture.

$$\frac{radius}{2} = \frac{Area_{circle}}{Perimetre_{circle}} \tag{3}$$

Apothem is 2 times the area divided by the perimeter of the object and represents the radius of the inscribing circle.

Most of the features were extracted using the regionprop command in Matlab. The length of major axis and minor axis was used as features, the eccentricity and the orientation was also used as features. Finger counting was used by [13] as features of the gesture. It was observed that the spacing's between consecutive fingers is approximately same as the width of the fingers at a point slightly above the base of the fingers. Thus a range of pixel value is used to find the number of fingers and thumbs present. The image ratio of 4:3, was divided into 40 equivalent intervals and the width and length between the extreme edges were found. The ratio of the length to width was calculated and termed as the gradient. This 40 gradients represented the nature of the gesture and represented in form of a graph. The area of the gradient plots were calculated and represented as a feature of the gesture. Figure 6 describes how the length and width of images were extracted at different intervals. The plot of gradients for gesture representing 'A' is shown in Fig. 7.

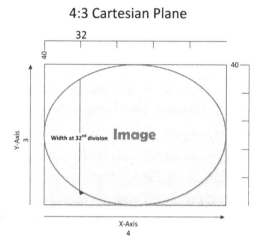

Fig. 6. Length and width of image at intervals

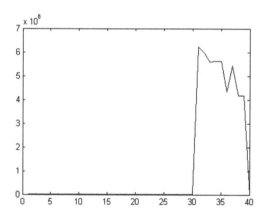

Fig. 7. Plot of ratio of length to width

To prevent the ratio from being infinity, the absolute value of the length and widths were taken and a very small value of 0.001 was added before calculating the ratio.

4 Classification Approach for Gestures

Classification was done based on ten features and upon observing the results, the classification was changed and modified slightly. First approach was finding the distance of the performed vector from the feature vectors obtained. The feature vectors were saved as mean of each features of a class. There are 10 features and 36 classes.

$$\begin{bmatrix} \mu_{1,1} & \cdots & \mu_{36,1} \\ \vdots & \ddots & \vdots \\ \mu_{1,10} & \cdots & \mu_{36,10} \end{bmatrix} \tag{4}$$

The test features were represented as column vector and subtracted element wise from each of the columns in the mean feature vector obtained. For every feature, the closest matching classes were found. This was done by finding the minimum value in the rows and noting its class. The Euclidean distance for the classes with closest match was calculated and compared.

$$\begin{bmatrix} f_1 - \mu_{1,1} & \cdots & f_1 - \mu_{36,1} \\ \vdots & \ddots & \vdots \\ f_{10} - \mu_{1,10} & \cdots & f_{10} - \mu_{36,10} \end{bmatrix} \tag{5}$$

The next classification approach was using KNN (K^{th} Nearest Neighbor), where the value of K was tested for 3, 5 and 7. A value of 7 was used to implement the system. In this classification the mean was not calculated but all the feature vector for each classes was used. The classes of 7 closest nearest neighbors are stored in an array and the unique class is found. If there existed two or more unique classes then the nearest neighbor is used where K is set to 1 (Fig. 8).

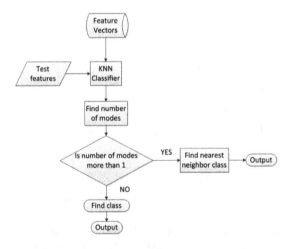

Fig. 8. Flowchart of KNN approach used

The third and fourth classification are same as the first and second approach but with reduced features. The feature representing the connectivity of the gesture or Euler's number [14] was eliminated. This was done since the variance of Euler's number between classes is very high. Thus if in a gesture, 9 features are extremely close enough while the feature showing connectivity is very far, then the Euclidean distance calculated is very high showing that the gesture is not closely matched. The final design was based on conditions of features. In this approach one of the features was given priority and used as condition to minimize the classes into subclasses. Feature which had a relatively high variance was chosen to act as a decision tree, thus determining the accuracy of the system based on decision of a less important feature. The finger count plus the spacing's between the fingers was the feature given priority. The values of this feature ranges from 0 to 5, thus the classes were divided into 6 sections. Table 1 shows the division.

Table 1. Spacing index for gestures

Spacing index	Gestures
0	B,H,Q
1	0,A,D,E,I,L,M,N,O,P,R,S,T,U,Y,Z
2	1,F,G,X
3	2,3,5,7,9,C,J,K,V
4	4,6,8
5	W

The spacing index represented new class and the gestures were sub classes. Classification was again done based on Euclidean distance for this approach.

5   Results and Accuracy

The classification results were checked for ten tests for each class. The characters were performed in orderly sequence 'a' to 'z' and '0' to '9'. Accuracy for single characters was tested first. ASL characters were then used to form words containing two, three or four characters. The results of the tests are given in Table 2.

Table 2. Results of classification (%)

Method	Number of characters in word			
	1	2	3	4
Mean Euclidean distance	23.6	22.5	21.9	21.1
KNN	31.9	31.1	30.8	30
Euclidean distance (reduced features)	35.2	32.5	31.1	28.1
KNN (reduced features)	83.8	83.6	82.2	82.25
KNN based on feature condition	71.1	68.3	67.5	67.5

Gestures were performed in orderly sequence and also randomly. The recognition rate was calculated by finding the ratio of correct classification and total tests. The total tests was 360, 10 tests for each 36 class of gestures.

$$recognition = \frac{total\ correct}{total\ tested} \times 100\% \tag{6}$$

Since the system is in real time, the algorithm was designed to show all the classification results in Matlab workspace thus the patterns noticed. Five classification methods which were expansion of Euclidean distance, was used to test for results.

The results obtained by the system compares relatively same with results obtained by (Kulkarni and Lokhande, 2010) [5] in which neural network was used as classification technique. Nearest neighbor classification is a simple classification technique compared to other state of art techniques.

6   Conclusions

Illumination correction of hand gesture resulted in a better and smoother binary image which was used to extract features to compare and classify gestures. Lighting conditions affect the results. Very dark environment with less illumination resulted in binary image with more noise thus required lots of image processing. High amount of features yielded good results but inclusion of a redundant feature affected the results largely. Eliminating the redundant features improved accuracy of classification. On the other hand, giving priority to a single feature of less importance also reduced the accuracy of the classification. Euclidean distance approach, nearest neighbor and K^{th} nearest neighbor are simple to implement and can be expanded with conditional algorithm to get good results. Implementing the system is very cheap and can be easily expanded to recognition of other objects or sign languages.

Classification using two camera inputs is possible future study. A hybrid classification and feature weighting is also area of exploration to obtain further improved result. The current research benefits by enabling communication with hearing impaired people easier by use of simple state of art. The algorithm can also be used in human machine interface for controlling devices and in any other non-verbal communication.

References

1. Bakaus, P., (n.d.).: https://paulbakaus.com/tutorials/performance/the-illusion-of-motion/
2. 28 October 2014. www.dixie.edu: http://www.dixie.edu/com/icl/File/disiplines/PALMISTRY%20101,%20SHAPES%20OF%20HANDS%20AND%20FINGERS.pdf. Accessed 2015
3. Garg, P., Aggarwal, N., Sofat, S.: Vision Based Hand Gesture Recognition. World Academy of Science, Engineering and Technology, 25 (2009)
4. Paansare, J.R., Gawande, S.H., Ingle, M.: Real time static hand gesture recognition for american sign language (ASL) in complex background. J. Sig. Process. 3(3), 364–367 (2012)
5. Kulkarni, V.S., Lokhande, S.D.: Appearance based recognition of american sign language using gesture segmentation. Int. J. Comput. Sci. Eng. 2(3), 560–565 (2010)
6. Rumyantsev, O., Merati, M., Ramachandran, V.: Hand Sign Recognition through Palm Gesture and Movement. Image processing, EE 368, Spring 2012
7. Stenger, B., Mendonca, P.R., Cipolla, R.: Model-Based 3D Tracking of an Articulated Hand 2, 310–315 (2001). doi:10.1109/CVPR.2001.990976
8. Nanda, A., Mishra, A.: Master Hand Technology For The HMI Using Hand Gesture And Colour Detection. Department of Electronics and communication Engineering National Institute of Technology, Rourkela (2012)

9. Fang, Y., Wang, K., Cheng, J., Lu, H.: A real-time hand gesture recognition method. In: 2007 IEEE International Conference on Multimedia and Expo, pp. 995–998 (2007). doi:10.1109/ICME.2007.4284820
10. Vese, L.: An Introduction to Mathematical Image Processing IAS, Park City Mathematics Institute, Utah (2010)
11. Smith, S.W.: Image formation and display. In: Smith, S.W. (ed.) The Scientists and Engineers Guide to Digital Signal Processing, pp. 373–396. Carlifornia Technical Publishing (1997)
12. Pedersen, J.T.: Study group SURF: Feature detection & description (2011)
13. Dey, S.K., Anand, S.: Algorithm for multi hand fingercounting: an easy approach. Adv. Vis. Comput. Int. J. (AVC) 1(1) (2014)
14. Gay, S.B.: Local properties of binary images in two dimensions. IEEE Trans. Comput. **20**(5), 551–561 (1971)

Unicast Routing Protocol Based on Attractor Selection Model for Vehicular Ad-Hoc Networks

Daxin Tian[1,4(✉)], Kunxian Zheng[1], Jianshan Zhou[1],
Zhengguo Sheng[2], Qiang Ni[3], and Yunpeng Wang[1,4]

[1] Beijing Advanced Innovation Center for Big Data and Brain Computing,
Beihang University, Beijing 100191, China
dtian@buaa.edu.cn
[2] Department of Engineering and Design, The University of Sussex, Richmond 3A09, UK
[3] School of Computing and Communications, Lancaster University, Lancaster LA1 4WA, UK
[4] Beijing Key Laboratory for Cooperative Vehicle Infrastructure Systems and Safety Control,
School of Transportation Science and Engineering, Beihang University, Beijing 100191, China

Abstract. As an important member of IOV, vehicular Ad Hoc Networks (VANETs) play a key role for many vehicular applications, which significantly rely on the vehicular routing. However, the frequently changed topology leads to great challenge to the routing protocol. In this work, inspired by the mechanism of cellular adaptive responses in a changing environment, called cellular attractor selection, we propose a novel bio-inspired unicast routing protocol, which can adapt vehicular message forwarding to the changing topology to guarantee the routing efficiency and reliability. The experimental results exhibit the robustness and effectiveness of the proposed method and the significantly improved performance over the conventional routing protocol.

Keywords: Vehicular ad-hoc networks · Unicast routing protocol · Self-adaptive mechanism · Biologically inspired networking · Attractor selection model

1 Introduction

There are many potential applications with IOV, such as traffic management, collision avoidance, cooperative driving [1–3]. As an important component of IOV, Vehicular Ad-Hoc Networks (VANETs) are different from traditional networks. The networking nodes of VANETs are vehicles with high mobility, which could cause rapid change in the network topology. Thus, the conventional routing protocols using routing table to forwarding packets may be infeasible in vehicular networks. Although VANETs have some common characteristics of Mobile Ad-Hoc Networks (MANETs), VANETs are characterized with some special features that should not be ignored of, such as the highly dynamic nature of network topology and more complexity of the vehicular scenarios. So conventional MANET routing protocols may fail in meeting the reliability demand imposed by the vehicular message forwarding.

The most commonly used routing protocols for mobile ad hoc networks are Dynamic Source Routing (DSR) [4], Ad-Hoc On-Demand Distance Vector (AODV) [5], Greedy

© Springer International Publishing AG 2016
C.-H. Hsu et al. (Eds.): IOV 2016, LNCS 10036, pp. 138–148, 2016.
DOI: 10.1007/978-3-319-51969-2_12

Perimeter Stateless Routing (GPSR) [6]. Different protocols have different routing processes. The nodes with the DSR protocol need to maintain and update their own routing buffer in real time. When the information stored in the routing buffer is available to construct a routing path, the message is forwarded by the hop-by-hop transmission. When there does not exist a feasible route, the nodes will discover a new route using flooding-like broadcasting mechanism and update the entries of their routing buffer. In the AODV protocol, a node uses a dynamic routing table to record the new path's information. In GPSR [6, 7], each forwarding node sends the packets to the next-hop node that is the closest to the destination node. GPSR depends on the information on the relative position between each neighbor node and the destination node to select the next-hop node from this forwarder's neighborhood. In some situations where no nodes are closer to the destination node than the current forwarding node, GPSR cannot use the greedy forwarding strategy to send the data packets to the next-hop node. To get around this problem, the current node uses the boundary forwarding strategy to send the data packets. However, this may result in high routing delay and low reliability [8].

As a new bio-inspired model [9], the attractor selection model has been successfully applied in many fields. For example, the adaptive vehicular epidemic routing method [10], the network selection method for multimode communications in heterogeneous vehicular telematics [11], the adaptive signal control for traffic networks [12], the epidemic broadcasting for vehicular ad-hoc networks [13]. Furthermore, the attractor selection mechanism offers a new choice of future mobile network management mechanism [14]. The attractor selection model has been shown effective for designing a self-adaptive decision making strategy. Compared to the traditional methods, the attractor selection model can achieve superior performance in terms of self-adaption and robustness. Because of the frequent change in VANET topology, static routing protocols cannot adapt to the changing network in real time. Different from the traditional method, the attractor selection model determines the next-hop node based on the route activity information. As shown in some existing works [11–15], the attractor selection model provides a self-adaptive and robust approach to boost the system performance in fluctuating environments. Inspired by the self-adaptive behavior of E. coli cells in dynamic environments, we propose a bio-inspired unicast routing protocol based on attractor selection (URAS), which can adjust the selection of the next-hop node according to the dynamic topology of a VANET in order to guarantee the message delivery reliability.

The rest of this paper is organized as follows. Section 2 discusses the attractor selection model incorporated in the URAS protocol. Section 3 presents the simulation situation we set up to evaluate our proposed URAS protocol and discusses the simulation results. Section 4 concludes this paper.

2 Unicast Routing Protocol Based on Attractor Selection Model

2.1 Cellular Attraction Selection Model

The attractor selection model is originally used to describe the adaptive regulation of E.coli's gene expression [9], in which the bi-stable switching mechanism of the operons affecting the gene expression in a dynamic environment is modeled by two stochastic nonlinear ordinal differential equations. This model can be expended to a high dimensional form by the following dynamic equations:

$$
\begin{cases}
\dfrac{dm_1}{dt} = \dfrac{S(A)}{1 + m_2^2} - D(A) \times m_1 + \eta_1 \\[2mm]
\dfrac{dm_2}{dt} = \dfrac{S(A)}{1 + m_1^2} - D(A) \times m_2 + \eta_2
\end{cases}
\tag{1}
$$

$$
\begin{cases}
S(A) = \dfrac{6A}{2 + A} \\[2mm]
D(A) = A
\end{cases}
\tag{2}
$$

where m_1, m_2 are the concentrations of two different RNAs or RNAs' protein products, which are produced by two mutual inhibitory operons, respectively. A is the cellular activity, which is a parameter indicating the comprehensive goodness of the cellular adaptation. $S(A)$ is the rate coefficient of producing the cellular activity, and $D(A)$ is the rate coefficient of degradation. The two functions are both effected by the cellular activity A. η_1 and η_2 are the independent white gene noises [9].

It can be found that as the cellular activity A increases, the effect of the white gene noises is reduced, so that the cellular gene expression becomes more deterministic. This implies that the cell adapts better to the current environment. As A decreases, the effect of the white gene noises becomes stronger, and the cellular gene expression is more random until the cell finds a new gene expression that can adapt to the environment well.

2.2 Unicast Routing Protocol

Let the set of all the nodes in a VANET be A, and current node's neighbor set be N_k, which contains the nodes within the communication coverage of the current node k, i.e.,

$$
N_k = \left\{ n \in A \mid dis(n, k) < r_k \right\}
\tag{3}
$$

where n is a neighbor node of the node k, and $dis(n, k)$ is the geographic distance between k and n, r_k is the node k's signal transmission range. In order to help the current node forward the data packet to the destination node while reducing the hop number, we consider that the data packet should be forwarded to the node that is much closer to the destination node d, and we let the candidate neighbor nodes that are suitable to serve as a next-hop node be the set B_k. The current node selects the next-hop node from the set B_k, i.e.,

$$
B_k = \left\{ n \in N_k \mid dis(n, d) < dist(k, d) \right\}
\tag{4}
$$

Furthermore, we assume that if B_k is an empty set, $B_k = N_k$.

We use the differential equations in (1) to formulate the possibility of selecting a node n from the set B_k as the next-hop node [11]:

$$\frac{d}{dt}m_n = \frac{s(\alpha)}{1 + (m_{max} - m_n)^2} - d(\alpha)m_n + \eta_n \tag{5}$$

where m_n is the possibility of the node n to be selected as the next-hop node, and the m_{max} is the maximum possibility among all of the nodes in B_k. α is the activity of the forwarding route, η_n is the white Gaussian noise, and $s(\alpha)$ is defined as follows

$$s(\alpha) = a\alpha^c + b\alpha \tag{6}$$

where a, b, c are real-number constants. $d(\alpha)$ is defined as follows:

$$d(\alpha) = \alpha \tag{7}$$

To show the adaptive mechanism underlying the attractor selection, we set the modeling parameters as $a = 8$, $b = 10$, $c = 4$ in Eq. (6), and then simulate the activity signal as shown in Fig. 1(a). We assume that there are 3 selection probabilities in the state vector $\boldsymbol{m}$ and update the state over time using the model (5). The evolution of each selection probability over time is illustrated in Fig. 1(b).

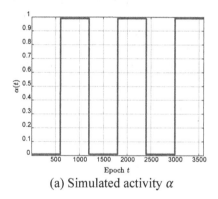

(a) Simulated activity α

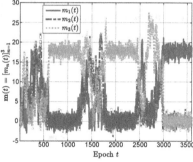

(b) Evolution of selection probabilities

Fig. 1. Simulation of the attractor selection model.

From Fig. 1, we can see that a relatively small activity α can lead to more obvious stochastic behaviors in the state evolution, in the situation of which the selection probabilities are fluctuating with an identical magnitude. By contrast, when the activity α increases, one of the entities in the state vector rises to a single highest value while the other two decrease to a lower level. This implies that the state switches from a shallow basin with low stability to a deep basin with high stability, called a stable attractor in the phase space. The stable attractor is associated with a high-level activity. The numerical experiment confirms that the attractor selection is driven by the activity parameter and the system state is always seeking for a stable state, randomly switching between different basins, until it is attracted into a stable state with high activity. This implies that once the goodness/fitness of a decision-making problem-specified solution can be mapped to the activity parameter, we can use the attractor selection mechanism to drive the decision maker in a dynamic environment to seek for an appropriate and stable solution with a high level of goodness/fitness in the solution space.

We design a self-adaptive unicast vehicular routing protocol based on the attractor selection model. To be specific, we treat the comprehensive performance of a routing path as the cellular activity parameter α and induce the forwarder (as a decision maker) to adapt its selection of a next-hop node to the changing vehicular network condition. In this way, a sequence of the next-hop nodes selected can construct a robust and effective vehicular routing path. In the attractor selection-inspired routing, if the activity parameter α is low, the current node is expected to select the next-hop node randomly. This means that the current routing path is not suitable for the current network condition, so that the node will seek for a new and more suitable routing path by random selection until the activity α becomes large enough. When a more stable routing path is constructed, it has a higher activity which can reduce the influence of the random term η_n. Thus, the network prefers using such a stable path to route the vehicular message in order to guarantee a high routing performance. An example is shown in Fig. 2. The current path 1 is not good, since it contains many hops that lead to a larger time delay. Thus, its corresponding activity α is low. With the effect of the random terms η_n, the forwarders in the situation are seeking for a better routing path, i.e., the path 2, which is more stable and contains less hops to forward the message to the destination node. It is worth pointing out here that the influence of the random terms will not disappear, which enables the node to find a better routing path. The selection of the next-hop node driven by the attractor selection mechanism is to some extent like the stochastic optimization.

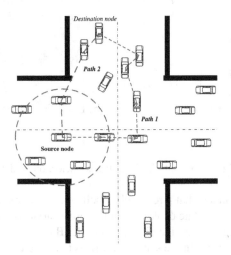

Fig. 2. An example for two different routing paths.

2.3   Cellular Activity Mapping

As aforementioned, we need to formulate a metric to quantify the comprehensive routing performance and then treat it as the cellular activity parameter α in the attractor selection model, such that we can adapt the bio-inspired model to the next-hop node selection decision making. Specifically, when the data packet is successfully delivered to the destination node, the destination node uses the attractor selection model to calculate the activity parameter α according to the condition of this current routing path. The formula is given as follows:

$$\alpha = (C^\mu D^\nu E^\sigma)/(\sum_{l \in J} C_l^\mu D_l^\nu E_l^\sigma) \tag{8}$$

where J is the set of all of routing paths, μ, ν, σ are the weights of C, D, E, respectively, and C is defined as follows:

$$C = hop_{min}/hop \tag{9}$$

where hop_{min} is the minimum hop number among the pervious routing paths, and hop is the hop count of the current routing path; C is the impact of the current hop count on the node activity α. As the current hop count increases, the activity α becomes low, and the node is encouraged to seek for a new routing path with less hops.

D is defined as follows:

$$D = time_{min}/time \tag{10}$$

where $time_{min}$ is the minimum time delay among the pervious routing paths, and $time$ is the delay of the current routing path; D is the impact of the current time delay on the node activity α. As the current time delay increases, the activity α becomes low, and the node is expected to find a shorter-delay routing path.

E is defined as follows:

$$E = \sum_{i=1}^{Y} a_i \tag{11}$$

where Y is the total number of hops in a routing path. This term is used to trade off the energy consumption over the stability of the routing path, and a_i is defined as follows

$$a_i = (FG)^2 / \sum_{l \in B} (F_l G_l)^2 \tag{12}$$

where B is the set of all the nodes that can be selected as the next-hop node of the current node, F is defined as follows:

$$F = 1/dis(n, k) \tag{13}$$

where the $dis(n, k)$ is the relative distance of the current node k and the next-hop node n. Because the energy consumption of a node is related to the distance of packet transmission, this term balances the energy consumption of the routing path.

G is defined as follows:

$$G = 1/v(n, k) \tag{14}$$

where the $v(n, k)$ is the relative velocity between the node n and k. The lower relative velocity is, the more stable the connection between these two nodes becomes. This term can be used to reflect the stability of a routing path. Once obtaining the activity α, the destination node sends a backward data packet to update the activity of all the nodes along the routing path.

In order to avoid the problem that the outdated activity α may mislead the selection of a next-hop node, we set the activity decay with time as follows

$$\alpha = \alpha_0 / (2^{t/x}) \tag{15}$$

where α_0 is calculated by the destination node, t is the time, and x is a real-number constant. After each node updates its own activity α, the activity will still decay with time. The selection of a next-hop node for forwarding vehicular messages as well as the update procedure of the activity information is detailed in the following Algorithms 1 and 2. We summarize the unicast routing protocol based on attractor selection model as follows:

Step 1: the current node k selects the next-hop node from B_k according to the possibility of the node being selected as the next-hop node;

Step 2: when a packet is successfully forwarded to the destination node, the system obtains a new activity α;

Step 3: the destination node sends a backward data packet containing the new α to update the activity of all the nodes along the routing path. The activity should decay with time during the process. Go to the first step to continue the sequential steps given above (Tables 1 and 2).

Table 1. Algorithm for selection of the next-hop node.

Algorithm 1. Selection of the next-hop node based on the attractor selection model
Input: positions of the current node, its neighboring nodes, and the destination node; speed of the current node and its neighbor nodes; the activity α
Output: the next-hop node; a
1: **If** the destination node is within the current node's neighborhood **Then**
2:      Select the destination node as the next-hop node
3:      Calculate a of the hop from k to the destination node
4:      **Return** the destination node; a
5: **Else**
6:      Construct a candidate set B_k
7:          **If** B_k is empty **Then**
8:              Set B_k to be N_k
9:          **End If**
10:      Evaluate m_n by using the attractor selection model for $\forall n \in B_k$
11:      Select $n^* = \text{argmax}_{n \in B_k} [m_n]$ as the next-hop node
12:      Calculate a of the hop from k to n^*
13:      **Return** n^*; a
14: **End If**

Table 2. Algorithm for updating the activity.

Algorithm 2. Update of the activity α by each node along a routing path
Input: the backward package;
Output: the new activity α of each node along a routing path
1: **If** a message arrives at the destination node successfully **Then**
2:     Calculate α associated with the forwarding path by the destination node
3:     Send a backward package carrying α by the destination node
4:         **If** the backward route does not fail at an intermediate node **Then**
5:             Update the activity of this intermediate node by $\alpha \leftarrow \alpha/2^{\frac{t}{c}}$
6:         **Else**
7:             Terminate the back propagation
8:         **End If**
9: **End If**

3 Experiments

3.1 Simulation Settings

In the simulation, we adopt the random walk model to simulate the mobility of vehicles in a region with 2250×450 m^2. The parameters of Eq. (6) $a = 8$, $b = 10$, $c = 4$. To balance the node energy consumption, the stability of routing path and routing delay, we set the parameters of Eq. (8) as $\mu = \nu = \sigma = 2$, and $c = 15$ in Eq. (15). To demonstrate the performance, we also carry out the simulation of GPSR with the same experimental settings. In the simulation, we compare URAS and GPSR in terms of the successful delivery rate under different node speeds, signal coverages, and the node numbers (node densities). The successful delivery rate is the ratio of the number of the packets that can be received by the destination node over that of all the packets sent by the source node.

3.2 Numerical Results and Analysis

We first analyze the impact of the dynamic nature of the environmental condition on the unicast vehicular routing protocol based on the attractor selection model. We randomly generate 200 vehicular nodes that are uniformly distributed within the specified region aforementioned. At the initialization of the simulation. Then, we vary the magnitude of the noise term η, i.e., the stochastic noise intensity. That is, the intensity of the white Gaussian noise term η, $\sigma(\eta)$, is set to 0.1, 0.01, and 0.001, respectively, and a simulation is carried out with each of these settings. The routing activity result obtained under different noise intensities is demonstrated in Fig. 3. Recall that the activity parameter is treated as a metric reflecting the comprehensive routing performance in terms of the hop number, the geographic routing distance and the routing delay. Figure 3 shows that on one hand, the stochastic fluctuations in the system really impair the routing performance represented by the activity parameter. On the other hand, even though the networking environment with stochastic noises is fluctuating all the time, the routing protocol based on the attractor selection can induce the activity to rise to a high level many times. This indicates that the bio-inspired routing mechanism enables seeking for a relatively robust routing path in a perturbing environment, which is of great significance in actual vehicular communication application scenarios.

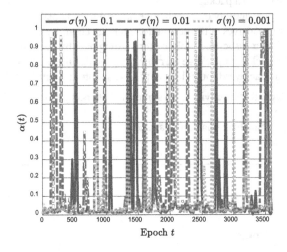

Fig. 3. Evolution of the activity α under different noise intensities.

Next, we compare our proposed solution with the conventional method, i.e., GPSR protocol in different simulation situations. Figure 4 shows the results obtained by the URAS and the GPSR with varying node number and varying signal coverage. It can be found that as the node number or the signal coverage increases, the successful delivery rate of both URAS and GPSR increases. However, when the network is sparse and the transmission distance small, URAS performs better than GPSR. The main reason is that as the node density is low, GPSR using the greedy forwarding strategy fails in getting the node closer to the destination. In this situation, it causes a high routing delay and failure rate. By comparison, our URAS outperforms the GPSR due to its adaptability to dynamic node density.

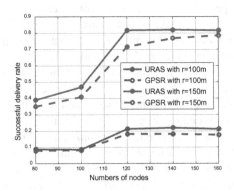

Fig. 4. Results of URAS and GPSR under different node numbers

Figure 5 gives the results of these two protocols under different node speeds and the transmission distances. The number of the nodes is fixed at 120. It can be found that with the increasing speed, the variation of the successful delivery rate is small, while the proposed URAS performs better than the GPSR, implying that our proposed algorithm can achieve better reliability in supporting a wider range of vehicular mobility.

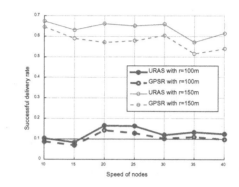

Fig. 5. Results of URAS and GPSR under different speeds

4   Conclusion

As the node density of VANETs as well as the node speed is changing all the time in reality, the traditional routing protocol may be infeasible to adapt to diverse vehicular application situations. In this paper, we propose a novel bio-inspired unicast routing protocol based on attractor selection (URAS), and this method demonstrates its superior advantage over the conventional protocol in VANETs. Specifically, the attractor selecting model-based vehicular unicast routing can adapt to the dynamic environments.

Acknowledgments. This research is supported by the National Natural Science Foundation of China under Grant nos. U1564212, 61672082, and Jiangsu Province Collaborative Innovation Center of Modern Urban Traffic Technologies.

References

1. Song, J., Hsu, C.-H., Dong, M., Zhang, D.: Vehicle cardinality estimation in VANETs by using RFID tag estimator. In: Hsu, C.-H., Xia, F., Liu, X., Wang, S. (eds.) IOV 2015. LNCS, vol. 9502, pp. 3–15. Springer, Heidelberg (2015). doi:10.1007/978-3-319-27293-1_1
2. Gao, Z., Chen, K., Zheng, J., Hao, Y., Yang, Y., Qiu, X.: Crossroads optimal geographic routing for vehicular ad hoc networks in City Scenario. In: Hsu, R.C.-H., Wang, S. (eds.) IOV 2014. LNCS, vol. 8662, pp. 201–210. Springer, Heidelberg (2014). doi: 10.1007/978-3-319-11167-4_20
3. Tian, D., Zhou, J., Wang, Y., Sheng, Z., Xia, H., Yi, Z.: Modeling chain collisions in vehicular networks with variable penetration rates. Transp. Res. Part C Emerg. Technol. **69**, 36–59 (2016)

4. Johnson, D.B.: The dynamic source routing protocol for mobile ad hoc networks. draft-ietf-manet-dsr-09.txt (1998)
5. Perkins, C., Belding-Royer, E., Das, S.: Ad hoc On-Demand Distance Vector (AODV) Routing. RFC Editor (2000)
6. Karp, B., Kung, H.T.: Gpsr: greedy perimeter stateless routing for wireless networks (2010)
7. Broch, J., Maltz, D.A., Johnson, D.B., Hu, Y.C., Jetcheva, J.: A performance comparison of multi-hop wireless ad hoc network routing protocols. In: ACM/IEEE International Conference on Mobile Computing and Networking, vol. 85–97, pp. 85–97. ACM (2001)
8. Dao-Quan, L.I., Liu, H.Y., Cao, Q.G.: New routing algorithm based on geographical location: GPSR-AD. J. Comput. Appl. **29**(12), 3215–3217 (2009)
9. Kashiwagi, A., Urabe, I., Kaneko, K., Yomo, T.: Adaptive response of a gene network to environmental changes by fitness-induced attractor selection. Plos One **1**(1), e49 (2006)
10. Tian, D., Zhou, J., Wang, Y., Zhang, G., Xia, H.: An adaptive vehicular epidemic routing method based on attractor selection model. Ad Hoc Netw. **36**(P2), 465–481 (2016)
11. Tian, D., Zhou, J., Wang, Y., Lu, Y.: A dynamic and self-adaptive network selection method for multimode communications in heterogeneous vehicular telematics. IEEE Trans. Intell. Transp. Syst. **16**(6), 3033–3049 (2015)
12. Tian, D., Zhou, J., Sheng, Z., Wang, Y., Ma, J.: From cellular attractor selection to adaptive signal control for traffic networks. Sci. Rep. **6**, 1–15 (2016)
13. Tian, D., Zhou, J., Wang, Y., Xia, H., Yi, Z., Liu, H.: Optimal epidemic broadcasting for vehicular ad hoc networks. Int. J. Commun. Syst. **27**(9), 1220–1242 (2014)
14. Motoyoshi, G., Leibnitz, K., Murata, M.: Proposal and evaluation of a future mobile network management mechanism with attractor selection. Eurasip J. Wirel. Commun. Netw. **2012**(1), 1–13 (2012)
15. Leibnitz, K., Murata, M.: Attractor selection and perturbation for robust networks in fluctuating environments. IEEE Netw. **24**(3), 14–18 (2010)

Social Networking and Big Data Analytics Assisted Reliable Recommendation System Model for Internet of Vehicles

Manish Kumar Pandey[(✉)] and Karthikeyan Subbiah

Department of Computer Science, Institute of Science,
Banaras Hindu University, Varanasi 221005, India
pandey.manish@live.com

Abstract. The devices are becoming ubiquitous and interconnected due to rapid advancements in computing and communication technology. The Internet of Vehicles (IoV) is one such example which consists of vehicles that converse with each other as well as with the public networks through V2V (vehicle-to-vehicle), V2P (vehicle-to-pedestrian) and V2I (vehicle-to-infrastructure) communications. The social relationships amongst vehicles create a social network where the participants are intelligent objects rather than the human beings and this leads to emergence of Social Internet of Vehicles (SIoV). The big data generated from these networks of devices are needed to be processed intelligently for making these systems smart. The security and privacy issues such as authentication and recognition attacks, accessibility attacks, privacy attacks, routing attacks, data genuineness attacks etc. are to be addressed to make these cyber physical network systems very reliable. This paper presents a comprehensive survey on SIoV and proposes a novel social recommendation model that could establish links between social networking and SIoV for reliable exchange of information and intelligently analyze the information to draw authentic conclusions for making right assessment. The future Intelligent IoV system which should be capable to learn and explore the cyber physical system could be designed.

Keywords: Big data · IoV · SIoV · Social recommendation system · Cyber physical systems

1 Introduction

Technology has drastically transformed our lives by bringing in huge benefits that reflects the beginning of our associated future, such as vehicles associated with computers, onboard sensors, sensors in wearable devices that notify the movements of objects and its current state of affairs. So, the internet of Vehicles (IoV) is an inevitable juxtaposition of the mobility and the Internet of things, in other words it is the Internet of things in the area of transport. The IoV aims at achieving an integrated smart transport system by improving traffic flow, preventing accidents, ensuring the road safety, and creating a comfortable driving experience. Mobility in transportation systems generates a huge amount of real data and it is a great challenge to deal with this data surge. So a

© Springer International Publishing AG 2016
C.-H. Hsu et al. (Eds.): IOV 2016, LNCS 10036, pp. 149–163, 2016.
DOI: 10.1007/978-3-319-51969-2_13

multi-dimensional approach is required to handle and study the vast amount of generated data in structured as well as unstructured formats both from the independent and connected sensors of the Internet of Vehicle (IoV) to obtain optimal results with safety measures [2]. The big data [1] technology provides a solution to this challenging problem to evolve such intelligent and smart vehicular system.

1.1 The IoV Technology

Hardware Infrastructure: Convergence of technologies in the design of vehicles is quickly making them as key devices in the Internet of Things (IoT) [3–5] with the capabilities to accept data as well as send data to the cloud, to the traffic infrastructure and to other vehicles. As a result, the Internet of Vehicle (IoV) becomes an emerging technology in data communication with definite protocols that facilitates data transfer between cars, roadside equipment, wearable devices and traffic data management centers. So the IoV is the next technological revolution, which integrated with sensor networks, camera [5], mobile communication [7], real-time localization [8], ubiquitous computing and other technologies [9] to realize the essential requirements for Intelligent Transportation Systems (ITS) applications [6].

Processing Needs: Now, it is an era of smart objects with sensor inputs that are able to communicate via the Internet based on the protocols and/or prototype standards of ICT. Therefore, advanced techniques are necessary for effectively handling huge data generated from IoV and to perform efficient online analytical query processing [2]. Thereby, the big data analysis outcomes are pertinent to the transportation benefits in terms of cost efficiency, time utilization in ensuring road safety, for effective traffic management, in automated tolling and providing other ITS services. The following facts supports big data paradigm as a promising technology for intelligent IoV systems: (i) Massive data streams produced by IoV audio, video and sensors must be handled and integrated [10], (ii) Spatial data of IoV objects in the context of the environments is described as location based and in time series and (iii) Integration of federated IoV smart objects' data are tended to have its own implicit semantics that need to be recognized for the inferring justifications.

The scalability and capability of big data analytics and predictions for IoV data management, exploration and exploitations lies in dynamic and scalable technological facts, which includes:

It is vitally significant to identify and address IoV smart objects in order to interact or query with various objects to realize each other's identity and address effectively.
Effective methods of data abstraction and compression should be developed for filtering out the redundant data.
Data indexing, archiving, access control and scalability for IoV data.
Data warehouse and its query language for multi-dimensional analysis, semantic intelligibility and interoperability for diverse data of IoV,
Time-series and event level data aggregation,
It is essential for privacy and protection of data management of IoV.

Communication Network's Needs: Wireless networks can be organized into three major categories. An infrastructure wireless network is the first one that mainly relies on a central station that coordinates all communications [11]. Second are ad hoc networks or non-structured networks that give equal roles to all stations in the network [12, 13]. Third, hybrid networks which combines the first two categories [14]. A case of hybrid networks is hybrid vehicular ad hoc networks (hybrid-VANETs) [15], which employ ad hoc networks for communication among vehicles and infrastructure networks, for example cellular systems for communication and wireless local area networks (WLANs) with a core network [16, 17]. Smart vehicles, through their finer communication potentiality, will be capable to work jointly not only with navigation and broadcast satellites, but also through passenger smart vehicles, smart phones and roadside units, making them an important component of IoT and the development of smart cities [18]. VANETs combine these with new applications and procedures to facilitate the intelligent communication among the connection to the Internet and the vehicles. VANETs rely on on-board units (OBU) and roadside units (RSU) and to facilitate the connectivity. The RSUs are communication infrastructure units that are positioned next to roads to communicate with vehicles and to a larger infrastructure or to a core network, depending upon metropolitan traffic topography. The OBU is a network device integrated with different sensors attached in vehicles that supports communication with different wireless networks, for example dedicated short-range communication (DSRC) and WLAN. A VANET has a varied range of applications, from road safety, through traffic management by the detection and avoidance of traffic accidents [19], traffic flow, reduction of traffic congestion [20], and infotainment to provide of driving comfort [21].

SIoV: The Fig. 1 shows different components of SIoV and the communication between them. The Social Internet of Things (SIoT) introduces social relationships between things, creating a social network where the participant entities are not humans, but intelligent things. In such networks, information about the traffic and road conditions is obtained from both humans as well as machines. As humans can be biased or may be forced to propagate false information for personal gains, the network should integrate mechanisms to assert the trust and reputation of the information sources.

The Social Internet of Things (SIoT) [22] is a network of intelligent things that have social interactions. The Social Internet of Vehicles (SIoV) [23, 24] is an example of a SIoT where the things are smart vehicles. Alam et al. [24] designed logical models of the subsystems occupied in the SIoV communication process and propose models that could be useful in order to set up safety, efficiency or comfort applications based Social Internet of Vehicles (SIoV).

Even though the basic rules are the same for both social networks of vehicles and social networks of humans, there are important differences in terms of the active character of the entities, the topology of the network, privacy concerns, their social interactions and security issues that arise.

Social Internet of Vehicles (SIoV) describes both the social interactions among vehicles [25] and among drivers [26]. As described in [26], a vehicular social network is produced when a driver goes to an area where additional public with familiar interests

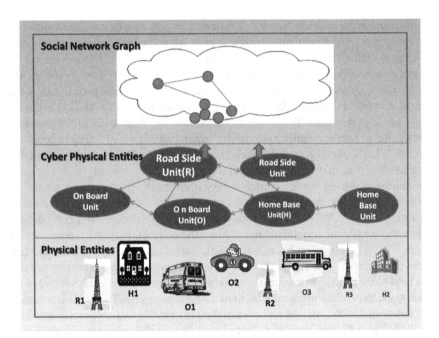

Fig. 1. Social Internet of Vehicles

or related content exist. Contrary to this, Nitti et al. [25] describe a vehicular social network as social interactions among cars, which converse alone to glance for update services and exchange messages relevant to traffic. As vehicles are autonomous and becoming more autonomous [27] and applications are already developed to support social interactions among drivers and passengers [28, 29].

1.2   The Next Generation Vehicles and SIoV

Recent advancements in technology that are context-aware and wireless vehicular communication techniques, such as Long-Term Evolution (LTE), Dedicated Short-Range Communications (DSRC), Worldwide Interoperability for Microwave Access (WiMax) and IEEE 802.11p [30] has boosted the design, development and deployment of vehicular networks. An increasing number of social network applications are being proposed for vehicular networks, which leads to a shift from traditional vehicular networks toward SIoV. The key aspects that enable SIoV in current vehicular networks are briefly discussed as follows.

Similar to [31], we focus on three main components, namely: next-generation vehicles; vehicle context-awareness; and SIoV context-aware applications.

Vehicular ad hoc networks (VANETs) are a class of mobile ad hoc network that has been anticipated to improve traffic protection and applications to provide comfort to drivers. The unique features of VANETs comprise of quick vehicles that follow predestined paths (i.e., roads) and message exchange having different priority levels. For example, messages for traffic safety applications require timely delivery of reliable message making it of high priority while messages for comfort and infotainment applications have low priority [32]. Vehicles can communicate among themselves (vehicle-to-vehicle, V2V) as well as with roadside units (vehicle-to-infrastructure, V2I) by using the on-board unit. The other forms of communication, such as vehicle-to-cloud broadband (V2B), where the vehicle communicate with a monitoring data centre, vehicle-to-human (V2H) to communicate with susceptible road users, and vehicle-to-sensor (V2S), where the vehicles converse with sensors embedded in the location [32] are enabled.

1.3 Interaction of SIoV with Social Network

Social network analysis (SNA) refers to the use of network theory to analyses social networks to discover important players in a network. Individual actors (either be vehicles or drivers or even passengers) within the network are represented as nodes, and the interactions or relationships among them are represented by the corresponding edges [33]. Based on the nature of interaction (either static or dynamic, metrics, like centrality, cohesion, degree and clustering coefficient among entities of the network) can reveal specific relations among nodes, as well as groups of entities that share common habits.

Cunha et al. [34] showed that vehicles tend to demonstrate a similar behavior and routines in terms of mobility. The vehicles mobility could be mapped in terms of social network, following the same basic laws of degree distribution and distance among nodes. Applying Social network analysis on vehicular networks can consequently improve the performance of communication protocols and services. Graph theory concepts, like centrality and clustering, can be applied in vehicular networks, as long as they integrate their specific features, such as mobility of nodes, channel conditions and drivers' behavior.

For information spreading in a network, the centrality of nodes has most important role to play [35, 36]. In a similar way, central nodes can serve as good spreaders of infections [37] or as good points for building defense mechanisms [38]. Furthermore, central nodes can be elected as the cluster head of groups that are created on the fly. A cluster head may act as a relay node for inter clusters traffic or as a relay node for intra-cluster communication [39].

1.4 Types of Attack in IoV

In information security, STRIDE Threat Model classifies attacks and threats into six main categories [40], specifically: tampering with data, spoofing identity, repudiation, disclosure of information, denial of service and elevation of privilege. Especially, Internet of Vehicles system is prone to different attacks like jamming, interference, eavesdropping and so on, These attacks and threats decease the stability, robustness, real-time, security and privacy of IoV, and make it lose the ability to provide effective services, even cause serious accidents [41–45], due to following constraints such as dynamic topology characteristics, bandwidth limitations, transmission power limitations, abundant sources, mobile limitation, non-uniform distribution of nodes, perception of vehicle dependent data on the trajectory, large scale network etc.

Following are various types of attacks in IoV.

Attacks on Authentication: This attack is categorized in to following sub-classes:

Sybil attack: In wireless networks, a single node with multiple identifications can damage the system by controlling most nodes in the system.
GPS deception: GPS deception can provide a node with fake information about its location, speed and some other GPS information.
Masquerading attack: In a network environment, this attack uses fake identity to gain the network access.
Wormhole attack: This kind of attack always have fatal influences on IoV system due to its characteristics of change and high dependence on efficient routing algorithm.

Availability Attacks: Denial of service and channel interference are common types of attacks on availability.

Secrecy Attacks: This steals data by eavesdropping or interception.

Routing Attacks: There are four different attack types in routing process [46, 47], which includes Eavesdropping [48], Denial of service [49], Masquerading [50], Route modification [51].

Data Authenticity Attacks: It is necessary to ensure that the source data has not been modified when data packets are transmitted through the network. Data authenticity attacks can be categorized into four subtypes namely: Replay attack, Camouflage attack, Fabricating and tampering with messages and Illusion attack [51–53].

1.5 Threats in SIoV

The security in vehicular network is a vital aspect of SIoV, because any negotiation in security could lead to life-threatening situations along with damage of other components that use the SIoV. Social vehicular network security contemplates social characteristics and human behavior in a similar manner [32]. This section reviews issues of security, trust along with reputation in vehicular networks with a specific focus on the social aspects.

SIoV Threats. Raya has reviewed the threats available in vehicular networks and categorized them into insider/outsider, malicious/rationale and active/passive categories [54]. Zeadally [55] has differently classified them into threats to availability, authenticity and to confidentiality.

Denial of Service (DoS) Attack aims to prevent legal users from accessing data or services in computer networks. In vehicular networks, large volumes of irrelevant messages will be flooded that result in jamming of the traffic that negatively impacts the communication between the network's nodes, on-board units and roadside units.

False Message Injection. An attacker from inside can mark a false message and broadcast it to the network. In this manner the attacker can falsify the traffic flow and could affect the decisions of other drivers, causing damage either through traffic jams or accidents.

Malware, such as viruses or worms, is typically introduced through outside unit software and firmware updates. Malware can contaminate vehicles and even permit remote adversaries to acquire control of individual vehicles.

Masquerading and Sybil. In a masquerading attack, a vehicle fakes its identity and pretends to be legal in the networks of the vehicle. Outsiders can carry out attacks, e.g. injecting false messages. In a Sybil attack, the attacker creates multiple identities and pretends to be multiple legitimate vehicles concurrently.

Impersonation Attack. In this, the attacker loots the identity of a legitimate vehicle to broadcast security messages on that vehicle's behalf. This could affect other drivers' decision making and create chaos in traffic.

1.6 Trust Issues in SIoV

There has been a detailed study of establishment of Trust in social networks. Original the concept of social trust was based on sociology. According to Golbeck, trust is defined as "a commitment to an action based on a belief that the future actions of that individual will lead to a good outcome" [56]. The social network as platforms to build mutual trust among entities was foreseen by Golbeck [57]. Wang et al. [58] has proposed a trustworthy Web service selection approach based on collaboration reputation by constructing a Web service collaboration network based on social networks. Zhang et al. [59] has proposed a newly-fashioned scheme BiFu, enabling the social media sites to alleviate the influence of the cold-start problem. Huang et al. [60] has proposed an approach that is capable of measuring the reputation of a single node effectively when the node suffers from malicious feedback ratings. Following are the trust issues in SIoV.

SIoV Trust Characteristics: There are five characteristics of Trust in the SIoV that makes them different from trust in customary social settings.

Uncertainty: Being dynamic trust is uncertain in SIoV.
Subjectivity: Trust in the SIoV depends on our actions consequences that is affected by the context [61] and that is what make it subjective.
Intransitivity: Trust in the SIoV is not always transitive
Context Dependence: Trust in the SIoV is context-dependent
Non-cooperativeness: Trust in the SIoV is need not be always cooperative

Reputation: Reputation management is component of trust management. Trust is dynamic and indicates whether an individual is to be believed on the basis of the trust value. Reputation is submissive and represents estimation about an individual. A reputation system could be classified into positive and negative reputation.

Overall trust is a multifaceted concept. SIoV faces two big challenges in form of trust-based management and decision making. For establishment of trust one needs to address the trust characteristics of the SIoV.

Security and privacy of IoV are serious issues because it will affect the lives of people on the roads. If network intrusion happens in IoV, the vehicles may be controlled by hackers, and this will lead to traffic havoc. So the security of IoV is a very serious issue. At the same time, driving tracks are the privacy of people. People may not want to let others know where and when they have been. However, the IoV could capture and driving track of vehicles, which will reveal the privacy. Some information in IoV could be public, while some information must be protected as privacy. Ensuring security could assure the safety of vehicle driving and also protect the privacy of people.

Thus we could see following queries for which we will try to find out answers in the context of SIoV:-

How trust recognition can be made in SIoV?
How to store, transform and analyze such a data surge?
Which are the technologies that should be capable of and scalable to in the era of ever increasing vehicular data?

This paper proposes an architecture wherein inter-vehicle recommendation system could be established with the assistance based on social networks by enabling reliable exchange of information.

The current paper is structured into four sections. The first section briefly introduces the concept of Internet of Vehicles, Social Internet of Vehicles, Security and Threats concerns in IoV as well as in SIoV and describes how the big data paradigm will be useful in analyzing the data generated in IoV. This Section also presents a comprehensive survey of previous research works in the area of IoV, SIoV as well as Big Data in IoV. Second section elucidates the proposed recommendation model and followed by discussion. Third section concluded with the essential features of the proposed model and future direction and followed by list of relevant references.

2   Proposed Architecture and Discussion

The current work proposes a recommender system model for IoV assisted by social networking recommendation system that uses reputation received in daily relationships, such as acquaintances meeting or helping other users. An acquaintance is a reliable person, previously known, who can provide the recommendation of others. A reputation acquaintance is a user having an indirect relationship with another user sent to the social network via reputations, so it is considered reliable by reputation.

Let's suppose that two previously known users Ride 1 and Ride 2 do not have any acquaintances in the social network. Their interaction through the social network makes them reliable users with HIGH trust level. They also trade their list of acquaintances. Upon having acquaintance with each other, the Ride 1 can exchange reliable messages with every acquaintance of Ride 2. Similarly, Ride 2 can exchange messages with acquaintances of Ride 1 as he has a path on the certification graph to the acquaintances of Ride 1. Figure 2 illustrates this situation. It can be depicted from the figure that Ride 2 has the users Ride 3 and Ride 4 as acquaintances, these users will be notified of the new relationship of Ride 1 and Ride 2.

The user receives messages and validates those messages using his likes and the followers-list stored in the user's equipment. The message will be considered as reliable

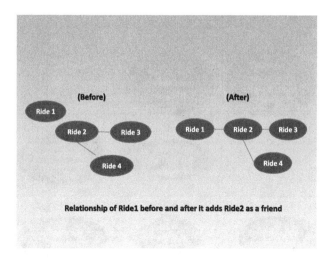

Fig. 2. Relationship of Ride 1 before and after adding Ride 2 as its friend

if the users on the receiver's social network has garnered a positive reputation for the sender or if its sender belongs to the social network of the receiver. Otherwise, the message is considered not reliable and ignored.

The operation of social networking recommendation as shown in Fig. 3 is based on PGP (Pretty Good Privacy) [62], and works as follows:

Step 1: The user generates a self-liked page.

Step 2: The page can be liked and followed by acquaintances in direct contact.

Step 3: The device of each user stores the likes and follower list of the added acquaintance and its acquaintances of acquaintances.

Step 4: The page of the new acquaintance is shared with the user's acquaintances to update their lists of acquaintances of acquaintances. Acquaintances of acquaintances recognize the page and thus receive reliable messages, giving out the conviction of the acquaintance that is a reliable user.

Step 5: After meeting a user, communication starts by searching a valid page address. Identification of a common acquaintance permits the users to verify their identities.

A Ride who does not trust a sender because he is not in his acquaintance, or even acquaintance of acquaintances, examines the page to determine if the sender is reliable. When receiving a message from a node that is neither an acquaintance nor a friend of his acquaintance then the receiving node considers the sender is reliable only when the number of its positive reputations is more than to the negative ones. The receiver takes into account the valuations of reliable users only when the users who are acquaintances or acquaintances of acquaintances of the receiver.

Linking reputation to the social network of the user restricts collusion attacks. Collusion can be produced when malicious users make a positive bonus for each other.

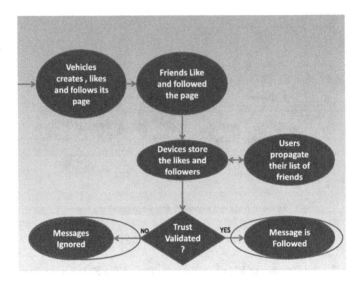

Fig. 3. Flow graph of the proposed model.

Thus, reputation is an additional prospect of trust acknowledgment, which permits users who are acquaintances or acquaintances of acquaintances to be measured trustworthy. Reputation can also have special feature to rate acquaintances or acquaintances of acquaintances.

Besides SIoV, the social networking also generates huge amount of data that needs to be analyzed to provide more reliable recommendation system. Thus we can see that sensor data along with data generated from social networking data is required to be processed for making vehicular system intelligent. This guides us to tap the potential of Big Data Analysis. It is clear that the IoT, IoV and SIoV applications can generate unprecedented amount of data for which big data provides promising tool [63, 64] to store and process these data.

The data sets generated from IoV have similar characteristics as that of big data i.e. volume, velocity, variability, variety, veracity, values, even visualization (i.e. Vi –where i = 1, 2, …, n) as shown in Fig. 4.

The algorithms for IoV big data set analysis can be grouped in many forms, which include heterogeneous, nonlinear, high-dimensional and distributed data processing [65].

As shown in Fig. 5, we could use this big data framework to analyze massive IoV and SIoV data for predicting congestion and free movements of traffic in making well-organized runtime traffic management. It is quite clear from proposed model that First Step is the pre-processing of raw data to ETL (Extract, Transform, Load), the second step is to analyze the pre-processed data using various Big Data Analytics tools to meet the defined objectives/goals and in the last and third step the outcomes of the analysis are to be used to generate desired results in form of reports, queries or future predictions. In future this model could be used with SIoV data for sentiment analysis for establishing the trust recognition.

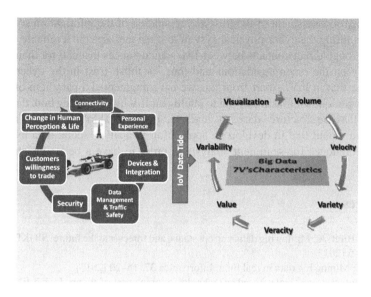

Fig. 4. Big data generation in IoV and its characteristics

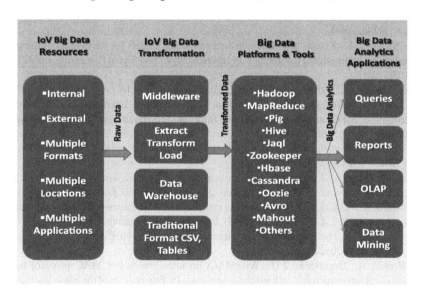

Fig. 5. The model of IoV massive data analytics framework

3 Conclusion

This current work has proposed a novel approach for processing an unprecedented amount of data from completely unrelated networks to create a reliable and trust worthy recommendation system. This social networking recommendation system incorporates mechanisms for assessment of the trust and reputation of the information sources and thereby permitting the cyber-physical system to trade messages in a reliable way. One can view through direct contacts between two acquaintances that call for their identity, so they rely on the recommendations and thus, establish trust in the cyber-physical systems like that in IoV. Apart from this we have augmented a paradigm of big data Analytics technique for making IoV in to intelligent IoV by processing both the unstructured as well as the structured data sets generated from Social IoV and Social networks. In future we would like to develop an application to analyze social data by big data analytics techniques for sentiment analysis in order to have a better insight of trust recognition.

References

1. Fan, W., Bifet, A.: Mining big data: current status, and forecast to the future. SIGKDD Explor. **14**(2), 1–5 (2013)
2. Bifet, A.: Mining big data in real time. Informatica **37**, 15–20 (2013)
3. Wu, B.: Internet-of-vehicles based on technologies of internet-of-things. In: ICLEM, pp. 348–356 (2012)
4. Vermesan, O., Friess, P.: Internet of Things: Converging Technologies for Smart Environments and Integrated Ecosystems. River Publishers, Aalborg (2013). ISBN 978-87-92982-96-4
5. Bin, S., Yuan, L., Xiaoyi, W.: Research on data mining models for the internet of things. In: Proceedings International Conference on Image Analysis and Signal Processing, pp. 127–132 (2010)
6. Leng, Y., Zhao, L.: Novel design of intelligent internet-of-vehicles management system based on cloud-computing and internet-of-things. In: Proceedings International Conference on Electronic & Mechanical Engineering and Information Technology, Harbin, Heilongjiang, China, vol. 6, pp. 3190–3193 (2011)
7. Goggin, G.: Driving the internet: mobile internets, cars, and the social. Future Internet **4**, 306–321 (2012). doi:10.3390/fi4010306
8. Guo, D., Mennis, J.: Spatial data mining and geographic knowledge discovery: an introduction. Comput. Environ. Urban Syst. **33**, 403–408 (2009). Elsevier
9. Crawford, K., Schultz, J.: Big data and due process: toward a framework to redress predictive privacy harms. B. C.L. Rev. **55**, 93 (2014). http://lawdigitalcommons.bc.edu/bclr
10. Dlodlo, N., et al.: The state of affairs in internet of things research. Electron. J. Inf. Syst. Eval. **15**(3), 244–258 (2012)
11. El-Hoiydi, A., Decotignie, J.D.: WiseMAC: an ultra low power MAC protocol for the downlink of infrastructure wireless sensor networks. In: Proceedings of the Ninth International Symposium on Computers and Communications (ISCC 2004), Alexandria, Egypt, vol. 1, pp. 244–251, 28 June–1 July 2004
12. Perkins, C.E.: Ad Hoc Networking. Addison-Wesley Professional, Boston (2008)
13. Caballero-Gil, P., Caballero-Gil, C., Molina-Gil, J.: How to build vehicular ad-hoc networks on smartphones. J. Syst. Architect. **59**, 996–1004 (2013)
14. Liu, B., Liu, Z., Towsley, D.: On the capacity of hybrid wireless networks. In: Proceedings of the Twenty-Second Annual Joint Conference of the IEEE Computer and Communications on IEEE Societies (INFOCOM 2003), San Francisco, CA, USA, vol. 2, pp. 1543–1552, 30 March–3 April 2003

15. Wang, M., Shan, H., Lu, R., Zhang, R., Shen, X., Bai, F.: Real-time path planning based on hybrid-VANET-enhanced transportation system. IEEE Trans. Veh. Technol. **64**, 1664–1678 (2014)
16. Tornell, S.M., Patra, S., Calafate, C.T., Cano, J.C., Manzoni, P.: GRCBox: extending smartphone connectivity in vehicular networks. Int. J. Distrib. Sens. Netw. **2015**, 478064 (2015)
17. Marquez-Barja, J.M., Ahmadi, H., Tornell, S.M., Calafate, C., Cano, J., Manzoni, P., Da Silva, L.: Breaking the vehicular wireless communications barriers: vertical handover techniques for heterogeneous networks. IEEE Trans. Veh. Technol. **64**, 5878–5890 (2014)
18. Gubbi, J., Buyya, R., Marusic, S., Palaniswami, M.: Internet of Things (IoT): a vision, architectural elements, and future directions. Future Gener. Comput. Syst. **29**, 1645–1660 (2013)
19. Joerer, S., Bloessl, B., Huber, M., Jamalipour, A., Dressler, F.: Demo: simulating the impact of communication performance on road traffic safety at intersections. In: Proceedings of the 20th Annual International Conference on Mobile Computing and Networking, Maui, HI, USA, pp. 287–290, 7–11 September 2014
20. Maglaras, L.A., Basaras, P., Katsaros, D.: Exploiting vehicular communications for reducing CO_2 emissions in urban environments. In: Proceedings of the 2013 International Conference on Connected Vehicles and Expo (ICCVE), Las Vegas, NV, USA, pp. 32–37, 2–6 December 2013
21. Cheng, H.T., Shan, H., Zhuang, W.: Infotainment and road safety service support in vehicular networking: from a communication perspective. Mech. Syst. Signal Process. **25**, 2020–2038 (2011)
22. Atzori, L., Iera, A., Morabito, G., Nitti, M.: The Social Internet of Things (SIoT)—when social networks meet the internet of things: concept, architecture and network characterization. Comput. Netw. **56**, 3594–3608 (2012)
23. Alam, K., Saini, M., El Saddik, A.: Toward social internet of vehicles: concept, architecture, and applications. IEEE Access **3**, 343–357 (2015)
24. Alam, K.M., Saini, M., Saddik, A.E.: Workload model based dynamic adaptation of social internet of vehicles. Sensors **15**, 23262–23285 (2015)
25. Nitti, M., Girau, R., Floris, A., Atzori, L.: On adding the social dimension to the internet of vehicles: friendship and middleware. In: Proceedings of the 2014 IEEE International Black Sea Conference on Communications and Networking (BlackSeaCom), Odessa, Ukraine, pp. 134–138, 27–30 May 2014
26. Luan, T., Lu, R., Shen, X., Bai, F.: Social on the road: enabling secure and efficient social networking on highways. IEEE Wirel. Commun. **22**, 44–51 (2015)
27. Schwarz, C., Thomas, G., Nelson, K., McCrary, M., Sclarmann, N., Powell, M.: Towards autonomous vehicles. Technical report 25-1121-0003-117, Mid-America Transportation Center, Lincoln, NE, USA (2013)
28. Squatriglia, C.: Ford's Tweeting Car Embarks on American Journey 2.0. Wired (2010). http://www.wired.com/2010/05/ford-american-journey/. Accessed 15 Jan 2016
29. Sha, W., Kwak, D., Nath, B., Iftode, L.: Social vehicle navigation: integrating shared driving experience into vehicle navigation. In: Proceedings of the 14th Workshop on Mobile Computing Systems and Applications, Jekyll Island, GA, USA, 26–27 February 2013
30. Wan, J., Zhang, D., Zhao, S., Yang, L., Lloret, J.: Context-aware vehicular cyber-physical systems with cloud support: architecture, challenges, and solutions. IEEE Commun. Mag. **52**, 106–113 (2014)
31. Vegni, A., Loscri, V.: A Survey on Vehicular Social Networks. IEEE Commun. Surv. Tutor. **17**, 2397–2419 (2015)

32. Al-Sultan, S., Al-Doori, M.M., Al-Bayatti, A.H., Zedan, H.: A comprehensive survey on vehicular ad hoc network. J. Netw. Comput. Appl. **37**, 380–392 (2014)
33. Scott, J.: Social Network Analysis. Sage Publications Ltd., Thousand Oaks (2012)
34. Cunha, F., Carneiro Vianna, A., Mini, R., Loureiro, A.: How effective is to look at a vehicular network under a social perception? In: Proceedings of the 2013 IEEE 9th International Conference on Wireless and Mobile Computing, Networking and Communications (WiMob), Lyon, France, pp. 154–159, 7–9 October 2013
35. Basaras, P., Katsaros, D., Tassiulas, L.: Detecting influential spreaders in complex, dynamic networks. Computer **46**, 24–29 (2013)
36. Borge-Holthoefer, J., Rivero, A., Moreno, Y.: Locating privileged spreaders on an online social network. Phys. Rev. E **85** (2011). doi:10.1103/PhysRevE.85.066123
37. Canright, G.S., Engø-Monsen, K.: Spreading on networks: a topographic view. Complexus **3**, 131–146 (2006)
38. Noel, S., Jajodia, S.: Optimal IDS sensor placement and alert prioritization using attack graphs. J. Netw. Syst. Manag. **16**, 259–275 (2008)
39. Souza, E., Nikolaidis, I., Gburzynski, P.: A new aggregate local mobility (ALM) clustering algorithm for VANETs. In: Proceedings of the 2010 IEEE International Conference on Communications (ICC), Cape Town, South Africa, pp. 1–5, 23–27 May 2010
40. Lazarevic, A., Srivastava, J., Kumar, V.: Cyber threat analysis–a key enabling technology for the objective force (a case study in network intrusion detection). In: Proceedings of the IT/C4ISR, 23rd Army Science Conference (2002)
41. Yu, L., Deng, J., Brooks, R.R., Yun, S.B: Automobile ECU design to avoid data tampering. In: Proceedings of the 10th Annual Cyber and Information Security Research Conference, p. 10. ACM (2015)
42. Sicari, S., Rizzardi, A., Grieco, L., Coen-Porisini, A.: Security, privacy and trust in internet of things: the road ahead. Comput. Netw. **76**, 146–164 (2015)
43. Singh, R., Singh, P., Duhan, M.: An effective implementation of security based algorithmic approach in mobile adhoc networks. Hum. Centric Comput. Inf. Sci. **4**(1), 1–14 (2014)
44. Othmane, L.B., Weffers, H., Mohamad, M.M., Wolf, M.: A survey of security and privacy in connected vehicles. In: Benhaddou, D., Al-Fuqaha, A. (eds.) Wireless Sensor and Mobile Ad-Hoc Networks, pp. 217–247. Springer, New York (2015)
45. Yan, G., Wen, D., Olariu, S., Weigle, M.C.: Security challenges in vehicular cloud computing. IEEE Trans. Intell. Transp. Syst. **14**(1), 284–294 (2013)
46. Kannhavong, B., Nakayama, H., Nemoto, Y., Kato, N., Jamalipour, A.: A survey of routing attacks in mobile ad hoc networks. IEEE Wirel. Commun. **14**(5), 85–91 (2007)
47. Cheng, J., Cheng, J., Zhou, M., Liu, F., Gao, S., Liu, C.: Routing in internet of vehicles: a review. IEEE Trans. Intell. Transp. Syst. **16**(5), 2339–2352 (2015)
48. Shah, N., Valiveti, S.: Intrusion detection systems for the availability attacks in ad-hoc networks. Int. J. Electron. Comput. Sci. Eng. (IJECSE) **1**(3), 1850–1857 (2012). ISSN 2277-1956
49. Ji, S., Chen, T., Zhong, S.: Wormhole attack detection algorithms in wireless network coding systems. IEEE Trans. Mob. Comput. **14**(3), 660–674 (2015)
50. Wallgren, L., Raza, S., Voigt, T.: Routing attacks and countermeasures in the RPL-based internet of things. Int. J. Distrib. Sens. Netw. 13(794326) (2013)
51. Xia, H., Jia, Z., Li, X., Ju, L., Sha, E.H.-M.: Trust prediction and trust-based source routing in mobile ad hoc networks. Ad Hoc Netw. **11**(7), 2096–2114 (2013)
52. Mejri, M.N., Ben-Othman, J., Hamdi, M.: Survey on vanet security challenges and possible cryptographic solutions. Veh. Commun. **1**(2), 53–66 (2014)

53. Rawat, D.B., Yan, G., Bista, B., Weigle, M.C.: Trust on the security of wireless vehicular ad-hoc networking. Ad Hoc Sens. Wirel. Netw. (AHSWN) J. **24**, 283–305 (2014)

54. Raya, M., Hubaux, J.P.: The security of vehicular ad hoc networks. In: Proceedings of the 3rd ACM Workshop on Security of Ad Hoc and Sensor Networks, Alexandria, VA, USA, pp. 11–21, 7 November 2005

55. Zeadally, S., Hunt, R., Chen, Y.S., Irwin, A., Hassan, A.: Vehicular ad hoc networks (VANETS): Status, results, and challenges. Telecommun. Syst. **50**, 217–241 (2012)

56. Golbeck, J.: Computing with trust: definition, properties, and algorithms. In: Proceedings of the 2006 Securecomm and Workshops, Baltimore, MD, USA, pp. 1–7, 28 August–1 September 2006

57. Golbeck, J.: Computing with Social Trust. HCI. Springer, London (2008)

58. Wang, S., Huang, L., Hsu, C.-H., Yang, F.: Collaboration reputation for trustworthy Web service selection in social networks. J. Comput. Syst. Sci. **82**(1), 130–143 (2016)

59. Zhang, D., Hsu, C.H., Chen, M., Chen, Q., Xiong, N., Lloret, J.: Cold-start recommendation using bi-clustering and fusion for large-scale social recommender systems. IEEE Trans. Emerg. Top. Comput. **2**(2), 239–250 (2014)

60. Huang, L., Wang, S., Hsu, C.H., et al.: J. Supercomput. **71**, 2190 (2015). doi:10.1007/s11227-015-1432-x

61. Gupta, S.: A general context-dependent trust model for controlling access to resources. Ph.D. thesis, Jadavpur University, Kolkata, India (2012)

62. Djamaludin, C., Foo, E., Corke, P.: Establishing initial trust in autonomous delay tolerant networks without centralised PKI. Comput. Secur. **39**(Part B), 299–314 (2013). Elsevier

63. Crawford, K., Schultz, J.: Big data and due process: toward a framework to redress predictive privacy harms. BCL Rev. **55**, 93 (2014). http://lawdigitalcommons.bc.edu/bclr

64. Tene, O., Polonetsky, J.: Big data for all: privacy and user control in the age of analytics. Nw. J. Tech. Intell. Prop. **11**, 239 (2013). http://scholarlycommons.law.northwestern.edu

65. Diebold, F.X.: Big Data Dynamic Factor Models for Macroeconomic Measurement and Forecasting, pp. 115–122. Cambridge University Press, Cambridge (2003)

V2V and M2M Communications

802.11p Wi-Fi Offloading from the Cellular Network to Vehicle-to-Infrastructure Communication Network Using the Software-Defined Network (SDN) Technique

Chung-Ming Huang[1(✉)], Meng-Shu Chiang[2], Duy-Tuan Dao[1], Hsiu-Ming Pai[1],
Shouzhi Xu[3], and Huan Zhou[3]

[1] Computer Science and Information Engineering,
National Cheng Kung University, Tainan, Taiwan
`{huangcm,daotd,paihm}@locust.csie.ncku.edu.tw`
[2] Dept. of Computer Science and Information Engineering,
Far East University, Tainan, Taiwan
`chiangms@cc.feu.edu.tw`
[3] College of Computer and Information Technology,
China Three Gorges University, Yichang, China
`xsz@ctgu.edu.cn, zhouhuan117@gmail.com`

Abstract. Wi-Fi offloading is a technique for reducing 3G/3.5G/4G cellular network's traffic load and users' expense spent in 3G/3.5G/4G cellular network. Nevertheless, it needs to judge whether the offloading from the cellular network to the Wi-Fi network is valuable or not by considering the target Wi-Fi network's situation. This paper proposed a Software Defined Network (SDN) –based method to pre-decide whether it is valuable to have offloading from the cellular network to the corresponding vehicle's ahead 802.11p Wi-Fi RSU network or not. By utilizing the centralization architecture and the information of the current contexts, including speed, position and direction, of vehicles, SDN Controller can calculate whether the networking situation of the corresponding vehicle's ahead 802.11p Wi-Fi RSU is good enough to offload or not before the vehicle enters into the signal coverage. The performance analysis shows that it can let vehicles have better networking situation and quality using our proposed scheme.

1 Introduction

Since more and more wireless mobile network's applications and service are devised/developed/invented, more and more traffic is directed into the 3G/3.5G/4G cellular network. To alleviate the 3G/3.5G/4G cellular network's load and users' expense spent in 3G/3.5G/4G cellular network, Wi-Fi offloading was proposed accordingly since several years ago [1, 2]. Offloading means that mobile users can connect with Wi-Fi network instead of the 3G/3.5G/4G cellular network when they are located within a heavily loaded cellular network and the Wi-Fi network is available. In this way, Wi-Fi network can distribute the loading to improve the 3G/3.5G/4G cellular network performance [3, 4].

© Springer International Publishing AG 2016
C.-H. Hsu et al. (Eds.): IOV 2016, LNCS 10036, pp. 167–178, 2016.
DOI: 10.1007/978-3-319-51969-2_14

Recently, there have been an increased demand for Vehicular Ad Hoc Network (VANET) to leverage the next generation's Intelligent Transportation Systems (ITS), which targets to support vehicle safety, entertainment service, and Internet of Vehicle (IOV) [5]. In the VANET for ITS, vehicles can access data from Internet using 3G/3.5G/4G cellular network using the On Board Unit (OBU) equipped inside a vehicle. Since some 802.11p Wi-Fi RSUs are located in roads, vehicles can also access data from Internet through these RSUs using the OBU equipped inside a vehicle. The aforementioned communication paradigm is called Vehicle to Infrastructure (V2I) communication in VANET. Therefore, offloading can also be laid out in VANET. That is, a vehicle X's V2I communication can handoff from the 3G/3.5G/4G cellular network, in which X's V2I communication is between X's OBU and a cellular network's BS, to the 802.11p Wi-Fi network, in which X's V2I communication is between X's OBU and the 802.11p Wi-Fi network's RSU. The challenge of offloading over VANET includes (1) how and when to have handover decision in advance? (2) how to make a suitable handover decision?

In this work, an Offloading with Handover Decision based on Software-Defined Network (OHD-SDN) control scheme is proposed to resolve the aforementioned issues for VANET's offloading. In our proposed OHD-SDN control scheme, each vehicle node should transmit its current context containing its speed, location, direction, sensed Wi-Fi/ 802.11p, etc., to SDN Controller [6] using its cellular network interface and transmits its data using either its cellular network interface or 802.11p Wi-Fi network interface, depending on its networking situation. Two main technical issues that SDN Controller in the proposed OHD-SDN control scheme are in charge of are as follows: (1) When to decide whether vehicle X needs to handoff from the cellular network to the ahead 802.11p Wi-Fi RSU for offloading X's data transmission or not? Let SDN Controller know the location of all 802.11p RSUs. SDN Controller can measure what the due time is for deciding whether X should have the offloading or not before X drives into the signal coverage of the corresponding 802.11p Wi-Fi RSU based on the received context of X and the location of the 802.11p Wi-Fi RSU. (2) How to decide whether vehicle X needs to handoff from the cellular network to the ahead 802.11p Wi-Fi RSU for offloading X's data transmission or not? SDN Controller can keep track networks quality inside the signal coverage of the 802.11p Wi-Fi RSU to decide whether it is suitable to have X to have offloading or not. When the decision making is positive, i.e., it should handoff to the 802.11p Wi-Fi network, X can have the handoff processing immediately after X has sensed the signal of the corresponding 802.11p Wi-Fi AP and thus can have longer communication time period using the 802.11p Wi-Fi RSU. When the decision making is negative, i.e., X should not handoff to the 802.11p Wi-Fi network, X can keep staying in the 4G cellular network without wasting the handoff decision time spent inside the 802.11p Wi-Fi network and then re-connect to the 4G cellular network using the traditional handoff method. To tackle the aforementioned two issues, SDN Controller in the proposed OHD-SDN control scheme can have related calculation after gathering vehicles' and RSU's context. When vehicle X is approaching an 802.11p Wi-Fi RSU, SDN Controller starts to make a decision for vehicle X using the proposed scheme. After the handover decision is made, the SDN Controller notifies vehicle X whether the ahead 802.11p Wi-Fi RSU is suitable for offloading or not. That is, for our proposed OHD-SDN, the SDN Controller can help vehicle X decide whether it is suitable to have the offloading from the 3G/3.5G/4G cellular network to the ahead 802.11p Wi-Fi network or not before X enters into the corresponding 802.11p Wi-Fi network.

The rest of this paper is organized as follows: Sect. 2 has related work of VANET offloading. Section 3 presents the architecture and functional flow of the proposed work. Section 4 describes the proposed control scheme in detail. Section 5 shows the performance analysis of the proposed control scheme. Finally, Sect. 6 has the conclusion remarks.

2 Related Works

There are several studies for vehicular offloading. The work of [7] proposed the Wiffler system, which is based on two key issues: (1) leveraging delay tolerance by a fix delay threshold and (2) the fast switching mechanism to 3G. Wiffler combined the estimation of the Wi-Fi throughput on vehicles' route and focused on the delay requirements of various kinds of applications for the Wi-Fi networks instead of cellular connectivity. However, due to the vehicle mobility affecting the Wi-Fi connectivity, the experimental results of this work shown that it has the low performance and suffers the experienced higher frequent disconnects. In [8], the authors proposed the prediction of vehicle's moving route and the geo-location of potential Wi-Fi hotspots for offloading. This prediction collects the information about (i) the number of available APs, with which vehicles can access, in the road and (ii) the time interval, which vehicles stay in APs' coverage range. The proposed mechanism tried to transfer the maximum amount data in a limit delay-tolerance time from the cellular network to the Wi-Fi network for offloading. Thus, this scheme based on the delay threshold for transferring data and is not effective for delay sensitive applications. In [9], the proposed scheme of APs' geographical distribution predicts the possible offloading using the semi-Markov, which models the problem as a time-homogeneous process to maximize a utility function based on both of the offloaded data and user satisfaction, i.e., connecting cellular network without changing to Wi-Fi for saving handover time. However, similar to the work depicted in [8], the prediction methods of this scheme faces the trade-offs issues between user satisfaction and the offloading to Wi-Fi connectivity of waiting a delay tolerance time. The aforementioned problems can be tackled by collecting information to the centralized unit and make a global prediction for offloading. It can be achieved with the SDN-based approach.

There are some works that tried to adopt the SDN offloading architecture in the regular wireless mobile network. In [10], authors proposed the SDN-based Mobile Offloading aRchitecturE (SMORE) that implemented the offloading in a real LTE/EPC mobile network. An SDN-based offloading is deployed with aggregation points and cloud infrastructures to make a selection for offloading. The SMORE Controller plays the role of a database that stores the registered offloading servers' IP addresses and IMSIs of UEs that subscribed to have the offloading services. However, the SMORE scheme only uses the cellular network quality to decide offloading no matter what the corresponding Wi-Fi network's situation is. In [11], it proposed a SDN working abstraction to integrate LTE/Wi-Fi architecture with a mobile backhaul of 5G mobile networks by enabling programmable offloading policies. Authors use the network entities, which are

Access Network Discovery and Selection Function (ANDSF). ANDSF helps MNs to discover Wi-Fi access networks for offloading. SDN Controller combines the information of network load, operator policy and signal threshold to derive offloading policy functions. However, this scheme is lack of the performance analytic, i.e., it just can be applied to MNs and not suitable to dynamic and fast changing topology like VANET. In summary, the previous SDN-based offloading schemes were not targeted for the VANET environment.

In this paper, we try to adopt the SDN-based offloading scheme, which is called OHD-SDN, in the VANET environment. The proposed OHD-SDN control scheme can improve the performance of offloading by gathering vehicles' and RSU's context into the SDN Controller to make a handover decision between the 802.11p Wi-Fi network and the 3G/3.5G/4G cellular network.

3   The Abstract Architecture and Control Flow

The main tasks of the proposed OHD-SDN control scheme are (1) when to decide whether vehicle X needs to handoff from the cellular network to the ahead 802.11p Wi-Fi RSU for offloading X's data transmission or not? and (2) how to decide whether vehicle X needs to handoff from the cellular network to the ahead 802.11p Wi-Fi RSU for offloading X's data transmission or not? Figure 1 depicts the abstract execution architecture of the proposed OHD-SDN control scheme. Each vehicle (i) transmits its current context to SDN Controller using its cellular network interface for offloading decision and (ii) transmits its data using its cellular network interface when it is not in an 802.11p Wi-Fi network's signal coverage, e.g., vehicle X1 in Fig. 1 or using its 802.11p Wi-Fi network interface when it is inside an 802.11p Wi-Fi network's signal coverage and the offloading is allowed. Four phases of the execution scenario in the proposed OHD-SDN control scheme are (1) approaching phase, (2) cellular to Wi-Fi's handoff phase, (3) data transmission's offloading phase and (4) Wi-Fi to cellular's handoff phase.

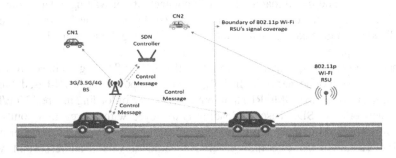

Fig. 1.   The abstract execution architecture of the proposed OHD-SDN control scheme

In the approaching phase, vehicle X is cruising on the road and X is connected to the cellular network. When X keeps going along the street, X transmits its context information to SDN Controller. SDN Controller gathers the information transmitted from vehicle X and calculates the time point t_{dk}, which is the due time to make decision of offloading for vehicle X. At the time point t_{dk}, SDN Controller has the handoff decision making based on the corresponding RSUs 802.11p Wi-Fi networks quality. If the decision is negative, then it keeps in phase 1, i.e., the approaching phase, for vehicle X; if the decision is positive, then it goes to phase 2 for vehicle X. In the Cellular to Wi-Fi's Handoff Phase, vehicle X executes the handoff processing from 3G/3.5G/4G cellular network to 802.11p Wi-Fi network using the MIH's messaging mechanism. In the data transmission's offloading phase, vehicle X (i) transmits its data using its 802.11p Wi-Fi network interface and (ii) transmits its current context to SDN Controller using its cellular network interface. With the time goes by, vehicle X is moving toward the edge of the 802.11p Wi-Fi network's signal coverage. When vehicle X is going to be out of the signal coverage of the 802.11p Wi-Fi network, it enters into the Wi-Fi to cellular's Handoff phase. In this phase, vehicle X executes the handoff processing from 802.11p Wi-Fi network to 3G/3.5G/4G cellular network using MIH's messaging mechanism. Figure 2 depicts the control flow of these 4 phases in the proposed OHD-SDN control scheme.

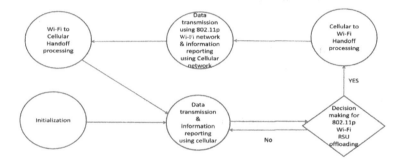

Fig. 2. The execution flow of the four phases in the proposed OHD-SDN control scheme

4 The Proposed OHD-SDN Control Scheme

This Section presents the methods for resolving related issues exist in the proposed OHD-SDN control scheme.

4.1 How to Derive the Due Time for Making the Offloading Decision?

To derive the due time for making the handoff decision, SDN Controller calculates the time point t_{dk}, which is the due time for making offloading decision, based on the periodically received context information transmitted by the vehicle. According to the periodically received context information of latitude & longitude and speed transmitted from the vehicle, SDN Controller calculates how far it is from vehicle's current location to the boundary of the ahead 802.11p Wi-Fi RSU and derives the corresponding driving time length time based on the vehicle's speed; then it measures what the final timing is for making the offloading decision. The final time for making the offloading decision, i.e., t_{dk}, is calculated as follows. For convenient explanation, Fig. 6 depicts the two cases that can exist and Table 1 contains the denotation and explanations of those parameters that are used for deriving time point t_{dk}. Let (1) P_c be the position of vehicle X's current GPS sampling, (2) P_n be the position of vehicle X's next GPS sampling, which can be estimated based on the position of vehicle X's current GPS sampling and X's speed, and (3) P_e be the entrance position of the ahead 802.11p Wi-Fi RSU's signal coverage, which is the intersection of the road and the ahead 802.11p Wi-Fi RSU's signal coverage. D_c denotes the distance from the current position to the entrance position of the ahead 802.11p Wi-Fi RSU's signal coverage, i.e., the distance between P_c and P_e; D_n denotes the distance from the next GPS sampling position, i.e., the next context report/transmitting position of the vehicle, to the entrance position of the ahead 802.11p Wi-Fi RSU's signal coverage, i.e., the distance between P_n and P_e; T_{RTT} denotes the round trip time delay between the vehicle and SDN Controller, for which one way delay is for transmitting vehicle's context to SDN Controller and one way delay is for transmitting SDN Controller's offloading decision message to the vehicle; T_{CO} is related computation time overhead for calculating offloading decision in SDN Controller; v is the speed of the vehicle; T_s is GPS sampling period.

Table 1. The notation of the expression

Variable	Meaning
P_c	current position of GPS's sampling
P_n	next position of GPS's sampling
P_e	entrance position of the 802.11p Wi-Fi RSU's signal coverage
d_c	distance between P_c and P_e
d_n	distance between P_n and P_e
T_S	GPS sampling period
T_{co}	the computing overhead in SDN Controller

In Fig. 3-(a), when D_n/v is greater than or equal to $T_{RTT} + T_{CO}$, which means that the offloading decision can be made in the next GPS sampling and context report/transmission time point and thus it still doesn't need to be made based on the currently reported/transmitted vechicle's context. In Fig. 3-(b), when D_n/v is smaller than $T_{RTT} + T_{CO}$, and D_c/v, which is equal to $v * T_s + D_n = T_s + D_n$, is greater than $T_{RTT} + T_{CO}$, which means that the offloading decision should be made in the current GPS sampling and context report/transmission time point.

4.2 How to Decide Whether the Ahead 802.11p Wi-Fi Network's Situation Is Good Enough to Have Offloading or not?

At time point t_{dk}, SDN Controller decides whether the ahead 802.11p Wi-Fi network's situation is good enough to have the corresponding vehicle to do data offloading from the 3G/3.5G/4G cellular network to the 802.11p Wi-Fi network or not. In order to measure the quality of 802.11p Wi-Fi network, the collision times in the carrier is used as an index to estimate the network quality, i.e., when the collision times is higher/

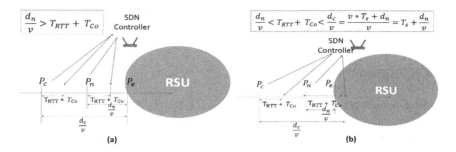

Fig. 3. The configuration of finding the time point for decision

smaller, it denotes that the network quality is better/worse. Thus, the network quality of an 802.11p Wi-Fi RSU is referred by the backoff counter's value for media access's contention window used in the 802.11p's CSMA/CA control scheme. In the CSMA/CA control scheme, initially, the backoff counter's value is set to 4 and thus the contention window can be 0–15 ($2^4 - 1$), i.e., the mobile node can wait for i time slots, for which i is randomly selected from 0–15, and then try to access the wireless medium. When the mobile node has transmission collision, the backoff counter's value is increased for 1 and thus the contention window size can be doubled for the re-transmission. The upper bound of re-transmission times is 6. That is, the upper bound of the backoff counter's value is 10 (4 + 6), for which the contention window can be 0–1023 ($2^{10} - 1$). That is, let the backoff counter's value be x when a mobile node MN gets the media access's privilege. Then, it implies that the retransmission times of MN is equal to x − 4. Each RSU that is involved in the data offloading can report/transmits the value of its backoff counter to SDN Controller when the value is changed. In this way, SDN Controller can have the up-to-date network situation of each 802.11p Wi Fi RSU. Then, SDN Controller can set a threshold for the value of its backoff counter to make the offloading decision.

4.3 How to Quantify the 802.11p Wi-Fi Network's Situation?

The 802.11p Wi-Fi network's situation is measured as follows. Since the bigger retransmission times result in the bigger backoff counter/contention window, it means that a mobile node has a higher chance to pick a bigger backoff counter when the retransmission times are becoming bigger. Thus, we deduce the following formula to represent the network quality. Let n be the number of vehicles connected to the RSU and CW_i be the contention window size of vehicle i, $CW_i = \{x \mid 2^4 - 1 \leq x \leq 2^{10-1}\}$, and let

$$N_{E=} = \frac{\sum_i^n \left(log_2^{(CW_{i+1})} - 4 \right)}{n} \tag{1}$$

denote the 802.11p Wi-Fi network's situation of RSU. At time point of T, if the value of N_E is greater than a threshold of N_E, then the corresponding vehicles cannot handoff to 802.11p Wi-Fi RSU and keep connecting LTE to maintain vehicles' networking quality; if the value of Ne value is smaller than a threshold, then the corresponding vehicles can have the handoff and connect to 802.11p Wi-Fi RSU.

5   Performance Analysis

This Section presents the performance analysis of the proposed scheme. Our proposed OHD-SDN control scheme is compared with the naïve scheme, which has a vehicle X to directly connect to the RSU when X enters into the signal coverage of the corresponding 802.11p Wi-Fi RSU without considering the networking situation of the corresponding 802.11p Wi-Fi RSU. The simulation is based on the NS-3 (Network Simulation 3–24) [12] which uses the C++ programming language. In the remaining part of this Section, we will explain how our simulation environment was built, how the mechanism works and show the results of the comparison.

5.1   Environment

The controller and SDN-based switch is the key component in a SDN-based network. Especially for controller, most of the SDN-based algorithm logic part is running on it. So, for our OHD-SDN control scheme, it needs a controller to simulate the control scheme as well. We just built a global network supervisor agent to take over the duty of SDN controller. All of the network selection mechanism and offloading judgment are inside that agent.

   We deploy 16 vehicles, a RSU and a cellular base station to provide the network services to those vehicles. The vehicles go back and forth around the RSU such that they can sometimes receive the RSU signal and are sometimes out of the signal coverage of the RSU. Our proposed OHD-SDN is aim at reducing the chance of switching to a heavily-loaded RSU, which makes the corresponding vehicle's networking situation and quality worse. Table 2 lists the parameters and their values in our simulation environment.

Table 2.   Configuration of the simulation environment

Parameter	Values
RSU coverage range	300 m
Number of vehicles	16
Speed	14 m/s
Simulation time	300 s
Packet payload	1490
RTS/CTS	Off
Data sending rate	1 Mbps
Packet payload	1490 Bytes
Traffic type	CBR
Cellular network type	LTE

5.2 Results of the Performance Analysis

For here, "Wi-Fi" means receiving data from Wi-Fi interface, and "LTE" means data from LTE interface. We accumulate the size of the packets receiving by each vehicle in every 0.1 s. In this way, we can get the throughput of every vehicle. Then, we sum up all vehicles' throughput to get the average throughput of the 802.11p Wi-Fi network. For the following figures, the X-axis denotes time, for which the unit is 0.1 s and Y-axis denotes the throughput, for which the unit is Kbps. The throughput represents the average throughput of all vehicles in the Wi-Fi network or LTE network.

Figure 4 shows the throughput of using the naïve scheme. Referring to Fig. 4, at the $1/4*50^{th}$ seconds, some vehicles start to enter into the signal coverage of RSU and handoff to the Wi-Fi network. As time goes by, there are more and more vehicles that try to connect the RSU, which makes the Wi-Fi network become congested. Since the naïve scheme doesn't constrain the vehicles to handoff and enter into the Wi-Fi network, the throughput goes down gradually when more and more vehicles share the bandwidth of the RSU.

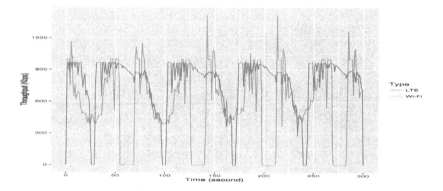

Fig. 4. The average throughput in 802.11p Wi Fi network and LTE network using the naïve control scheme.

The performance of setting different thresholds for N_E is depicted in Figs. 5, 6 and 7, for which the threshold is set as 0.5, 0.25 and 0.125 respectively. Figure 5 shows the throughput of using our proposed OHD-SDN scheme. Since our proposed OHD-SDN scheme can evaluate the loading of the RSU before vehicles enter into the signal coverage of the ahead 802.11p Wi-Fi RSU, vehicles would not connect to the Wi-Fi network and just stay in LTE when the controller detects that the RSU cannot support more vehicles. The main concern is to do a reasonable offloading, but not request the vehicles as a victim to go into a cheap network and congest in it. Figure 6 shows the comparison of the average throughput in Wi Fi network between the proposed OHD-SDN scheme average and the naïve scheme. At very beginning of the Fig. 6, the average throughput of both naïve and OHD-SDN control schemes are the same because both schemes don't reach the limit. From the $1/4*50^{th}$ second, the vehicles that plan to go into the 802.11p Wi-Fi RSU become more. Our proposed OHD-SDN control scheme can have the better average throughput for each vehicle because the number of vehicles that can enter into the signal coverage of 802.11p Wi-Fi network is under control, but it is not controlled in the naïve scheme.

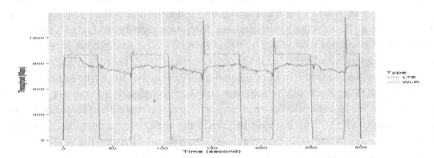

Fig. 5. The average throughput in 802.11p Wi-Fi network and LTE network using the proposed OHD-SDN control scheme.

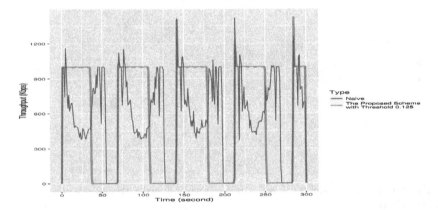

Fig. 6. The comparison of the average throughput in 802.11p Wi-Fi network between the proposed OHD-SDN scheme average and the naïve scheme.

Figure 7 shows the comparison of the average throughput in 802.11p Wi-Fi network among our proposed OHD-SDN schemes with 3 different thresholds of N_E and the naïve scheme. From Fig. 7, we can observe that the bigger threshold it is set, the smaller average throughput it has. But no matter which threshold value the proposed OHD-SDN control scheme is set, it still better than naïve control scheme.

Figure 8 shows the comparison of the average packet loss among our proposed OHD-SDN schemes with 3 different thresholds of N_E and the naïve scheme. It can be observed that our proposed OHD-SDN control scheme with threshold 0.125 has better situation than the naïve method for almost 40%.

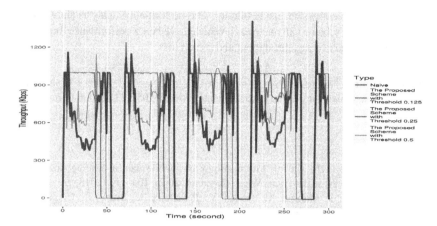

Fig. 7. The comparison of the average throughput in 802.11p Wi Fi network among our proposed OHD-SDN schemes with 3 different thresholds of N_E and the naïve scheme.

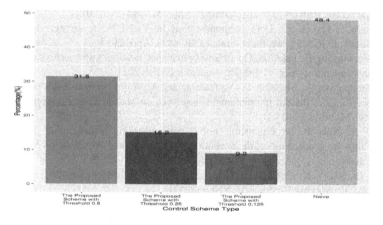

Fig. 8. The comparison of the average packet loss rates in Wi-Fi.

6   Conclusion

This paper has proposed an SDN-based control scheme to help vehicles decide whether it is suitable to handoff to the ahead 802.11p Wi Fi RSU to have offloading from the 3G/3.5G/4G cellular network or not. In this way, each vehicle can handoff to the ahead 802.11p Wi Fi RSU when the networking situation of the ahead 802.11p Wi Fi RSU is still good and can stay in its currently connected 3G/3.5G/4G cellular network when the networking situation of the ahead 802.11p Wi Fi RSU is not good. The main benefit of using the SDN-based method for making the offloading decision is twofold. The 1st one is that the 802.11p Wi-Fi RSU is relieved from the computing overhead for making the offloading decision and thus is only in charge of the processing of transmission and handoff. The 2nd one is that vehicles can maintain its networking situation because it won't go into a cheap Wi Fi network and become congested inside blindly. The performance analysis shows that our proposed OHD-SDN scheme can make each vehicle have better performance that the naïve scheme in terms of the average throughput and packet loss.

Acknowledgement. This research was supported by the National Science Council of the Republic of China, Taiwan, under the contract number MOST 105-2221-E-006-063.

References

1. Aijaz, A., Aghvami, H., Amani, M.: A survey on mobile data offloading: technical and business perspectives. IEEE Trans. Wirel. Commun. **20**(2), 104–112 (2013)
2. Rebecchi, F., Dias de Amorim, M., Conan, V., Passarella, A., Bruno, R., Conti, M.: Data offloading techniques in cellular networks: a survey. IEEE Commun. Surv. Tutor. **17**(2), 580–603 (2014)
3. Wu, X., et al.: Vehicular communications using DSRC: challenges, enhancements, and evolution. IEEE J. Sel. Areas Commun./Suppl. **31**(9), 399–408 (2013)
4. Al-Sultan, S., Al-Doori, M.M., Al-Bayatti, A.H., Zedan, H.: A comprehensive survey on vehicular ad hoc network. J. Netw. Comput. Appl. **37**, 380–392 (2014)
5. Da Cunha, F.D., et al.: Data communication in VANETs: a survey, challenges and applications, INRIA Saclay, Paris, France, RR-8498, April 2014
6. Open Networking Foundation: OpenFlow switch specification. http://archive.openflow.org/documents/openflow-spec-v1.1.0.pdf, Accessed 28 Feb 2011
7. Balasubramanian, A., Mahajan, R., Venkataramani, A.: Augmenting mobile 3G using Wi-Fi. In: Proceedings of the 8th International Conference on Mobile Systems, Applications, and Services - MobiSys 2010 (2010)
8. Siris, V.A., Kalyvas, D.: Enhancing mobile data offloading with mobility prediction and prefetching. In: Proceedings of the Seventh ACM International Workshop on Mobility in the Evolving Internet Architecture - MobiArch 2012 (2012)
9. Zhang, D., Yeo, C.K.: Optimal handing-back point in mobile data offloading. In: 2012 IEEE Vehicular Networking Conference (VNC) (2012)
10. Cho, J., Nguyen, B., Banerjee, A., Ricci, R., Van der Merwe, J., Webb, K: SMORE: software-defined networking mobile offloading architecture. In: Proceedings of the 4th Workshop on All Things Cellular, pp. 21–26, August 2014
11. Amani, M., Mahmoodi, T., Tatipamula, M., Aghvami, H.: SDN-based data offloading for 5G mobile networks. In: Proceedings of the ZTE Communications (2014)
12. Dupont, B.: Improvements in VANET Simulator in ns-3. Masters project, Department of Computer Science, Old Dominion University, December 2011

Distance Assisted Information Dissemination with Broadcast Suppression for ICN-Based VANET

Yuhong Li[1(✉)], Xiang Su[2], Anders Lindgren[3,4], Xinyue Shi[1], Xiang Cai[1], Jukka Riekki[2], and Xirong Que[1]

[1] State Key Laboratory of Networking and Switching Technology, Beijing University of Posts and Telecommunications, Beijing, China
hoyli@bupt.edu.cn
[2] Centre for Ubiquitous Computing, University of Oulu, Oulu, Finland
[3] SICS Swedish ICT, Kista, Sweden
[4] Luleå University of Technology, Luleå, Sweden

Abstract. Information-centric networking (ICN) is being applied to the vehicular networks by more and more researchers on account of its lightweight and connectionless networking paradigm and in-network caching characteristics, making it suitable for the dynamic environments of vehicular networks. However, wireless transmission of interest packets to find content in the network may lead to broadcast storms that can affect the performance of information dissemination severely. This paper proposes a distance assisted data dissemination method with broadcast storm suppressing mechanism (DASB) for supporting rapid and efficient information dissemination in ICN-based vehicular ad hoc networks (VANETs). Geo-position data of vehicles are used to accelerate packet forwarding, and vehicular nodes in certain areas are restricted to forward packets in order to suppress the broadcast storm. Simulation results show that the proposed method can greatly reduce the total number of packets transmitted in the network, and the successful information delivery ratio and information delivery time can also be improved.

Keywords: Information-centric networking · VANET · Broadcast storm suppression

1 Introduction

By connecting vehicles to people, other vehicles, and their surrounding environment, data about road and environmental conditions can be obtained by any vehicle and personal and entertainment offerings can be provided to passengers. To that end, vehicular ad hoc networks (VANETs) have been regarded not only as a key technology for increasing road safety and transport efficiency, and providing infotainment for people in mobile environments, but also as a method for increasing revenue for service providers and car manufacturers. Nevertheless, due to the highly dynamic mobile environment and the resulting wireless transmission conditions, some problems still need to be solved in order to bring VANET into reality.

© Springer International Publishing AG 2016
C.-H. Hsu et al. (Eds.): IOV 2016, LNCS 10036, pp. 179–193, 2016.
DOI: 10.1007/978-3-319-51969-2_15

Information-centric Networking (ICN) is a novel networking paradigm [1] that does not require global IP address allocation and management, setup of data delivery paths, or session establishment and management. Focus in the network is moved from named end-points to distribution of named data from producers or intermediate caches in the network. Thus, many major requirements of VANETs can be matched by the ICN paradigm. For example, the receiver-driven and name-based data delivery mode reduces the high overhead of mobility management and session maintenance. Asynchronous ICN communication suits the intermittent links of VANETs well. The in-network caching mechanism of ICN provides help to reduce the latency of obtaining data by vehicles, in particular for data of limited geographic interest. Additionally, most applications in VANET are information oriented and in many cases, vehicles and people on board do not need to directly interact with each other, but are satisfied with obtaining the needed information, and do not mind who provides the information and how and from where it comes from. At the same time, the computing and storage resources required by ICN, such as name-based data forwarding and in-network caching can be provided at low cost by vehicles which do not have restrictions on battery size, volume, or weight that many other mobile devices suffer from. Hence, the ICN paradigm is a suitable candidate for realizing VANETs.

However, introducing ICN in VANET also faces challenges. We address a typical VANET using wireless transmission technology such as IEEE 802.11p, where broadcasting data over a network interface is the basic communication mode between two nodes. We assume that nodes make use of the possibility to overhear packets to facilitate efficient multicasting of Interest packets such that they can spread quickly throughout the network. However, in the receiver-driven ICN paradigm, if an information request (e.g., the Interest packet in NDN [2]) is broadcasted, multiple copies of the request will be transmitted through the network, with the risk for routing loops and other redundant transmissions. When in-network caching mechanism is used, multiple copies of the responded data will also be produced and spread over the network. This not only wastes the valuable wireless transmission resources, but also, due to interference, decreases transmission reliability. Moreover, the density of the vehicle nodes and the applications running in the vehicles may change heavily and frequently, leading to unbalanced data traffic. Hence, a broadcast storm may heavily influence the quality of data transmission. In addition, the inherent feature of VANET, that is, short-lived intermittent connectivity, reduces the possibility of data dissemination. As a result, all vehicular nodes having transmission opportunity take part in the data forwarding in most routing mechanisms [3, 4]. This makes the problem of broadcast storm even worse.

In this paper, we introduce DASB, a distance assisted data dissemination method with a broadcast storm suppression mechanism, to realize efficient and fast data dissemination in ICN-based VANETs. Our work aims at making the ICN paradigm viable for VANETs by designing an efficient data dissemination mechanism with low packet redundancy. Specially,

- We propose a packet forwarding strategy to reduce the numbers of hops of packet forwarding and at the same time to suppress the forwarding of the nearby nodes, by making use of the geo-position information of the vehicles;
- We introduce a mechanism to suppress the broadcast storm while keeping the successful packet delivery ratio by limiting the amount of nodes around the current forwarding node that broadcast the data further;

- We evaluate the proposed mechanisms through implementation and carrying out simulations. Especially, we use real world traffic and a vehicle mobility model to validate the proposed mechanism.

The rest of the paper is organized as follows. In Sect. 2, the distance assisted packet forwarding scheme for ICN-based VANETs is described. In Sect. 3, the method of broadcasting suppression and the corresponding suppression angle are introduced. Following this the implementation and simulation environment are described, and the performance of the proposed method is evaluated and discussed in Sect. 4. We discuss the related work in Sect. 5. Finally, Sect. 6 concludes the paper.

2   Distance Assisted Packet Forwarding

Work in [5–7] has investigated the advantages of introducing information centric networking into VANETs, and made some improvements to the basic NDN architecture to implement the name-based data dissemination in VANETs. In short, we borrow ideas from these works and keep the following functions: (i) packets are allowed to be broadcast over the same wireless network interface from which the packets were received; (ii) the CS (Content Storage) and PIT (Pending Interest Table) functionality remains as for normal NDN operation; (iii) a timer based mechanism that allows forwarding of packets after waiting a certain time is used in each intermediate node.

A problem with previous solutions is that the mechanisms proposed have the potential to create broadcast storms in the network, leading to high overhead and waster of network resources. In order to suppress such broadcast storms, we reduce the data transmitted in the network, and therefore improve data dissemination efficiency. We introduce the following features in our system: (i) the data structures Forwarded Table (FT) and Waiting Table (WT) in the nodes; (ii) a modified format of Interest and Data packets, carrying geo-position information; (iii) a method for calculating the retransmission deferral timer and packet forwarding method based on internode distance; and (iv) a broadcast storm suppression mechanism. The first three features are described below, and the fourth feature will be explained in Sect. 3.

2.1   Packet Forwarding According to Distance

All data is transmitted through broadcasting it over the wireless network interface. Since many nodes are able to receive the packets by overhearing the wireless channel, this allows Interest and Data packets to be forwarded by intermediate nodes to increase the likelihood of reaching the destination, but this can also lead to loops and repeated forwarding. This may in turn cause heavy packet loss due to serious interference in the physical layer and network layer congestion.

To avoid loops and repeated forwarding of Interest packets, we introduce a *Forwarded Table* (FT) in each node which records the Nonce, a unique identifier used when creating an Interest, and the forwarding time of the Interest by the current node. The table is subsequently used to ensure that an Interest packet is forwarded at most once. A node frees table entries according to a local strategy, for example, after a certain time, when it can be assumed that possible local forwarding of the packet in the neighbourhood has ceased.

To shorten the data response time and to reduce the amount of packets transmitted in the network, we use a greedy geo-position based forwarding strategy. Namely, we allow the vehicular nodes furthest away from the current node to forward the packet first. This is because that node will propagate the packet the furthest physical distance and thus is likely to bring the packet closer to a remote destination that is not in range of the first node. In this way, fewer vehicular nodes are involved in packet forwarding, and fewer hops between the content requestor and responder are needed. This can be expected to decrease the latency of requesting content and also the interference and therefore also improve the content delivery ratio.

In order to be able to estimate the distance between the previous node that broadcasts the packet and the nodes receiving the packets by overhearing the wireless channel, we modify the original Interest and Data packets in NDN to include geo-position information of the previous node, as shown in Fig. 1. Thus, when a node receives, for example, an Interest packet, it can calculate the distance between itself and the previous forwarder, according to its own position information and the position information carried in the packet. In vehicular networks, it is common that all vehicles have a GPS navigator, so including the location of the node in the message is a feasible requirement.

Name	Selectors	Nonce	Guiders	*PreNode_ position*

Fig. 1. Format of interest packets

In order to enable the furthest node to forward the packet without knowing the distance information of other nodes, we introduce two types of retransmission deferral timers, T_i and T_d in each vehicle node. When a node receives an Interest packet that is not listed in its FT, it calculates the distance to the previous node that sent the packet. Then it sets the retransmission deferral time for timer T_i according to a "waiting time function", where the value of the timer is dependent on the distance, and adds the packet information to its *Waiting Table* (WT). The longer the distance, the shorter the deferral time. As a result, the timer in the node furthest away will expire first, and the node will forward the Interest first. During the deferral time of T_i, all the nodes listen for other transmissions of the same Interest packet. Upon overhearing the same Interest transmitted by another node, the nodes will discard the Interest and stop the timer T_i. The same mechanism is applied when a Data packet is received by a node, using timer T_d.

2.2   Waiting Time Function and Waiting Table

Considering the case that multiple vehicle nodes may have the same distance to the previous node, the deferral time t consists of two parts $t = t_1 + t_2$, where t_1 is the time related to the distance, t_2 is a random time, and $t_2 \ll t_1$ (i.e., t_2 is far smaller than t_1). Thus, one of the nodes having the longest distance will have the smallest t, and will forward the Interest or Data first, by broadcasting it through the wireless network interface.

The longest distance for a vehicle being able to forward packets is determined by the maximum distance of wireless transmission. In order to determine the deferral time for each node, we assume:

R is the reliable radio transmission distance. For simplicity, here we suppose all the vehicles have the same R.

D_m is the longest distance between two vehicles to send and receive data, i.e., no data transmission errors are caused by the distance. V_m is the maximum velocity of the vehicles and L_m is the maximum tolerated latency for one hop. Considering the movement of the vehicles $D_m = R - 2V_m \times L_m$, which is the case that two vehicles travel to the opposite directions at the maximum speed.

The deferral time is a decreasing function of the distance, and depending on the geographical distribution of the vehicular nodes in the network, different functions can be used. In this paper, we assume that vehicles are randomly distributed. We assign a simple linear decreasing function to the deferral time, as shown in Fig. 2.

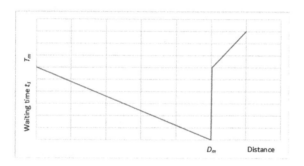

Fig. 2. Deferral time function

The maximum time T_m when the distance is 0 may eventually have influence on the data response latency. If it is too big and the network density is lower, vehicular nodes nearby the forwarding node may have relatively long deferral time. Theoretically, T_m should be $T_{hop} < T_m < 2T_{hop}$, where T_{hop} is the maximum transmission and processing delay of one hop. In practice, the maximum time can be determined by considering the average density of the vehicles in selected scenarios and the accuracy of the clocks. Figure 8 in Sect. 4 illustrates the relationship between T_m, the density of the vehicular nodes and the data response latency obtained by our simulations.

It should be noted that the synchronization of clocks among vehicles will not play a role in our method because the deferral time is used and it only requires measuring relative time intervals.

3   Forwarding Suppression

3.1   Forwarding Suppression Angle

As shown in Fig. 3, when an Interest is sent by node A, both node B and node C will receive the packet. Since the distance from B to A (d_{BA}) is longer than that from C to A (d_{CA}), B will forward the packet before C. In other words, C's forwarding is suppressed. However, if node D has the requested content, as shown in Fig. 3, the content can be obtained only when node C forwards the Interest. Here we assume that D is the nearest node having the requested information when multiple copies of the requested information exist. To avoid forwarding a packet far away from the content holder, when the position of such a node D is known, we introduce a suppression angle α_{SA}, to determine a sector within which packet forwarding is suppressed. In the case presented in Fig. 3, node C is outside this sector and hence forwards the packet and node B is the only node inside the sector forwarding the packet.

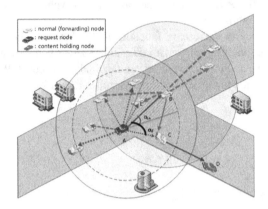

Fig. 3. Forwarding suppression angle

As shown in Fig. 3, after node C overhears the Interest from B during the deferral time, the angle α_F formed by line AB and AC can be calculated, namely: $\alpha_F = \arccos \dfrac{d_{BA}^2 + d_{CA}^2 - d_{CB}^2}{2d_{BA} \cdot d_{CA}}$. Here, d_{BA}, d_{CA}, d_{CB} are the distances between node B and A, node C and A, and node C and B, respectively. These distances can be calculated when node B and C receive the Interest from node A and when C receives the same Interest from B again. In this case, node C will first calculate the angle α_F according to the geo-position information carried in both Interest packets. If $\alpha_F < \alpha_{SA}$, it means that C is in a direction similar enough to B, and since B is expected to be closer to the content holder, C will discard the Interest received both from B and A, stop the deferral timer, and delete the corresponding entry from its waiting table WT. In This way, redundant Interest packet forwarding will be suppressed, but the forwarding of the Interests will not be restricted only to a certain direction, all directions may receive the Interest. If multiple copies of requested information are cached in the network, the suppression of Interests will greatly reduce the amount of the responded Data packets. Similarly, certain amount of Data packets will also be suppressed.

3.2   Suppression Angle and Information Delivery Ratio

Since the successful delivery of an Interest packet to a node holding the requested information is related to the suppression angle α_{SA}, we calculate the maximum failure probability of forwarding the Interest as a function of α_{SA}.

We start by re-drawing the situation described in Fig. 3 as Fig. 4. To study the situation in which an Interest is not forwarded, we place point D at the intersection of circles A and B. They all have the same radius R, which denotes the radio transmission distance of the vehicular nodes A and B. d_{AB} is the distance between A and B. As shown in Fig. 4, the following situation will lead to a cessation of packet forwarding: (i) there are no nodes in the grid area; (ii) nodes exist in the stripe area, in other words, there are nodes that can receive the forwarded packets; (iii) all nodes that received the forwarded packets are distributed in the suppressed area. In this case, all the nodes that have the possibility to forward packets further are suppressed.

Suppose the vehicles are randomly distributed in the considered area with an average density of ρ. Then the probability of the above condition (ii) is $P(D) = \dfrac{4\pi - 3\sqrt{3} - 6\sin^{-1}\dfrac{d_{AB}}{2R}}{5\pi - 3\sqrt{3}}$. The probability of the above condition (iii) is $P(C) = \dfrac{6\alpha_{SA}d_{AB}^2}{(4\pi - 3\sqrt{3})R^2}$. Suppose m, n are the number of nodes in the grid and the stripe area respectively, therefore, $m = \rho \times (\dfrac{\pi}{6}R^2 + \sin^{-1}\dfrac{d_{AB}}{2R} \cdot R^2)$;

$n = \rho \times (\dfrac{2}{3}\pi R^2 - \dfrac{\sqrt{3}}{2}R^2 - \sin^{-1}\dfrac{d_{AB}}{2R} \cdot R^2)$.

Thus, the probability of failing forwarding is $P = P(D)^m.P(C)^n$. For example, when $d_{AB} = R$, $\alpha = \dfrac{\pi}{3}$, $\rho = 9/\pi R^2$, $m = 3$, $n = 2$; $P = 4.7\%$;   and   when $d_{AB} = R$, $\alpha = \dfrac{\pi}{6}$, $\rho = 9/\pi R^2$, $m = 3$, $n = 2$; $P = 1.1\%$. The relationship among suppression angle, the delivery ratio of Interest packets and the density of vehicular nodes is shown in Fig. 9.

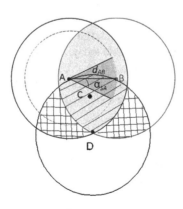

Fig. 4. Suppression angle and probability of packet loss

3.3 Packet Processing at Vehicular Nodes

A node wishing to retrieve data from the network broadcasts an Interest packet expressing its wish through the name of the requested data. The processing at an intermediate node is as follows. As shown in Fig. 5(a), each node receiving an Interest ("new instance") first checks if the same Interest ("old instance") is already in the Waiting Table (WT) matching the Nonce field of the Interest. If yes, the node next decides if the Interest should be suppressed based on the forwarding angle α_F of the new instance and the suppressing angle α_{SA}. If $\alpha_F > \alpha_{SA}$, which means the node is in a location different from the "new" previous node (i.e., Node B in Fig. 3), it will continue running the old deferral timer, until it times out and forwards the Interest (i.e., the Interest it received earlier from node A in Fig. 3). If $\alpha_F < \alpha_{SA}$, the node will stop the old timer, delete the corresponding entry in the WT and discard the Interest (e.g. node E in Fig. 3).

If no entry is found in the WT, the node will check if the Interest is in the Forwarded Table. If yes, the packet is discarded. Otherwise, the node searches the information name in its CS, similarly to the original NDN mechanism. If a match is found, the node starts the Data response procedure. If not, it will check if there is already an entry exist in the PIT. If a match is found, the node will not forward the Interest, since the same Interest has been forwarded already. Otherwise, the node will add an entry in the WT by initiating a new timer t_I according to the waiting time function and register it in the PIT. The node will schedule the Interest forwarding when the timer expires.

Similar processing is used when a Data packet is received at a node, except caching is done at the intermediate node, as shown in Fig. 5(b).

4   Performance Evaluation

We implemented the proposed method in ndnSIM [8], which realizes the basic mechanisms of NDN in the network simulator ns-3 [9]. We extended the ndnSIM implementation with support for the functionality described in this paper (Forwarded Table, Waiting Table, waiting time function and the corresponding broadcast suppression method).

To evaluate the performance of the proposed method, we use the tool OpenStreetMap (OSM) [10] and Simulation of Urban Mobility (SUMO) [11] to create different mobility scenarios. OSM provides freely exportable maps of cities. The OSM road information is generated and validated by satellite images and GPS traces, and is commonly regarded as the highest quality road data publicly available today. SUMO is an open-source traffic simulator with continuous space and discrete time. SUMO is capable of importing maps in multiple formats, including OSM. In our simulation, we use OSM to create the real-world map, and use SUMO to generate vehicle nodes and traffic, and mobility model in the real-world road maps.

We evaluate the proposed method using the metrics total number of messages transmitted in the network, data request and response (i.e., round-trip) time and successful information delivery ratio by comparing our approach with basic NDN. Figure 6 shows the parameters of ndnSIM used in our simulations.

Figure 7 illustrates the map obtained by using OSM and imported in SUMO. This is the map of Solna in Stockholm, Sweden, with an area of about 8.05 km². We measure the

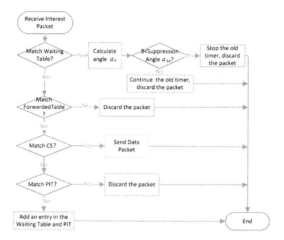

(a) Processing of Interest Packet

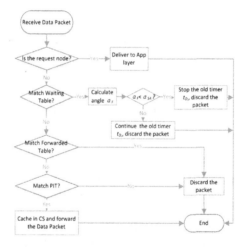

(b) Processing of Data Packet

Fig. 5. Processing of interest packet and data packet

performance of the proposed method when there are 100, 200, 400 and 600 vehicles respectively distributed in the sections of roads randomly. In our tests, 10% of the nodes send Interests with different names (i.e., asking for different content) every 0.5 s. The test time is 10 s. Another 10% of the nodes serve as content providers, holding the requested content and are randomly distributed in the network. In order to analyse the effects of the distance assisted routing and broadcast suppression, we disabled caching in the intermediate nodes. We assume that the nodes are able to know their own position and for evaluation of broadcast suppression, we also assume that nodes know the position of the content provider.

Parameters	Value
WLAN Protocol	IEEE 802.11p
Data Link Types	DLT_IEEE802_11_RADIO
Wireless transmission model	ConstantSpeedPropagationDelayModel
Signal propagation loss model	RangePropagationLossModel
Receiving gain	0db
Remote station manager	ConstantRateWifiManager
Data transmission rate	10packets/s
Time	50s

Fig. 6. Parameter set during simulations

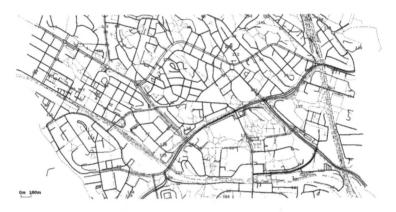

Fig. 7. Map for the simulations

4.1 Results

To evaluate the influence of the maximum deferral time T_m to the latency of packet forwarding, we measure the average round-trip latency of information requests with different T_m values. Here, we measure latency as the elapsed time from sending an Interest packet until receiving a Data packet as response under different vehicular densities in the network. Figure 8 illustrates the results. Here we can see that with the increase of T_m, the round-trip latency increases. This is because each forwarding node will wait a relatively longer time on average when T_m increases. However, with the increase of the number the nodes in the fixed area, the distance between two nodes becomes shorter, the average deferral time of each forwarding node becomes longer, and therefore the round-trip latency increases. However, the distance-based routing does not increase the number of hops of data forwarding when the number of vehicles increases and thus, the round-trip latency will not increase in general.

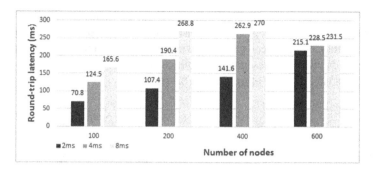

Fig. 8. Relationship among round-trip latency, Tm and node density

Figure 9 illustrates the relationship between suppression angle, information delivery ratio and density of vehicular nodes. Here the delivery ratio is defined as $D_r = N_{sent}/N_{rec}$, where N_{sent} is the total number of Interest packets sent by nodes in the network and N_{rec} is the total number of received Data packets requested by the nodes. We can see that increasing the suppression angle will result in the reduction of the information delivery ratio when the density of the vehicles is fixed. In addition, with the increase of the density of vehicles, the information delivery ratio may decrease further. This is because more vehicles are in the radio transmission area, therefore there will be more nodes to take part in the packet forwarding, and there will be more congestion and more packet loss. However, by using our proposed method, the delivery ratio decreases not as radically as the basic NDN method and it can be seen that it is at higher node densities that the suppression of broadcasts become more important.

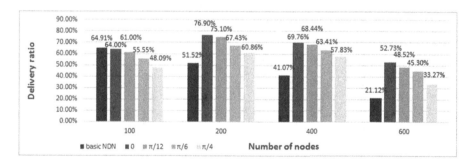

Fig. 9. Relationship among suppression angle, delivery ratio and node density

Figure 10 illustrates the total number of Interest and Data packets transmitted in the network with different node density (i.e., different number of nodes in the fixed area) compared with the basic NDN mechanism. Note that all the requested information are different, and there is only one copy of each information in the network. In other words, no caches of information are available. We compare also the effects when different suppression angles are used. The total amount of traffic in the network increases with a higher number of nodes since that corresponds to a larger number of content requests in our model, but we can see that the same trend holds true for all node densities. Our broadcast suppression mechanisms decreases the number of packets radically, reducing the traffic volume with 70–97% depending on node density, when compared with the original NDN method. In addition to the general gain in delivery ratio that we could see in Fig. 9, this also means that the overhead and resource usage for each piece of delivered content is significantly lower, leaving room for other traffic in the network.

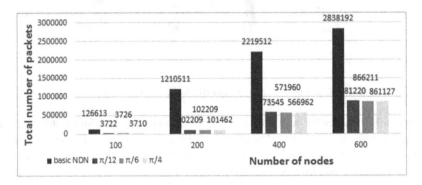

Fig. 10. Number of packets forwarded in the network

Figure 11 illustrates the average latency for obtaining data compared with the basic NDN mechanism, i.e., the time between an Interest is sent and the first Data packet is received. Here we can see that in general our proposed method performs comparable to basic NDN at very low or high node densities and has over 30% shorter latency for obtaining information than the basic NDN method in medium-density scenarios.

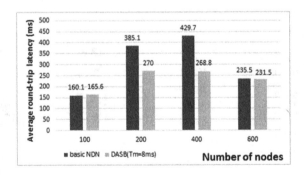

Fig. 11. Average latency of information request and response

5 Related Work

VANET and MANET (Mobile ad hoc networks) share the same principle not re-lying on fixed infrastructure for communication. They have many similarities, such as self-organization, low bandwidth and short range of radio transmission. Hence, most ad hoc routing protocols are still applicable for VANET, such as AODV (Ad-hoc On-demand Distance Vector) [12] and DSR (Dynamic Source Routing) [13] etc. However, VANET differs from

MANET in its highly dynamic topology. A number of studies [14–16] have been have shown that most ad hoc routing protocols (e.g., AODV and DSR) suffer from highly dynamic nature of node mobility. Therefore, some routing protocols have been presented for VANET, including position-based routing [15, 17], broadcast routing [18] and cluster-based routing [17, 19].

Among them, GPSR (Greedy Perimeter Stateless Routing) [20] is one of the most known position-based protocols. It combined the greedy routing with face routing by using face routing to get out of the local minimum where greedy fails. It works best in a free open space scenario with evenly distributed nodes. In this paper, we use geo-graphical location information and greedy algorithm in the context of ICN, since vehicular nodes' movement is normally constrained along roads and streets. Geographical information can be easily obtained from street maps and modern navigation systems. In addition, by using the greedy methods, packets suffers less latency in general.

Broadcast is a frequently used routing method in VANETs. Broadcast is also used in unicast routing protocols during the routing discovery phase to find an efficient route to the destination. The simplest way to implement a broadcast service is flooding, where each node broadcasts message to all its neighbours except the one from which it got this message from. Through flooding the message will eventually reach all nodes in the network. Flooding performs relatively well when there are a certain small number of nodes in the network and is easy to be implemented. However, when the number of nodes in the network increases, the bandwidth needed for one message transmission may increase exponentially. In the wireless environment, this may also cause heavy contentions and collision. Thus, the performance of transmission will decrease heavily. Flooding may has also a significant overhead. In this paper, the flooding mechanism is used to deliver the messages in the context of ICN, and we concentrate on reducing the number of broadcasted messages in order to reduce the overhead and increase the bandwidth usage.

Several researchers have investigated the possibilities of using the ICN paradigm in VANETs. For example, the ICN Research Group of the Internet Research Task Force (IRTF) has identified vehicular networks as a key scenario in which ICNs are likely to play an important role and outlines some challenges and existing work in the area in [21]. In [5, 6], authors report studies on the advantages of using Named Data Networking (NDN) [22] in vehicular networks. Here, the focus has been on introducing basic NDN mechanisms in VANETs, such as where and how to implement NDN concepts like the PIT (Pending Interest Table), and CS (Content Store) and how to combine it with flooding mechanisms to distribute data. Work reported in [7] takes this one step further. A counter-based broadcast scheme and two transmission defer timers are introduced to counteract the broadcast storm phenomena, by reducing packet collision events on the wireless medium. However, no advanced mechanism is presented to suppress the broadcast storm. [23, 24] present methods for Interest forwarding in NDN. We borrow from V-NDN [23] the idea of using a simple greedy forwarding method to spread Interest. However, instead of spreading Interests to all directions, we restrict the spreading of Interest in certain area to suppress the broadcasting storm. Navigo in [24] coupled names with the locations where the data reside: Interests are either forwarded according to the FIB with a probability p or simply flooded with a probability of $1 - p$, in order to avoid the packets focusing on a single destination area for a long time. However, the purpose of the mechanism is to balance the traffic among different sources, not suppress broadcast storm. In addition, both [23, 24] discuss only forwarding Interests, forwarding the responses carrying the requested data is not discussed. The mechanism proposed in this paper applies to forwarding of both Interest and Data packets.

6   Conclusions and Future Work

An information dissemination method for ICN-based VANETs has been proposed in this paper. Through the retransmission deferral timing function and the geo-position information, a broadcast suppression sector can be formed and distance assisted packet forwarding can be realized. By prohibiting packet forwarding in the suppression sector, large amount of packet forwarding can be eliminated, especially when in network caching is used in an ICN network. In this way, our method can reduce the interference of broadcasting data in the wireless environment, which may potentially increase the throughput of the whole network. Our simulation results show that the proposed method can greatly reduce the total number of packets forwarded in the network, while keeping a good delivery ratio of the requested data and a low data response time.

There are still some assumptions in our method, such as random distribution of vehicles. Our next step is to evaluate our method more thoroughly and improve our method by considering the distribution of vehicles along certain roads and the density of vehicles on the road. In our current results, we could see the importance of broadcast suppression at higher node densities. By estimating the density of vehicles, for example like in [25], it may be possible to adjust the angle used for the broadcast suppression sector to further improve performance for a wide range of scenarios. While the focus in this paper has been on the forwarding of interest messages, we also want to study the impact of utilizing caching in the network, and in particular infrastructure assisted caching and forwarding.

Acknowledgement.   The work in the paper was partly supported by the Chinese National High Technology Research and Development Program (863 Program) under Grant No. 2015AA016101.

References

1. Ahlgren, B., Dannewitz, C., Imbrenda, C., et al.: A survey of information-centric networking. IEEE Commun. Mag. **50**(7), 26–36 (2012)
2. Zhang, L., Afanasyev, A., Burke, J., Jacobson, V., et al.: Named data networking. In: ACM SIGCOMM Computer Communication Review (CCR), July 2014
3. Sharef, B.T., Alsaqour, R.A., Ismail, M.: Vehicular communication ad hoc routing protocols: a survey. J. Netw. Comput. Appl. **40**, 363–396 (2014)
4. Daraghmi, Y.A., Yi, C.W., Stojmenovic, I.: Forwarding methods in dissemination and routing protocols for vehicular ad hoc networks. IEEE Netw. **27**(6), 74–79 (2013)
5. Wang, J., et al.: DMND: collecting data from mobiles using name data. In: IEEE Vehicular Networking Conference (2010)
6. Wang, L., et al.: Rapid traffic information dissemination using named data. In: ACM MobiHoc NoM Workshop (2012)

7. Amadeo, M., Campolo, C., Molinaro, A.: Enhancing content-centric networking for vehicular environments. Comput. Netw. **57**(16), 3222–3234 (2013)
8. NS-3 based Named Data Networking (NDN) simulator. http://ndnsim.net/2.0/
9. NS-3: a discrete-event network simulator. http://www.nsnam.org/
10. OpenStreetMap. http://www.openstreetmap.org
11. Simulation of Urban Mobility. http://sumo.sourceforge.net
12. Perkins, C.E., Royer, E.M.: Ad-hoc on demand distance vector routing. In: 2nd IEEE Workshop on Mobile Computing Systems and Applications, pp. 90–100, February 1999
13. Johnson, D.B., Maltz, D.A.: Dynamic source routing in ad hoc wireless networks. Mob. Comput. **353**, 153–181 (1996)
14. Liu, G., Lee, B.S., Seet, B.C., Foh, C.H., Wong, K.J., Lee, K.K.: A routing strategy for metropolis vehicular communications. In: International Conference on Information Networking (ICOIN), pp. 134–143 (2004)
15. Füßler, H., Mauve, M., Hartenstein, H., Kasemann, M., Vollmer, D.: Location based routing for vehicular ad-hoc networks. ACM SIGMOBILE Mob. Comput. Commun. Rev. (MC2R) **7**(1), 47–49 (2003)
16. Santos, R.A., Edwards, A., Edwards, R., Seed, L.: Performance evaluation of routing protocols in vehicular ad hoc networks. Int. J. Ad Hoc Ubiquit. Comput. **1**(1/2), 80–91 (2005)
17. Lochert, C., Mauve, M., Füßler, H., Hartenstein, H.: Geographic routing in city scenarios. ACM SIGMOBILE Mob. Comput. Commun. Rev. (MC2R) **9**(1), 69–72 (2005)
18. Korkmaz, G., Ekici, E., Özgüner, F., Özgüner, Ü.: Urban multi-hop broadcast protocol for inter-vehicle communication systems. In: ACM International Workshop on Vehicular Ad Hoc Networks, pp. 76–85 (2004)
19. Little, T.D.C., Agarwal, A.: An information propagation scheme for VANETs. In: 8th International IEEE Conference on Intelligent Transportation Systems (ITSC 2005) (2005)
20. Karp, B., Kung, H.T.: GPSR: greedy perimeter stateless routing for wireless networks. In: 6th Annual International Conference on Mobile Computing and Networking, pp. 243–254. ACM (2000)
21. Pentikousis, K., Ohlman, B., Corujo, D., Boggia, G., Tyson, G., Davies, E., Molinaro, A., Eum, S.: Information-centric networking: baseline scenarios, RFC7476, March 2015. https://tools.ietf.org/html/rfc7476
22. Jacobson, V., Smetters, D.K., et al.: Networking named content. In: 5th International Conference on Emerging Networking Experiments and Technologies, December 2009
23. Grassi, G., Pesavento, D., Pau, G., Vuyyuru, R., Wakikawa, R., Zhang, L.: VANET via named data networking. In: INFOCOM Workshop on Name Oriented Mobility (NOM), Toronto, Canada, April–May 2014
24. Grassi, G., Pesavento, D., Pau, G., Zhang, L, Fdida, S.: Navigo: interest forwarding by geolocations in vehicular named data networking. In: IEEE World of Wireless Mobile and Multimedia Networks (WoWMoM), Boston, USA, June 2015
25. Wennerström, H., Rohner, C.: Towards even coverage monitoring with opportunistic sensor networks. In: Proceedings of ACM MobiCom Workshop on Challenged Networks (CHANTS), New York, USA, October 2016

A Cooperative Route Choice Approach via Virtual Vehicle in Internet of Vehicles

Tao Lei$^{(\boxtimes)}$, Shangguang Wang$^{(\boxtimes)}$, Jinglin Li$^{(\boxtimes)}$,
and Fangchun Yang$^{(\boxtimes)}$

State Key Laboratory of Networking and Switching Technology,
Beijing University of Posts and Telecommunications,
No. 10 Xitucheng Road, Haidian District, Beijing, China
{leitao,sgwang,ljli,fcyang}@bupt.edu.cn

Abstract. Popular navigation services are used by drivers both to plan out routes and to optimally navigate real time road congestion in internet of vehicles (IoV). However, the navigation system (such as GPS navigation system) and apps (such as Waze) may not be possible for each individual user to avoid traffic without creating congestion on the clearer roads, and it might even be that such a recommendation leads to longer aggregate routes. To solve this dispersion, in this paper, we first apply a concept of virtual vehicle in IoV, which is an image of driver and vehicle. Then, we study a setting of non-atomic routing in a network of m parallel links with symmetry of information. While a virtual vehicle knows the cost function associated with links, they are known to the individual virtual vehicles choosing the link. The virtual vehicles adapt the cooperation approach via strategic concession game, trying to minimize the individual and total travel time. How much benefit of travel time by the virtual vehicles cooperating when vehicles follow the cooperation decisions? We study the concession ratio: the ratio between the concession equilibrium obtained from an individual optimum and the social optimum. We find that cooperation approach can reduce the efficiency loss compared to the non-cooperative Nash equilibrium. In particular, in the case of two links with affine cost functions, the concession ratio is at most 3/2. For general non-decrease cost functions, the concession ratio is at most 2. For the strategic concession game, the concession ratio can approach to 1 which is a significant improvement over the unbounded price of anarchy.

Keywords: Internet of vehicles · Route choice · Virtual vehicle · Strategic concession game

1 Introduction

Optimal route choice not only can decrease the travel time for drivers, but also can solve or reduce the traffic congestions [1], particularly in metropolitan areas. To provide an optimal route, most navigation systems (such as Google Maps) and traffic apps (such as Waze) are used by drivers both to plan out routes and to optimally navigate real time road congestion [2].

© Springer International Publishing AG 2016
C.-H. Hsu et al. (Eds.): IOV 2016, LNCS 10036, pp. 194–205, 2016.
DOI: 10.1007/978-3-319-51969-2_16

Navigation systems and traffic apps calculate the best route taking into account real-time traffic flow data, as well as historic data to predict traffic flow [3]. For example, Google Maps calculates the current traffic condition using both real-time data from anonymous GPS-enabled device users and historic traffic data to provide optimal routes [2]. Waze collects aggregate traffic information in areas of interest and so can take real time traffic conditions, which are incalculable to individual drivers, into account when computing optimal route recommendations [3].

Despite this, drivers may still not satisfy the recommendations of the route from navigation systems and traffic apps. And the recommendations always not consider the possible for each individual driver to avoid traffic without creating congestion on the clearer roads, and it might even be that such a recommendation leads to longer aggregate routes.

Consider a simplistic example according to [3]. Suppose that a thousand drivers want to route from city Source to city Destination, which is reachable from Source through two parallel roads. The travel time in each of these roads depends on whether or not an accident has occurred. Specifically, suppose that in each of these roads, in the absence of accidents, each driver's trip takes $n/1000$ h, where n is the number of driver on the road (e.g., if half of the drivers take a road with no accident, then the travel time of each driver is half an hour). However, if an accident occurs, then the road becomes clogged, and each driver's trip takes one $2n/1000$ h, independently of the number of drivers on the road. Suppose that an accident occurs on each road with some probability p, which is known to all drivers, but whether or not an accident has occurred on a given road is unknown. Now, we analyze the travel time expectation of each driver cloud spend in different cases:

- Case 1: If there is no any real-time traffic information exist, then each driver would choose a road random. To a first order approximation, we assume that the exactly half of drivers would take each road. In this case, the travel time expectation can be obtained easily, i.e., $3p(1 - p)/2$.
- Case 2: If there is exist navigation system or traffic app, suppose that each driver can knows exactly which road has had an accident, and can route each driver to his individually optimal. In this case, in every situation except one where no accident occurs on either road, each driver would spend two hours on the road. The travel time expectation of each driver is $2p(1 - p)$ which is larger than Case 1.
- Case 3: Now suppose that each driver not only knows which road has had an accident, and also can negotiate with others to choose road cooperatively. In this case, a part of drivers would choose the road which has had accident. Assuming n drivers chooses the accident road, then the travel time expectation of each driver can be obtained, i.e., $(6n^2 - 4000n + 2 \times 10^6)p(1 - p)/10^6$.

Taking a closer look at this example, we observe that Case 2, in which each driver chooses the road selfishly, maybe is the worst selection, even is worse than Case 1. This implies recommendations form the navigation systems and traffic apps may not decrease the travel time for driver, and even lead to a new traffic congestion. In Case 3, it is same as Case 2 when $n = 0$, or is same as Case 1 when $n = 500$. For the Case, we know that the travel time expectation of each driver is the least when $n = 1000/3$, that is say the socially optimal routing when drivers cooperate to choose the road. Hence, drivers cooperate with each other can optimal the travel time.

According to the above analysis, we know drivers choose road cooperatively can optimal socially welfare. However, drivers always cannot know others choices in reality, and they also cannot negotiate with each other when they choose the route.

To study this question, in this paper, we first propose a vehicle agent-based [4] in cloud to help drivers negotiate with others. In this paper, we called agent virtual vehicle (VV). Suppose each driver has a corresponding VV, and it has the prats of driver's knowledge which can replace the driver to make decision in cloud.

Then we consider a bargaining routing approach [5] to optimal the travel time to solve the cooperative problem. In this game, we set a source node, a target node, and m parallel links, known to all players. The players (who know the others' strategy) decide which route to take, and incur the travel cost realized on their route. Because the VV may exist selfish behavior and we cannot inextricably compel VV to cooperate with others. However, if there has any benefit from the cooperation, the VVs may willing cooperate with others to decrease the cost. In this paper, we restrict attention to bargaining policies which performed by VVs themselves - that is, policies that induce an equilibrium in which all VVs are best off by perform the strategic concession game [6]. We refer to such equilibria as concession equilibria.

In the strategic concession game model, we establish several results. First, we show a revelation principle, which implies that restricting attention to bargaining policies is without loss of generality. Second, we quantify the efficiency loss in this setting using the concession ratio, which is the ratio between the concession equilibrium and the socially optimal one. Clearly, the Nash equilibrium of the non-cooperative game can always be obtained to implementing the full-information by VVs. Therefore, the mediation ratio is always bounded from above by the price of anarchy (PoA) [7]. We show that if all cost functions are affine, then the concession ratio is at almost 3/2 for the case of two parallel links, and is almost at $(2m - k)\backslash 2(m - k)$ for the case of m parallel links with k accident links. For general (non-decreasing) cost functions, we show that the concession ratio for m parallel links is at almost 2.

The rest of this paper is organized as follows. In Sect. 2, we introduce the virtual vehicle, and describe the basic knowledge of strategic concession game. The affine cost function case of concession ratio is analyzed in Sect. 3. In Sect. 4, the concession ration in general cost function is presented. Finally, we conclude in Sect. 5.

2   Model and Preliminaries

2.1   Virtual Vehicle

Like the agent bridge the gap between cyber and physical [8], the proposed VV can make decisions to replace driver, and have the detailed of driver information: preferences (such as which lane the driver is likely to select) and route plans are together considered as driver's behavior.

In order to effectively describe and obtain the personalization navigation, we construct the VV that encompasses both a vehicle and its driver. VVs can both locally sense data and directly access social network data and physical sensor data from the cloud. VV can communicate with the corresponding human and vehicle through the existing telecommunication systems, such as LTE. Navigation systems and traffic apps can connect with VVs through the network communication in cloud.

VV can interact with other VVs, navigation systems and traffic apps in the cloud, where it is not limited by communication and computation resources. VV can obtain big-picture real-time traffic data, both sensed locally and from the cloud; by interacting with other VVs, VVs can predict other drivers' behavior and proactively work to plan a route. VVs for driverless vehicles can make decisions about path planning and about interaction with other vehicles; VVs for common vehicles can help drivers make decisions by mining other drivers' behavior. By obtaining social and sensor data directly from the cloud to learn, and by actively communicating with other VVs, the VV can coordinate with others to select a best route for driver. In other words, the VV acts like a brain, allowing a physical vehicle and driver to interact and coordinate with others in the cloud; the physical vehicle behaves like an actuator on the road, acting upon directions from the VV. Control actually happens at the virtual level, in the cloud, instead of at the physical level, on the road.

VVs in cloud can obtain full-information including traffic information and other VVs decisions from the navigation systems and traffic apps. Hence, VVs can cooperate with each other to achieve a concession equilibrium via strategic concession game, and they can choose a more suitable route for driver.

2.2 Preliminaries

Let $N = \{1, 2, \ldots, n\}$ be the set of players, which are the VVs in this paper. A nonatomic unit of flow must be passed from a source node to a sink node through a parallel-links network on a set of links $L = \{1, 2, \ldots, m\}$, and each link can be chosen by an arbitrarily player. Hence, each player has m strategies denoted by $x_i \in \{1, 2, \ldots, m\}$, the aggregate decisions of all VVs yield a feasible flow, $X = (x_1 x_2 \ldots x_n)$. From the example describe in Sect. 1, we know that each vehicle's travel time is decided by all vehicles choices, and the cost function of VV i can be denoted by $\varphi_i(x) = \varphi_i(x_1, \ldots x_i, \ldots, x_n)$. The *social cost* of a given tuple of cost functions and flow is given by $cost(X) = \sum_{i=1}^{n} \varphi_i(x)$. We consider a *Strategic Concession Game* (SCG) in which VVs have incomplete information regarding the cost function on the link. We call all games that follow the description above, SCG, and focus on the *concession* model.

In non-cooperative game, there exists *Nash Equilibrium* (NE) when all players denoted $\left(x_1^{NE}, \ldots, x_n^{NE}\right)$, such as in the example described in Sect. 1, the travel time expectations are two NEs in Case 1 and Case 2, respectively. Let $S_j \in [0, x^{NE}]$, $j \in \{1, 2, \ldots, n\}$ denotes the discount of player j from its NE. Then the concession principle is that player i executes concession if its discount satisfies:

$$S_i = \begin{cases} \alpha_i S_j, & \text{if } \alpha_i S_j \leq x_i^{NE} \\ x_i^{NE}, & \text{if } \alpha_i S_j > x_i^{NE} \end{cases}, \tag{1}$$

where $\alpha_i \in R$ denotes the offer from player i.

We further endow the game with an informed, benevolent VVs who observe the realization of cost functions before any flow is routed, and can communicate with each other. Hence, all players can execute the SCG to achieve a new equilibrium via communication. However, players how make decision in SCG? What principles players should be obeyed? The following we discuss the detail of SCG principles [9].

- **Principle 1.** The offer from player i has more attractive than all other players, i.e., for $\forall j (\neq i) \in \{1, 2, \ldots, n\}$, if

$$\frac{\alpha_i S_j / x_i^{NE}}{S_j / x_j^{NE}} > \frac{\alpha_j S_i / x_j^{NE}}{S_i / x_i^{NE}} \Leftrightarrow \alpha_i \frac{x_j^{NE}}{x_i^{NE}} > \alpha_j \frac{x_i^{NE}}{x_j^{NE}} \Leftrightarrow \alpha_i > \alpha_j \left(\frac{x_i^{NE}}{x_j^{NE}}\right)^2.$$

- **Principle 2.** We say a player is winner if its offer has more attractive other players. If the player i is a winner, other players must receive the offer α_i. Hence, the aim of other player $j (\neq i) \in \{1, 2, \ldots, n\}$ is choose the maximum S_j when the winner i gives the offer α_i. And when the player j making concession, the player i must reduce its discount, i.e., $S_i = \alpha_i S_j$.

- **Principle 3.** If $\alpha_i \frac{x_j^{NE}}{x_i^{NE}} = \alpha_j \frac{x_i^{NE}}{x_j^{NE}}$ for all $j (\neq i) \in \{1, 2, \ldots, n\}$, the player i is the winner if it satisfies, for $\forall j (\neq i) \in \{1, 2, \ldots, n\}$, it has $\{U_i^W(\alpha_i), U_j^L(\alpha_i)\} \geq \{U_i^W(\alpha_j), U_j^L(\alpha_j)\}$, where

$$U_i^W(\alpha_i) = \varphi_i(x_1^{NE}, \ldots, x_i^{NE} - \alpha_i S_j(\alpha_i), \ldots, x_j^{NE} - S_j(\alpha_i), \ldots, x_n^{NE}),$$
$$U_j^L(\alpha_i) = \varphi_j(x_1^{NE}, \ldots, x_i^{NE} - \alpha_i S_j(\alpha_i), \ldots, x_j^{NE} - S_j(\alpha_i), \ldots, x_n^{NE}).$$

Otherwise, select another player as the winner via random device.

- **Principle 4.** If the offer α_i from the winner i satisfies $U_i^W(\alpha_i) < U_i^L\left(\alpha_i \left(\frac{x_i^{NE}}{x_i^{NE}}\right)^2\right)$, the player j can replace i to be a new winner. If player j does that, it can select an arbitrary α_i^P if its satisfies $U_i^W\left(\alpha_j^P \left(\frac{x_j^{NE}}{x_i^{NE}}\right)^2\right) \leq U_i^L(\alpha_j^P)$.

- **Principle 5.** If $\alpha_i^m > \alpha_i^0$, and player I give the discount offer α_i^s, then player j has a right to be a winner via selecting an offer α_j^P which satisfies $U_i^L(\alpha_j^P) \geq \min\left\{U_i^W(\alpha_i^s), U_i^L\left(\alpha_i^s \left(\frac{x_i^{NE}}{x_i^{NE}}\right)^2\right)\right\}$. Or player i to be the winner and its offer α_j^Q is selected by player j which satisfies $U_i^W(\alpha_j^Q) \geq U_i^W(\alpha_i^s)$. For $i, j \in \{1, 2, \ldots, n\}$, $i \neq j$, α_i^0 and α_i^m can be described as follows.

$$\alpha_i^0 = \max \left\{ \alpha_i \in R^+ \, | \, U_i^W(\alpha_i) = U_i^L \left(\alpha_i \left(\frac{x_j^{NE}}{x_i^{NE}} \right)^2 \right) \right\},$$

$$\alpha_i^m = \arg \max_{\alpha_i \geq \alpha_i^0} \left\{ U_i^W(\alpha_i) \right\}.$$

In those principles, the Principle 1 and 2 defined a player how to be a winner, and Principle 3 limits the benefits between winner and loser. Otherwise, Principle 4 and 5 can prevent the hostile offer.

Each VV can be able to use his knowledge of cost realizations to maximum the benefit, but he cannot compel VVs to take his advice. Hence, VVs can perform SCG with each other to achieve a concession equilibrium (CE).

Definition 1 (CE). Given an aggregate offer $\Lambda = \{\alpha_1, \alpha_2, \ldots, \alpha_n\}$, if there is no player change its offer and all players agree the present benefit, we say the $\Lambda = \{\alpha_1, \alpha_2, \ldots, \alpha_n\}$ is a concession equilibrium.

Obviously, there may more than one CE in SCG due to the CE is decided the offer of winner. As we shall soon show, in some cases the unconstrained social optimal flow cannot be implemented as a CE. To measure the difference from the optimal solution, we introduce the *concession ratio* (CR), defined as the ratio of the expected costs of CE flow and the globally optimal flow.

Definition 2 (CR). Give a CE $\Lambda = \{\alpha_1, \alpha_2, \ldots, \alpha_n\}$, suppose the corresponding decisions $X = (x_1 x_2 \ldots x_n)$, the *concession ratio* (CR) with respect to Λ is defined as:

$$CR(\Lambda) = \frac{E_\Lambda[cost(X)]}{E[cost(X_{optimal})]}.$$

The globally optimal decisions known by all VVs, but they may not make that decision due to some VVs cannot obtain a satisfactory benefit, but the optimal can be calculated according to the full information of VVs and flow. Hence, we can use the CR to measure the difference between SCG and other approaches. To understand our approach more convenience, we show several more properties of our models:

Lemma 1. In the non-cooperative games, if the decisions of all players are NE, and the CR is not the optimal, then if players cooperate and perform a SCG, a new CE can be achieved, and the CR cloud be better than NE.

Proof. Assume the NE is $X^{NE} = (x_1^{NE} x_2^{NE} \ldots x_n^{NE})$, $CR(X^{NE}) > CR(X_{optimal})$. Then, players perform SCG and players give the offers. According to the Principle 1, 2 and 3, there is a winner and other players would calculate their offer, until achieve a CE which implies the benefits of players are increased. Hence, the globally cost could be decreased, and the CR decrease. $\qquad \square$

From the Lemma 1, we know that the globally of CE from the SCG is better than NE from non-cooperative games. In the SCG, players may give the different offers, and the discounts vary from different players, hence there exists more than one CE in a same CE, and we have the following results.

Lemma 2. In the SCG, there may exist k CEs $\{CE_1, \ldots, CE_k\}$, for an arbitrary CE_i, $i = \{1, 2, \ldots, k\}$ with the corresponding aggregate decisions X_i, and the CR satisfies

$$CR(X_{optimal}) \leq CR(X_i) < CR(X^{NE}).$$

From the Lemma 1, we know $CR(X_i) < CR(X^{NE})$. According to the Principle 4 and 5, there is no any player can provide a hostile offer, hence the decisions cannot be better than the globally optimal decisions, then the results of Lemma 2 can be obtained.

3   Affine Cost Function

In the full-information case, VVs in same link have same travel time, if the cost functions in each link only decided by the number of VVs affine cost function in this paper, i.e., the cost functions in a no accident road is n/N, and with accident road is $2n/N$. We show that the concession ratio bounded away from the PoA in the case of two links, and for any fixed number of links. We begin with the case of two parallel links.

Proposition 1. The CR of SCG with affine cost function on two links is at most 3/2.

Proof. Consider N VVs in the full-information case with two links with the accident probability p in each link, and link 1 has an accident, the cost functions of the two links is $\varphi_1(X_1) = (2\sum_{X_1} 1)/N$ and $\varphi_2(X_2) = (\sum_{X_2} 1)/N$, then the NE of non-cooperative game is $X^{NE} = \{x_i^{NE} | x_i^{NE} = 2p(1-p), i = 1, 2, \ldots, N\}$. Then, all VVs perform the SCG and give the offers $\Lambda = \{\alpha_1, \alpha_2, \ldots, \alpha_n\}$. Because of the offer of VV should make the all benefits of players increasing, there must exist at least one VV changes its selection. Assume the player 1 is winner, then according to the Principles 3 of SCG, others should compute their benefits and make a new decision. Since their benefits increase, they must agree with the concession, then the cost could be less than the X^{NE}. According to definition of CR, we have

$$CR(X) = \frac{(6n^2 - 4Nn + 2N^2)p(1-p)/N^2}{(4/3)p(1-p)},$$

where n denote the number of players which selection the link 1. Since the Principle 4 and 5 limited the hostile offer, hence the benefits should be higher than NE, in other words the cost should decrease and we have:

$$CR(X) = \frac{(6n^2 - 4Nn + 2N^2)p(1-p)/N^2}{(4/3)p(1-p)} \leq \frac{2p(1-p)}{(4/3)p(1-p)} = \frac{3}{2}. \qquad \square$$

VVs know all other VVs' decisions and the accident information, the SCG can be performed if there are VVs willing concession, then all VVs can decrease the cost. From the Proposition 1, the bound of CR in SCG can be obtained, i.e., in the full-information case with the affine cost function, the CR in SCG has the upper bound 3/2 and the lower bound 1.

Proposition 2. The CR of SCG with affine cost function on two links can achieve at 1, if all VVs has no any selfish behavior and seek to maximize their benefit cooperatively.

Proof. The main objective of SCG is that player maximize its benefit via concession from the NE. In the non-cooperative games, players not always satisfy the benefits in the case of NE, such as the Case 2 in the example in Sect. 1. If all players willing to cooperate with each other, then the SCG can be performed. From the offers $\Lambda = \{\alpha_1, \alpha_2, \ldots, \alpha_n\}$, assuming player i is the winner, then we have

$$U^L(\alpha_i) = \varphi(x_1^{NE} - s_1(\alpha_i), \ldots, x_i^{NE} - \alpha_i \prod_{j=1,j\neq i}^{N} s_j(\alpha_i), \ldots, x_N^{NE} - s_N(\alpha_i)),$$

$$U_i^W(\alpha_i) = \varphi_i(x_1^{NE} - s_1(\alpha_i), \ldots, x_i^{NE} - \alpha_i \prod_{j=1,j\neq i}^{N} s_j(\alpha_i), \ldots, x_N^{NE} - s_N(\alpha_i)).$$

Since the benefit only decided by the VVs' decisions, and there only two selections for VVs, hence the benefit can be described as follows.

$$U^L(\alpha_i) = \frac{w_1(x_1^{NE} - s_1(\alpha_i)) + \ldots + (x_i^{NE} - \alpha_i \prod_{j=1,j\neq i}^{N} s_j(\alpha_i)) + \ldots + w_N(x_N^{NE} - s_N(\alpha_i))}{N},$$

where $w_j \in \{0, 1\}$, and $w_j = 1$ denotes VV i and VV j have the same decision, otherwise $w_{ji} = 0$. Then the first order of benefit is:

$$\frac{\partial U^L(\alpha_i)}{\partial s_j} = \frac{w_j - \alpha_i \prod_{k=1,k\neq i,k\neq j}^{N} s_k(\alpha_i)}{N} = 0, \ j(\neq i) \in \{1, 2, \ldots, N\}$$

To solve the above equations, we have $\alpha_j/\alpha_i = 1$ if player j has the same selection with player i, and $\alpha_j/\alpha_i = (2\sum_{X_1} 1)/(\sum_{X_2} 1)$ if player j has different selection with player i. When the final equilibrium achieved, then the discount can be obtained $s(\alpha_j) = \frac{2\alpha_j x_j^{NE}}{\alpha_j + 2\alpha_j}$, and $x_j^{NE} = 2p(1-p)$, we have $s(\alpha_j) = \frac{4}{3}p(1-p)$. According to the definition of CR, the CR is 1 and the proof is finish. □

From the Proposition 2, the optimal equilibrium can achieve and each player can obtain the maximum benefits when all players willing cooperate in the full-information case. In other words, VVs can minimize their travel time cooperatively, and the social cost also cloud be achieved.

Now we complement this positive result by a negative one, showing that when m is large. For each link, the cost functions in a no accident road is n/N, and with accident road is $2n/N$. Before presenting the results of m is large, we introduce a helpful lemma.

Lemma 3. Consider N VVs with m links, if there is a link has accident, VVs can select a link random in the full-information case. In the non-cooperative games, there only exist one NE, i.e., $x^{NE} = mp(1 - p)^{m-1}$.

In the non-cooperative games, each VV knows the traffic information. They will choose a link random in the rest $m-1$ links, then the N VVs cloud be distribute in $m-1$ links uniformly. Then, assume the i link has an accident, the NE can be calculated:

$$x^{NE} = \binom{m}{1} \left(\sum_{L/i} \frac{N/(m-1)}{N} \cdot \frac{N}{m-1} \right) p(1 - p)^{m-1} = \frac{m}{m-1} p(1 - p)^{m-1}.$$

We are now ready to present our negative result, by constructing an affine SCG to observe the number of links how impacts the CR.

Proposition 3. The CR of SCG with affine cost function is irrelevant with the number of links, and the CR also is at most $\frac{2m-1}{2(m-1)}$.

According to the Lemma 3, we can obtain the NE of non-cooperative games in the full-information case. Then, we can calculate the optimal equilibrium, i.e., $(2/3)mp(1 - p)^{m-1}$, similar with Proposition 1, we have

$$CR(X) \leq \frac{\frac{m}{m-1} p(1 - p)^{m-1}}{\frac{2m}{2m-1} p(1 - p)^{m-1}} = \frac{2m - 1}{2(m - 1)}.$$

Now, we extend the one accident link to $k(\leq m)$ accident links, and the results of the general case of affine cost function can be described as follows.

Theorem 1. For the m links with $k(\leq m)$ accident links, N VVs perform the SCG with affine cost function, the value of CR is limited in the range of $\left[1, \frac{2m-k}{2(m-k)}\right]$.

Proof. In the SCG, each VV willing cooperative to obtain maximum benefit which implies the minimum travel time in our considering case. According to the Proposition 2, we know that VV can make the best decision to cooperate with each other, and the optimal decisions can be obtained when all VVs make the best the decision. Hence, the minimum of CR is 1 according to its definition. Similar with the proof of Proposition 2, we can calculate the expected costs of each VV as follows.

$$\binom{m}{k} \frac{((2m - k)(n - Nk/(2m - k))^2 - 2k(m - k)N^2/(2m - k))p^k(1 - p)^{m-k}}{k(m - k)p^k(1 - p)^{m-k}N^2},$$

then the optimal costs is $\binom{m}{k}\frac{2}{2m-k}$. In the non-cooperative games, we can obtain the

NE is $\binom{m}{k}\frac{1}{m-k}$. According to the definition of CR and the Lemma 2, the maximum of

CR is $\frac{2m-k}{2(m-k)}$. □

4 General Cost Function

As established in the previous section, when the cost functions are restricted to the set of affine functions, the MR in m links with k accident links can be converged the optimal cost.

In this section, we discuss the MR in case of general cost function. For the cost function, we know the travel time cannot decrease with the number of vehicles increasing in a road, hence the general cost function must be a non-decrease function. Then, we show the results has some difference with the affine cost function case. Before presenting the results, we fist introduce a definition of partition.

Definition 3 (Partition). For the m links and with k accident links, assume the cost functions of m links are $c_1, c_2, \ldots, c_m (c_1 \le c_2 \le \ldots \le c_m)$, we can divide the m links into l sets $L_1, L_2, \ldots, L_l$ such that:

1. The links i, j in the same set if $c_i(n) = c_j(n)$, n denotes the number of VVs;
2. For arbitrary two sets L_i and L_j, $i \neq j$, they satisfy $L_i \cap L_j = \emptyset$;
3. For $c_i \in L_h$ and $c_j \in L_k$, if $h < k$, $c_i(n) < c_j(n)$.

Note that the link in same set has same cost function, and VVs cloud choose the links of L_1 random in non-cooperative game, hence the NE could be $c_1(N\backslash|L_1|)$, $|L_1|$ denotes the number of links in L_1.

Lemma 4. Let $c_1, c_2, \ldots, c_m$ be a cost functions than can be divided into a partition $L_1, L_2, \ldots, L_l$. In the SCG with N VVs, let $n_1, n_2, \ldots, n_m$ be the optimal number of VVs in the corresponding links, and let $\sum_{i=1}^{m} c_i(n_i) = \gamma$. Then $\sum_{i=1}^{m} n_i c_i(n_i) \le \gamma N/|L_1|$.

Proof. Since $n_1, n_2, \ldots, n_m$ are the optimal number of VVs in links, hence we have

$$n_i c_i(n_i) = n_j c_j(n_j), \ \forall i, j \in \{1, 2, \ldots, m\}.$$

According to the definition of partition, the cost functions satisfy $c_1 \le c_2 \le \ldots \le c_m$, hence $n_1 \ge n_2 \ge \ldots \ge n_m$. Then, we have follow result:

$$\sum_{i=1}^{m} n_i c_i(n_i) \le \sum_{i=1}^{m} n_1 c_i(n_i),$$

$$\sum_{i=1}^{m} n_i c_i(n_i) \le n_1 \sum_{i=1}^{m} c_i(n_i) = n_1 \gamma.$$

Besides, in the NE of non-cooperative game, the number of VVs in each link of L_1 is $N/|L_1|$. Since the n_1 is the number of VVs in each link of L_1 in the optimal case, hence $n_1 \leq N/|L_1|$. ▢

In the full-information case, VVs cooperate with each other to decrease the cost using SCG. When VVs perform the SCG, they will calculate the discount according to the offers, then they exchanged their offers until achieve a CE, and we use the CR to measure the CE referred to its definition. For the CR with the non-decrease cost function case, we have the following result.

Theorem 2. For the m links with $k(\leq m)$ accident links, N VVs perform the SCG with non-decrease cost function $c_1, c_2, \ldots, c_m$, and assume it can be divided into a partition $L_1, L_2, \ldots, L_l$. Then, the upper bounds of CR can be limited in $\left[\max\left\{1, \frac{|L_1|}{m}\right\}, 2\right]$.

Proof. In the non-cooperative game, the NE is $c_1(N \backslash |L_1|)$, and according to the Lemma 4, then we have

$$CR_{\max} = \frac{c_1(N \backslash |L_1|)}{\left(\sum_{i=1}^{m} n_i c_i(n_i)\right)/N} \geq \frac{c_1(N \backslash |L_1|)}{\gamma N |L_1|/N},$$

$$CR_{\max} = \frac{|L_1| c_1(N \backslash |L_1|)}{\gamma} \geq \frac{|L_1| c_1(N \backslash |L_1|)}{m c_1(n_1)} \geq \frac{|L_1|}{m}.$$

According to the SCG, VVs make discounts $d_1, d_2, \ldots, d_m$ to achieve a new CE, and we have $c_1(N \backslash |L_1|) = c_1(n_1) + d_1$. Then, we have

$$CR_{\max} = \frac{c_1(N \backslash |L_1|)}{\left(\sum_{i=1}^{m} n_i c_i(n_i)\right)/N} = \frac{N c_1(N \backslash |L_1|)}{m n_1 c_1(n_1)} \leq \frac{N c_1(N \backslash |L_1|) + m n_1 d_1}{m n_1(c_1(n_1) + d_1)},$$

$$CR_{\max} \leq \frac{N}{m n_1} + \frac{d_1}{c_1(n_1) + d_1}.$$

Since $c_1 = \min\{c_1, c_2, \ldots, c_m\}$ and $n_i c_i(n_i) = n_j c_j(n_j)$, hence $n_i \geq N/m$, then

$$CR_{\max} \leq \frac{N}{m n_1} + \frac{d_1}{c_1(n_1) + d_1} \leq \frac{N}{mN/m} + 1 = 2.$$

From the definition of CR, we know that $CR \geq 1$, hence we have CR can be limited in $\left[\max\left\{1, \frac{|L_1|}{m}\right\}, 2\right]$. ▢

5   Conclusion

In this paper, we first apply a concept of virtual vehicle in IoV, which is an image of driver and vehicle, to solve the optimal route choice problem when drivers willing cooperate with each other. We study a class of strategy concession game with parallel-links routing in which VVs have incomplete information about the costs of the links and other VVs decisions. We define the concession ratio: the ratio between the concession equilibrium arising from cooperation recommendations and the social optimum, which is always bounded from above by the PoA. We find that the concession ratio is at most 3/2 for two links with affine cost functions, the concession ratio is at most 2 for general non-decrease cost functions. The main open question left by our work is verity the concession ratio in the road networks.

Acknowledgments. This work is supported by the Natural Science Foundation of Beijing under Grant No. 4132048, National Natural Science Foundation of China under Grant No. 61202435 and 61272521

References

1. Sha, W., Kwak, D., Nath, B., Iftode, L.: Social vehicle navigation: integrating shared driving experience into vehicle navigation. In: Proceedings of the 14th Workshop on Mobile Computing Systems and Applications, Jekyll Island, Georgia (2013)
2. Large, D.R., Burnett, G., Benford, S., Oliver, K.: Crowdsourcing good landmarks for in-vehicle navigation systems. Behav. Inf. Technol. **35**(10), 1–10 (2016)
3. Vasserman, S., Feldman, M., Hassidim, A.: Implementing the wisdom of waze. In: Proceedings of the 24th International Joint Conference on Artificial Intelligence (IJCAI 2015), pp. 660–666 (2015)
4. Qin, Y., Huang, D., Zhang, X.: VehiCloud: cloud computing facilitating routing in vehicular networks. In: Proceedings of 11th IEEE International Conference on Trust, Security and Privacy in Computing and Communications, pp. 1438–1445 (2012)
5. Roth, A.E.: Game-Theoretic Models of Bargaining. Cambridge University Press, Cambridge (1985)
6. An, B., Lesser, V., Sim, K.M.: Strategic agents for multi-resource negotiation. Auton. Agent. Multi Agent Syst. **23**, 114–153 (2011)
7. Roughgarden, T., Tardos, É.: Bounding the inefficiency of equilibria in nonatomic congestion games. Games Econ. Behav. **47**, 389–403 (2004)
8. Semwal, T., Nikhil, S., Jha, S.S., Nair, S.B.: TARTARUS: a multi-agent platform for bridging the gap between cyber and physical systems. In: Proceedings of the International Conference on Autonomous Agents & Multiagent Systems, pp. 1493–1495 (2016)
9. Jørgensen, S., Yeung, D.W.: A strategic concession game. Int. Game Theory Rev. **1**, 103–129 (1999)

A Digital Diary Making System Based on User Life-Log

Yechan Park[(✉)], Byungseok Kang, and Hyunseung Choo

College of Software, Sungkyunkwan University, Suwon, Korea
{dpcks001,byungseok,choo}@skku.edu

Abstract. A common digital diary system is a software technology that proactively suggests contents of interest to users based on various kinds of context information. It provides benefits to users and meets their satisfaction. This research was motivated by our interest in understanding the criteria for measuring the success of a diary making system from users' point of view. Even though existing work has introduced a wide range of criteria such as users' biological information, picture, movie, etc. In this paper, we propose a digital diary making system which aimed at measuring the user emotion from their life-log data (daily-life photos). We can get those life-log data from user's smartphone storage. The final product of digital diary includes feeling, time, and physical location information.

Keywords: Life-log · Digital diary · User emotion · Diary making system

1 Introduction

Smartphones are rising the mobile phone market [1]; they are not just phones; they also act as media players, gaming consoles, personal calendars, storage, etc. They are small size portable computers with fewer computing capabilities than PCs. However, unlike PCs, users can carry their smartphone with them at all times. The ubiquity of mobile phones and their computing capabilities provide an opportunity of using them as a life-logging device. Life-logs [2, 3] are used to record user daily life events and assist them in memory augmentation. In a more technical sense, life-logs sense and store users contextual information from their environment through sensors, which are core components of life-logs.

A life-logging by digital system [4, 5] means to record our daily life in detail. To date we have only relied on our human memory to record and remember our daily experience. The human brain tends to quickly lose the details of his/her experiences. Therefore, we record special events such as party and travel with photos and videos. Excluding such special events, we rarely record the daily experiences that are the major part of our life; what we do at most is write a short diary. Because of developing technologies related to information and communication technology (ICT), ubiquitous and high bandwidth 4G/LTE mobile networks we believe that we will be able to automatically capture and record our daily experiences. With this context, research on the capture and retrieval of life-logs is emerging quickly.

Several works introduce capturing a life-log [6–9] by audio and video with various sensors such as a GPS (location), gyros, physiological sensors (brain wave), acceleration

© Springer International Publishing AG 2016
C.-H. Hsu et al. (Eds.): IOV 2016, LNCS 10036, pp. 206–213, 2016.
DOI: 10.1007/978-3-319-51969-2_17

sensors (motion), documents, annotations and emails. Retrieval is the most important problem for the life-log system. The amount of multimedia data captured is very large, and the problem is to find valuable photo/image through the data. Remembering the feeling or emotion of our experiences is easier than remembering details of them, so the emotion can provide valuable keys for life-logging system. We have developed a user emotion based life-logging system, by which we can take a photo by parameters such as time, location, and emotion. In the following sections, a literature review on life-logging system and platform technologies are presented in Sect. 2. In Sect. 3, we detail our proposed digital diary making system. Finally, we conclude the paper in Sect. 4.

2 Related Work

The field of life-logging is a relatively new but rapidly expanding area of research and it has been recognize that a visual life-log should be segmented into manageable shots, activities and events to make it manageable. In this section we discuss the most known contributions of life-logs in the literature. Life-log sources can be classified into sub categories from various perspectives. From one view point, they can be classified into biological data, multimedia data, etc. Figure 1 shows the categorization of previous works for life-log sources.

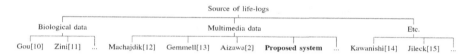

Fig. 1. Classification of life-log

In [10], they introduced a smartphone-based personal data management and personality analysis system. In their system, the smartphone functions as not only a source of personal data but also a gateway to manage other wearable and communicate with a server that keeps personal data in a larger amount and a longer period. In [11] investigated how life-logs from commercial wearable trackers and smartphone sensors can be leveraged to automatically provide patients with knowledge for self-reflection on their disease. In this paper, they present an architecture for the acquisition of life-logs, fusion, storage and prototype GUI for the visualization of quality of life indicators.

The work of [12] introduced state-of-the-art literature on wearable diaries and life-logging systems, and discuss the key issues and main challenges. The multimedia-based diary system offers an aesthetic user interface that encourages users to reflect on their day, to evaluate their emotional reactions which are measured by wearable bio-sensors and visualized as colorful images. In [13], they developed a platform for recording, storing, and accessing a personal lifetime archive. The goals of proposed system included understanding the effort to digitize a lifetime of legacy multimedia contents. In [2] presented continuous capture of life-log with various sensors and additional data. Furthermore, they proposed an effective retrieval methods using multimedia contents. Their life-log system contains video, audio, acceleration sensor, gyro, GPS, annotations, documents, web pages, and emails.

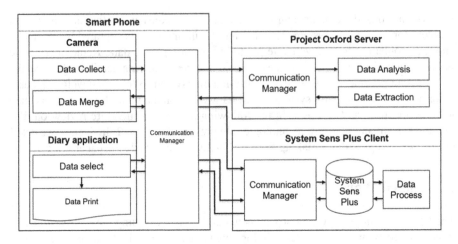

Fig. 2. Basic architecture and modules of proposed system

In [14] presented an application to support users to do their homework, especially self-monitoring of user behaviors. By collecting life-logs of users via smart phones, their proposed application estimates user activities based on life-logs. The work of [15] described digital diary concept in more detail and also provide an overview of related diary and timeline applications. Additionally, they presented a proof of concept implementation as well as results of an early user experience evaluation.

3   Proposed System

This section presents the software implementation of the life-log based digital diary making system. Our system mainly classified into three parties: user smartphone, project Oxford [16] server and System Sens Plus (SSP) server. We adapt Oxford server for image processing and modified standard source of System Sens [17] system for storing user photos.

3.1   Architecture and Modules

Our system has adopted the client/server mode where the smartphone acts as a client and project Oxford and System Sens acts as a server. The general system architecture and modules in both client and server sides are shown in Fig. 2. For the client, the smartphone itself can provide a plenty of usage data and sensing data. For instance, an iPhone has two integrated interfaces, HomeKit and HealthKit. In addition, sensors embedded in a smartphone can also be used to get GPS, light, acceleration, pressure and other data. Currently many wearable offer a network such as Bluetooth to connect a smartphone. Thus, a smartphone can take the data from wearable such as smart watch, bracelet, ring, etc. Further, a smartphone can be used to get information such as weather from outside APPs and SNS via the Internet.

In our system, smartphone client includes two main modules such as camera and dairy application. In case of camera, this module equipped high-quality sensors, powerful shooting modes and multitude of camera settings, smartphones have shown point-and-shoot cameras the door. The main function of this module is collecting and merging user photos. The other main module of smartphone is diary application module. This module associated with data select and data retrieval. We developed this application under the Android 6.0 code name Marshmallow [18].

The Project Oxford server is developed by Microsoft. We use the API of this server to provide user emotion based on "Face Recognition" technology. This Oxford server automatically recognizes faces in photos, group faces that look alike and verifies whether two faces are the same. It can be used for things like easily recognizing which users are in certain photos and allowing a user to log in using face authentication. It's the same technology that guesses how old a person looks based on a photograph. This server includes communication manager, data analysis and data extraction module. Data analysis module is the key in Oxford server.

System Sens [17] is developed by UCLA research center. This system help researcher capture usage context in their deployments in an extendible way. System Sens is designed to be unobtrusive-it has no user interface to minimize impact on usage, and it has a small footprint in terms of memory, CPU, and energy consumption. The DB module is for persistently keeping all data from many users. The communication module provides stable and safe communications between a smartphone and two servers are essential in the system. We modified original source code of System Sens for effectively managing the user photos and related tagging information. Therefore, we called this system as System Sens Plus.

3.2   Photo Collection and Diary Making Process

The personal data in our system is from various sources in different forms. It is thus necessary to control and coordinate the data collections from the multiple sources. The data collection control is according to a file of the collection schedules that is stored in the System Sens Plus. The schedules specify that when data will be captured or acquired for user smartphone. Due to the data heterogeneity, the schedule for a data source is decided with considerations of data change rate, collection condition, local DB capacity, upload situation, etc. Another factor to be considered in setting the schedules is the energy consumption of a smartphone battery. It is necessary to make some tradeoff between the frequency of data collection and the reduction of power usage.

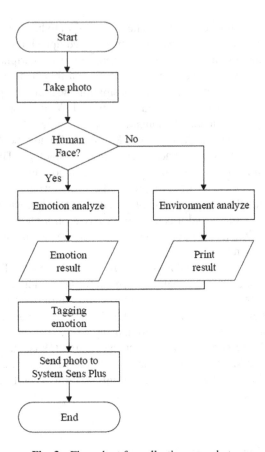

Fig. 3. Flow chart for collection user photos

To collect user photos, smartphone takes a photo and sends it to the Oxford server. After that, Oxford server analyzes received photo whether human face or not based on the rules of its image processing engine. Next, the server tags emotion information based on analyzing result of receiving photo. Finally, System Sens Plus stores user photo and its tagging data (emotion, time, and location). The detail data collection process is described in Fig. 3.

To provide life-log diary, we developed Android base diary application and installed it to the user smartphone. Android is an open source and Linux-based operating system for mobile devices such as smartphones and tablet computers. Android was developed by the Open Handset Alliance, led by Google, and other companies. For this experimental study, we use newly published Android Marshmallow. Figure 4 shows basic step of producing digital diary. Firstly, user executes diary application from his/her mobile device and selects one event. Secondly, diary application requests associated data to System Sens Plus server. Finally, user application retrieves the results. Figure 5 shows the screenshot of life-log diary. We divide user emotion into three categories [19, 20] such as happiness, neutral, and sadness. Our system also provides daily emotion

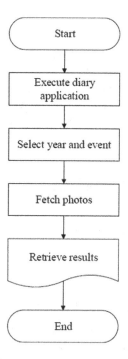

Fig. 4. Flow chart for producing life-log diary

information and Google Map service based on physical location of user photos (see Fig. 5).

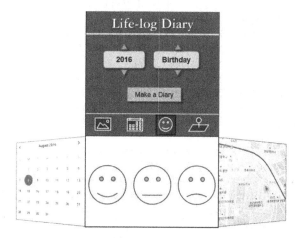

Fig. 5. Output of digital diary

4   Conclusion

To overcome the limitation of making digital diary, we implemented an emotion based life-logging which is familiar to user. We proposed digital diary system reflecting user preference based on emotion and context information which can obtain from mobile devices. For future works, we will verify the usefulness from usability tests, and enlarge the data set including the number of case samples as well as the types of various user activities.

Acknowledgments. This work was supported in part by the Ministry of Science, ICT and Future Planning, South Korea, Institute for Information and Communications Technology Promotion through the G-ITRC Program under Grant IITP-2015-R6812-15-0001 and in part by the National Research Foundation of Korea within the Ministry of Education, Science and Technology through the Priority Research Centers Program under Grant 2010-0020210.

References

1. Goasduff, L., Pettey, C.: Gartner says worldwide smartphone sales soared in fourth quarter of 2011 with 47 percent growth, April 2012
2. Aizawa, K., Tancharoen, D., Kawasaki, S., Yamasaki, T.: Efficient retrieval of life log based on context and content. In: Proceedings of the 1st ACM Workshop on Continuous Archival and Retrieval of Personal Experiences, pp. 22–31. ACM (2004)
3. Hori, T., Aizawa, K.: Context-based video retrieval system for the life-log applications. In: Proceedings of the 5th ACM SIGMM International Workshop on Multimedia Information Retrieval, pp. 31–38. ACM (2003)
4. Tancharoen, D., Yamasaki, T., Aizawa, K.: Practical experience recording and indexing of life log video. In: Proceedings of the 2nd ACM Won Continuous Archival and Retrieval of Personal Experiences, pp. 61–66. ACM (2005)
5. Minamikawa, A., Kotsuka, N., Honjo, M., Morikawa, D., Nishiyama, S., Ohashi, M.: Rfid supplement for mobile-based life log system. In: 2007 International Symposium on Applications and the Internet Workshops (2007)
6. Hwang, K.-S., Cho, S.-B.: Landmark detection from mobile life log using a modular Bayesian network model. Expert Syst. Appl. **36**(10), 12065–12076 (2009)
7. Abe, M., Morinishi, Y., Maeda, A., Aoki, M., Inagaki, H.: A life log collector integrated with a remote-controller for enabling user centric services. IEEE Trans. Cons. Electron. **55**(1), 295–302 (2009)
8. Ryoo, D.-W., Bae, C.: Design of the wearable gadgets for life-log services based on utc. IEEE Trans. Cons. Electron. **53**(4), 1477–1482 (2007)
9. Makino, Y., Murao, M., Maeno, T.: Life log system based on tactile sound. In: Kappers, A.M.L., Erp, J.B.F., Bergmann Tiest, W.M., Helm, F.C.T. (eds.) EuroHaptics 2010. LNCS, vol. 6191, pp. 292–297. Springer, Heidelberg (2010). doi:10.1007/978-3-642-14064-8_42
10. Guo, A., Ma, J.: A smartphone-based system for personal data management and personality analysis. In: 2015 IEEE International Conference on Computer and Information Technology; Ubiquitous Computing and Communications; Dependable, Autonomic and Secure Computing; Pervasive Intelligence and Comput ing (CIT/IUCC/DASC/PICOM), pp. 2114–2122. IEEE (2015)

11. Zini, F., Reinstadler, M., Ricci, F.: Life-logs aggregation for quality of life monitoring. In: Proceedings of the 5th International Conference on Digital Health 2015, pp. 131–132. ACM (2015)
12. Machajdik, J., Hanbury, A., Garz, A., Sablatnig, R.: Affective com - puting for wearable diary and lifelogging systems: an overview. In: Machine Vision-Research for High Quality Processes and Products-35th Workshop of the Austrian Association for Pattern Recognition. Austrian Computer Society (2011)
13. Gemmell, J., Bell, G., Lueder, R.: Mylifebits: a personal database for everything. Commun. ACM **49**(1), 88–95 (2006)
14. Kawanishi, N., Tamai, M., Hasegawa, A., Takeuchi, Y., Tajika, A., Ogawa, Y., Furukawa, T.: Lifelog-based estimation of activity diary for cognitive behavioral therapy. In: Adjunct Proceedings of the 2015 ACM International Joint Conference on Pervasive and Ubiquitous Computing and Proceedings of the 2015 ACM International Symposium on Wearable Computers, pp. 1251–1256. ACM (2015)
15. Jilek, C., Maus, H., Schwarz, S., Dengel, A.: Diary generation from personal information models to support contextual remembering and reminiscence. In: 2015 IEEE International Conference on Multimedia & Expo Workshops (ICMEW), pp. 1–6. IEEE (2015)
16. Microsoft Cognitive Services. https://www.microsoft.com/cognitive-services/. Accessed 23 Aug 2016
17. Mahajan, F.R., Estrin, D.: Systemsens: a tool for monitoring usage in smartphone research deployments. In: Proceedings of the Sixth International Workshop on MobiArch, pp. 25–30. ACM (2011)
18. Android6.0 Marshmallow. https://www.android.com/. Accessed 23 Aug 2016
19. Lopes, P.N., Salovey, P., Coté, S., Beers, M., Petty, R.E.: Emotion regulation abilities and the quality of social interaction. Emotion **5**(1), 113 (2005)
20. Gross, J.J., Thompson, R.A.: Emotion regulation: conceptual foundations (2007)

Miscellaneous Issues

Accurate Part-of-Speech Tagging
via Conditional Random Field

Jinmei Zhang[1(✉)] and Yucheng Zhang[2]

[1] Nanjing Technician College, Nanjing 210023, China
zjm6363@vip.163.com
[2] Institute of Computing Technology of the Chinese Academy of Sciences,
Beijing 100190, China
zhangyucheng@ict.ac.cn

Abstract. POS tagging (i.e. part-of-speech tagging) is an important component of syntactic parsing in the field of natural language processing. While CRF (i.e. conditional random field) is a class of statistical modelling method often applied in pattern recognition and machine learning, where it is used for structured prediction. As POS tagging can be considered as a structured prediction task to some extent, so in this paper, we proposed to utilize the inherent advantages of CRF, and apply it to POS tagging task to get more accurate. The subsequent experiments are introduced to validate our proposed method.

Keywords: POS tagging · CRF · Part-of-Speech · Conditional random field · Accurate, prediction

1 Introduction

We discuss POS tagging, or part-of-speech tagging using the well-known conditional random field (CRF) model introduced originally by Lafferty et al. [1]. POS tagging plays an important role in the field of natural language processing [1–4, 11, 13]. To the best of our knowledge, there exist several methods to solve this problem [21–23], such as hidden markov chain based POS tagger in [18] which adapted the hidden markov chain to POS tagging, decision forests based POS tagger [19] which adapted decision forests model to POS tagging, and maximum entropy model based model [20] which adapted maximum entropy model to POS tagging.

While CRF is a class of statistical modelling method, which is often applied in pattern recognition and machine learning, and it is used for structured prediction [4, 7, 11]. To some extent, POS tagging can be considered as a sort of structured prediction task. From a technical perspective, we accomplish this by making use of the fundamental ability of the CRFs to incorporate arbitrarily defined feature functions. The newly defined features are expected to alleviate data sparsity problems caused by the fine-grained labels. As a result, we proposed to utilize the inherent advantages of CRF, and apply it to POS tagging task to get better performance in this paper. We present experiments on an open dataset, and the experimental results show that our proposed method is promising in POS tagging.

© Springer International Publishing AG 2016
C.-H. Hsu et al. (Eds.): IOV 2016, LNCS 10036, pp. 217–224, 2016.
DOI: 10.1007/978-3-319-51969-2_18

The rest of the paper is organized as follows. Section 2 listed two preliminary concepts, namely POS tagging and conditional random field. Then based on these two concepts, we describe in detail how to use the proposed method to utilize the inherent advantages of CRF, and apply it to POS tagging task to get more accurate in Sect. 3. In Sect. 4, we conduct simulation experiments to validate our proposed method. At last, the conclusion and the future work discussion are listed in Sect. 5.

2   Preliminary

In this section, we mainly describe two concepts related to this paper, namely POS tagging and CRF.

2.1   POS Tagging

In corpus linguistics, POS tagging is the process of marking up a word in a text as corresponding to a particular part of speech, based on both its definition and its context—i.e., its relationship with adjacent and related words in a phrase, sentence, or paragraph [1–4, 11, 13]. A simplified form of this is commonly taught to school-age children, in the identification of words as NN, VB, DT, VBZ, etc.

Once performed by hand, POS tagging is now done in the context of computational linguistics, using algorithms which associate discrete terms, as well as hidden parts of speech, in accordance with a set of descriptive tags. POS-tagging algorithms fall into two distinctive groups: one is rule-based tagger, which need large numbers of hand-crafted rules; the other is probabilistic tagger, which use a tagged corpus to train some sort of models. Obviously, to some extent, POS tagging can be considered as a structured prediction task.

In POS tagging, the goal is to label a sentence (a sequence of words or tokens) with tags like NN, VB, DT, VBZ, etc. For example, given the sentence "Book that flight. Does that flight serve dinner?", the labeling might be "Book (VB) that (DT) flight (NN). Does (VBZ) that (DT) flight (NN) serve (VB) dinner (NN)". This process is as shown in Fig. 1.

2.2   CRF

Conditional random field (CRF) is a class of statistical modelling method often applied in pattern recognition and machine learning, where it is used for structured prediction [3, 4, 11, 13]. Whereas an ordinary classifier predicts a label for a single sample without regard to neighboring samples, a CRF can take context into account; e.g., the linear chain CRF popular in natural language processing predicts sequences of labels for sequences of input samples [4, 7, 11]. In fact, the linear chain CRF is a special case of CRF, where the hidden variables form a straight line, which is as shown in Fig. 2.

CRF is a type of discriminative undirected probabilistic graphical model. It is used to encode known relationships between observations and constructs consistent interpretations. It is often used for labeling or parsing of sequential data, such as natural

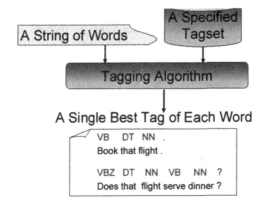

Fig. 1. POS tagging.

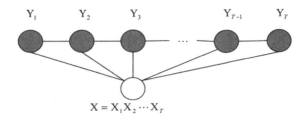

Fig. 2. A special case of CRF, i.e. linear-chain CRF.

language text or biological sequences and in computer vision. Specifically, CRFs find applications in shallow parsing, named entity recognition, gene finding and peptide critical functional region finding, among other tasks, being an alternative to the related hidden Markov models.

3 POS Tagging via CRF

As POS tagging can be considered as a structured prediction task to some extent, so in this paper, we proposed to utilize the inherent advantages of CRF, and apply it to POS tagging task to get better performance.

3.1 Feature Function and Conditional Probability

Each feature function of CRF is a function that takes in as input: a sentence s, the position i of a word in the sentence, the label l_i of the current word and the label l_{i-1} of the previous word, and outputs a real-valued number (though the numbers are often just either 0 or 1). For example, one possible feature function could measure how much we suspect that the current word should be labeled as an adjective given that the previous word is "very".

Next, we assign each feature function f_j a weight λ_i. Given a sentence s, we can now score a labeling l of s by adding up the weighted features over all words in the sentence:

$$score(l|s) = \sum_{j=1}^{m} \sum_{i=1}^{n} \lambda_j f_j(s, i, l_i, l_{i-1}), \tag{1}$$

where the first sum runs over each feature function j, and the inner sum runs over each position i of the sentence. To make more clear the constructing process of feature function f_j and the effects of the corresponding weight λ_i. in POS tagging tasks via CRF, we list several examples by the following:

(1) *feature $f_1(s, i, l_i, l_{i-1}) = 1$ if $l_i = ADJ$ and the ith word ends in "-ly"; 0 otherwise. If the weight λ_i associated with this feature is large and positive, then this feature is essentially saying that we prefer labelings where words ending in -ly get labeled as ADV.*

(2) *feature $f_2(s, i, l_i, l_{i-1}) = 1$ if $i = 1$, $l_i = VB$, and the sentence ends in a question mark; 0 otherwise. Again, if the weight λ_2 associated with this feature is large and positive, then labelings that assign VERB to the first word in a question (e.g., "Is this a sentence beginning with a verb?") are preferred.*

(3) *feature $f_3(s, i, l_i, l_{i-1}) = 1$ if $l_{i-1} = ADJ$ and $l_i = NN$; 0 otherwise. Again, a positive weight for this feature means that adjectives tend to be followed by nouns.*

To build a conditional random field, you just define a bunch of feature functions (which can depend on the entire sentence, a current position, and nearby labels), assign them weights, and add them all together, transforming at the end to a probability if necessary. Finally, we can transform these scores into probabilities $p(l|s)$ between 0 and 1 by exponentiating and normalizing as follows:

$$p(l|s) = \frac{exp[\sum_{j=1}^{m} \sum_{i=1}^{n} \lambda_j f_j(s, i, l_i, l_{i-1})]}{\sum_{l'} exp[\sum_{j=1}^{m} \sum_{i=1}^{n} \lambda_j f_j(s, i, l'_i, l'_{i-1})]} \tag{2}$$

Based on the functions defined in Eqs. 1 and 2, we can proceed to form a CRF problem, and solve it use the learning and prediction algorithm in CRF. In conclusion, we can perform a POS tagging task via CRF.

3.2 Model Training Process

Assume we have a bunch of training examples (sentences and associated part-of-speech labels). Randomly initialize the weights of our CRF model. To shift these randomly initialized weights to the correct ones, for each training example:

(1) *Go through each feature function f_i, and calculate the gradient of the log probability of the training example with respect to λ_i:*

$$\frac{\partial}{\partial w_j} \log p(l|s) = \sum_{j=1}^{m} f_i(s,j,l_j,l_{j-1})$$
$$- \sum_{l'} p(l'|s) \sum_{j=1}^{m} f_i(s,j,l'_j,l'_{j-1}) \tag{3}$$

(2) *Note that the first term in the gradient is the contribution of feature f_i under the true label, and the second term in the gradient is the expected contribution of feature f_i under the current model. This is exactly the form you'd expect gradient ascent to take.*
(3) *Move λ_i in the direction of the gradient:*

$$\lambda_i = \lambda_i + \alpha \left[\sum_{j=1}^{m} f_i(s,j,l_j,l_{j-1}) \right.$$
$$\left. - \sum_{l'} p(l'|s) \sum_{j=1}^{m} f_i(s,j,l'_j,l'_{j-1}) \right], \tag{4}$$

where α is some learning rate.
(4) *Repeat the previous steps until some stopping condition is reached (e.g., the updates fall below some threshold).*

In other words, every step takes the difference between what we want the model to learn and the model's current state, and moves λ_i in the direction of this difference.

3.3   Finding the Optimal POS Tagging

The naive way is to calculate $p(l|s)$ for every possible labeling l, and then choose the label that maximizes this probability. However, since there are k^m possible labels for a tag set of size k and a sentence of length m, this approach would have to check an exponential number of labels.

A better way is to realize that CRFs satisfy an optimal substructure property that allows us to use a dynamic programming algorithm to find the optimal label, similar to the Viterbi algorithm for HMMs [3, 4, 11, 13].

4   Experiments

In this section, we conduct simulation experiments to validate our proposed method.

4.1 Experiment Setup

We adopt the dataset that can be obtained through the Internet, i.e. Turku Dependency Treebank[1]. This dataset contains text from 10 different domains. The treebank does not have default partition to training and test sets. Therefore, from each 10 consecutive sentences, we assign the 9th and 10th to the development set and the test set, respectively. The remaining sentences are assigned to the training set.

Major code is implemented in Python, while model training procedure is written in C++ for efficiency promotion. The experiments are all performed in a server with a 16-core 2.6 GHz Intel Xeon processor with 32 GB RAM.

4.2 Experimental Results

The performance at each iteration number during the training process is as shown in Fig. 3. Once the parameters are updated using the training set at each iteration number, we test the performance of the model with the test set. Figure 3 is plot with the experimental results of 100 iteration number. As we can see, in the first 40 iterations, the performance improves significantly; while after that, the performance will not change much. So in practical application scenarios, we must choose a appropriate iteration number to balance the performance and the cost. Simple though, the experiment results validate that our proposed method is promising in performing a POS tagging task.

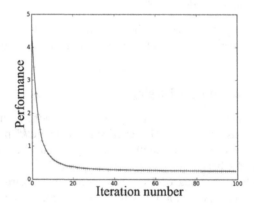

Fig. 3. Performance at each iteration number during the training process.

---

[1] http://bionlp.utu.fi/fintreebank.html.

5 Conclusion

In this paper, we proposed to utilize the inherent advantages of CRF, and apply it to POS tagging task to get more accurate. The subsequent experiments are introduced to validate our proposed method.

In the future, we will study how to consider our model in service computing environment [5, 8, 10, 12, 13, 16] and cloud computing system [6, 9, 15], which may bring about effectiveness and efficiency.

References

1. Lafferty, J., McCallum, A., Pereira, F.: Conditional random fields: probabilistic models for segmenting and labeling sequence data. In: Proceedings of the 18th International Conference on Machine Learning (ICML), pp. 282–289. MIT Press (2001)
2. Gross, S.S., Russakovsky, O., Do, C.B., Batzoglou, S.: Training conditional random fields for maximum labelwise accuracy. In: Proceedings of the Advances in Neural Information Processing Systems (NIPS), pp. 529–536. MIT Press (2006)
3. Zhong, P., Wang, R.: Learning sparse CRFs for feature selection and classification of hyperspectral imagery. IEEE Trans. Geosci. Remote Sens. 46(12), 4186–4197 (2008)
4. Sutton, C., McCallum, A.: An introduction to conditional random fields. Mach. Learn. 4(4), 267–373 (2011)
5. Wang, L., Sun, Q., Wang, S., Ma, Y., Xu, J., Li, J.: Web service QoS prediction approach in mobile internet environments. In: Proceedings of the IEEE International Conference on Data Mining Workshop (ICDM), pp. 1239–1241. IEEE (2016)
6. Xu, J., Wang, S., Zhou, A., Yang, F.: Machine status prediction for dynamic and heterogenous cloud environment. In: Proceedings of the IEEE International Conference on Cluster Computing (CLUSTER), pp. 136–137. IEEE (2016)
7. Ding, C., Zhang, L.: Double adjacency graphs-based discriminant neighborhood embedding. Pattern Recogn. 48(5), 1734–1742 (2015)
8. Wang, S., Zheng, Z., Zhengping, W., Yang, F.: Context-aware mobile service adaptation via a co-evolution eXtended classifier system in mobile network environments. Mob. Inform. Syst. 10(2), 197–215 (2014)
9. Liu, Z., Wang, S., Sun, Q., Zou, H., Yang, F.: Cost-aware cloud service request scheduling for SaaS providers. Comput. J. 57(2), 291–301 (2014)
10. Wang, S., Zhu, X., Yang, F.: Efficient QoS management for QoS-aware web service composition. Int. J. Web Grid Serv. 10(1), 1–23 (2014)
11. Sha, F., Pereira, F.: Shallow parsing with conditional random fields. In: Proceedings of the Association for Computational Linguistics on Human Language Technology, pp. 134–141. Association for Computational Linguistics (2003)
12. Wang, S., Zhou, A., Hsu, C., Xiao, X., Yang, F.: Provision of data-intensive services through energy- and QoS-aware virtual machine placement in national cloud data centers. IEEE Trans. Emerg. Top. Comput. 2(4), 290–300 (2016)
13. Gupta, R.: Conditional random fields. In Unpublished report, IIT Bombay, pp. 1–24 (2006)
14. Zhou, A., Wang, S., Li, J., Sun, Q., Yang, F.: Optimal mobile device selection for mobile cloud service providing. J. Supercomput. 8(72), 3222–3235 (2016)
15. Wang, S., Sun, L., Sun, Q., Wei, J., Yang, F.: Reputation measurement of cloud services based on unstable feedback ratings. Int. J. Web Grid Serv. 11(4), 362–376 (2015)

16. Xu, J., Wang, S., Su, S.: Latent interest and topic mining on user-item bipartite networks. In: Proceedings of the IEEE International Conference on Services Computing (SCC), pp. 778–781 (2016)

17. Klinger, R., Tomanek, K.: Classical probabilistic models and conditional random fields. J. Mol. Evol. **48**(5), 532–543 (2013)

18. Sastry, G.M.R., Chaudhuri, S., Reddy, P.N.: An HMM based part-of-speech tagger and statistical chunker for 3 Indian languages. In: Proceedings of the Proceedings of the IJCAI Workshop on Shallow Parsing for South Asian Languages, pp. 29–32. Morgan Kaufmann (2007)

19. Pammi, S.C., Prahallad, K.: POS tagging and chunking using decision forests. In: Proceedings of the IJCAI Workshop on Shallow Parsing for South Asian Languages, pp. 33–36. Morgan Kaufmann (2007)

20. Dandapat, S.: Part of speech tagging and chunking with maximum entropy model. In: Proceedings of the IJCAI Workshop on Shallow Parsing for South Asian Languages, pp. 136–137. Morgan Kaufmann (2007)

21. Freitag, D., McCallum, A.: Information extraction with HMM structures learned by stochastic optimization. In: Proceedings of the 26th Innovative Applications of Artificial Intelligence (IAAI), pp. 584–589. AAAI (2000)

22. Malouf, R.: A comparison of algorithms for maximum entropy parameter estimation. In: Proceedings of the 6th Conference on Natural Language Learning, pp. 1–7 (2002)

23. Keskin, C., Kıraç, F., Kara, Y.E., Akarun, L.: Hand pose estimation and hand shape classification using multi-layered randomized decision forests. In: Fitzgibbon, A., Lazebnik, S., Perona, P., Sato, Y., Schmid, C. (eds.) ECCV 2012. LNCS, vol. 7577, pp. 852–863. Springer, Heidelberg (2012). doi:10.1007/978-3-642-33783-3_61

Performance Evaluation for Traditional Virtual Machine Placement Algorithms in the Cloud

Ruo Bao[✉]

Beijing University of Posts and Telecommunications, Beijing, China
br@bupt.edu.cn

Abstract. The virtual machine placement problem can be described as designing optimal placement scheme for virtual machine in cloud environment. Cloud data centers are facing increasingly virtual machine placement problems, such as high energy consumption, imbalanced utilization of multidimensional resource, and high resource wastage rate. In this paper, typical exact and heuristic algorithms as solution to the virtual machine placement problem in the cloud are surveyed in terms of energy consumption and resource wastage. The purpose of this paper is to evaluate the performance of both the exact and approximate algorithms developed by using the WebCloudSim sytem.

Keywords: Cloud computing · Virtual machine placement · WebCloudSim

1 Definition

The virtual machine placement problem is to map the virtual machines to the physical machines is called the VM placement. In other word, VM placement is the process to select the appropriate host for the given VM. More specifically, given a data center consists of a set of physical machines and a corresponding queue of user requests for virtual machine instantiation, the scheme solving virtual machine placement problem aims at determining a host of the data center to place each virtual machine in the queue, dedicated to one or more of the following objectives: (1). To minimize the electric energy consumed by the data center, because the costs of powering and cooling accounts much for the total operational expenditure of datacenters; (2). To minimize the resource wastage in datacenter when virtual machine placement is conducted; (3). To minimize the overall systems computing time caused by virtual machine placement.

2 Exact Algorithms

Under the condition that the scale of the problem is not large, exact algorithms for the virtual machine placement problem can be classified into many categories like primordial search methods and dynamic programming. Primordial search methods aims at searches all over the solution space with various kinds of pruning method while dynamic programming focus on insight on characteristic of sub problem. Because the

© Springer International Publishing AG 2016
C.-H. Hsu et al. (Eds.): IOV 2016, LNCS 10036, pp. 225–231, 2016.
DOI: 10.1007/978-3-319-51969-2_19

number of proposed algorithms is very large in this field, we will provide two representative examples.

2.1   First Fit Algorithm

The classic Bin Packing Problem [5] is often adapted to the context of virtual machine placement in the following way: a whole set of virtual machines (objects) of different sizes should be placed into a series of hosts (bins) such that the minimum number of hosts are employed to place all virtual machines, thus saving energy. The First Fit Algorithm accomplishes that by activating a single host at a time as they get filled up with virtual machines. Each virtual machine is placed in the first host where it fits, according to a predefined order between active hosts. In addition, just one virtual machine – the first one in the queue – is taken at a time, and then placed on a host. For that reason, the First Fit Algorithm is suitable for the single delivery mode.

2.2   Round Robin Algorithm

The Round Robin algorithm mainly focuses on distributing the load equally to all the nodes. Using this algorithm, the scheduler allocates one VM to a node in a cyclic manner. The round robin scheduling in the cloud is very similar to the round robin scheduling used in the process scheduling. The scheduler starts with a node and moves on to the next node, after a VM is assigned to that node. This is repeated until all the nodes have been allocated at least one VM and then the scheduler returns to the first node again. Hence, in this case, the scheduler does not wait for the exhaustion of the resources of a node before moving on to the next. As an example, if there are three nodes and three VMs are to be scheduled, each node would be allocated one VM, provided all the nodes have enough available resources to run the VMs. The main advantage of this algorithm is that it utilizes all the resources in a balanced order. An equal number of VMs are allocated to all the nodes which ensure fairness. However, the major drawback of using this algorithm is that the power consumption will be high as many nodes will be kept turned on for a long time. If three resources can be run on a single node, all the three nodes will be turned on when Round Robin is used which will consume a significant amount of power.

3   Heuristic Algorithms

By definition, heuristic is a technique designed for solving a problem more quickly when classic methods are too slow, or for finding an approximate solution when classic methods fail to find any exact solution. This is achieved by trading optimality, completeness, accuracy, or precision for speed. Hence virtual machine placement problem is a non-deterministic problem in the strict sense. Numbers of heuristic virtual machine placement algorithms have been proposed that run under cloud computing environment. This section explains some of the existing heuristic virtual machine placement approaches.

3.1 Single Dimensional Best Fit

This method uses the single dimension (CPU, memory, bandwidth etc.) for placing a VM. When a VM arrived, scheduler visit the physical machines in the decreasing order of their capacity used in a single dimension and place the VM to the first PM that has the enough resources. That means VM place to the PM which used the maximum capacity along with the given dimension. Problem with approach is that it can increase the resource misbalancing because resource in the cloud is multi-dimension (CPU, memory, bandwidth etc.). So there may be a situation where a host utilizes their full CPU capacity while other resources such as memory and bandwidth are underutilized. N. Rodrigo et al. [6], proposed a heuristic for the mapping between VM and PM. Main aim of this approach is to balance the CPU utilization on each PM. Only CPU utilization is consider as a load metric, so after the mapping only amount of available CPU is check instead of whole PM. Objective function of this method is to minimize the standard deviation of residual CPU in each PM.

If there are n hosts in the data center and m is the number of VM in each host then objective function can be defined as

$$\text{Min} \left(\sqrt{\frac{\sum_{i=1}^{n} \left(rcpu_i^{PM} - rcpu_{mean}^{PM} \right)^2}{n}} \right) \tag{1}$$

$$rcpu_i^{PM} = cpu_i^{PM} - \sum_{j=1}^{m} cpu_j^{VM} \tag{2}$$

$$rcpu_{mean}^{PM} = \frac{\sum_{i=1}^{n} rcpu_i^{PM}}{n} \tag{3}$$

Where $rcpu_i^{PM}$ is the remaining CPU capacity of the i-th PM, cpu_i^{PM} is the total CPU capacity of the i-th PM and $\sum_{j=1}^{m} cpu_j^{VM}$ is the CPU used by the j-th VM. Problem with this approach is that they only consider the CPU capacity for mapping between the PM and VM. So other resource can be imbalance.

3.2 Genetic Algorithm

Genetic algorithm (GA) is a search technique used to find exact or approximate solutions to optimization and search problems. Genetic algorithms are categorized as global search heuristics. They are inspired by evolutionary biology such as inheritance, mutation, selection, and crossover. A typical genetic algorithm requires: a genetic representation of the solution domain and a fitness function to evaluate the solution domain. The solution domain can be represented as the physical machines with a resource provisioning capacity. With the hint of classic Bin Packing Problem Model, the fitness function can be defined over the number of bins in the solution. The aim would be to deliver a solution that is nearly optimal in terms of the number of bins used and the efficiency of packing of the bins. A variation to genetic algorithm known as Grouping Genetic Algorithm can also be applied to the VM Placement problem. These algorithms can take into account additional constraints while optimizing the cost function. This is particularly useful in cases where we need to operate on groups. The Grouping Genetic Algorithm can be thought of as a bin packing problem where the aim is to not only find a solution with highest packing efficiency but also to satisfy the constraints.

4   Performance Evaluation

In this section, we evaluate the efficiency and effectiveness of those approaches via the simulation experimentation in WebCloudSim [9–12]. WebCloudSim is a cloud data-center environment simulation system developed for performance evaluation.

4.1   Simulation Setup

All of the experiments are conducted on a 16-port fat-tree data center network with 64 core switches and 16 pods. Each pod is comprised of 8 aggregation switches and 8 edge switches. That is, there are 128 aggregation switches and 128 edge switches in the cloud data center, in which each edge switch can connect to 8 PMs, and each PM can host one or more VMs. In our experiment, we simulate a cloud data center comprising 1024 heterogeneous PMs and 2000 heterogeneous VMs. Each PM is modeled to have dual-core CPU with performance equivalent to 3720 MIPS, 10 GB of RAM, 10 GB/s network bandwidth and 1 TB of storage. In this simulation experimentation, we compare those four approaches: First Fit (FF), Round Robin Algorithm (RR), Single Dimensional Best Fit (SDBF), and Genetic Algorithm (GA) in terms of the overall energy consumption and the overall resource wastage, and then analyze the related parameter.

4.2   Experimental Results and Evaluation

In this section, we analyze the performance of the four approaches via comparing to each other in term of the overall energy consumption and the overall resource wastage.

4.2.1   Comparison of Overall Energy Consumption

The first set of experiments aims at estimating the overall energy consumption after when the 2,000 VMs are allocated to the 1,024 PMs. The overall energy consumption is decided by the number of PMs used and the number of VMs hosted by these PMs.

As depicted in Fig. 1, the experiment aims at estimating the overall energy consumption incurred due to the PMs used and the VMs hosted by these PMs. The experimental results indicate that GA has the least amount of the overall energy consumption, this is because that GA is a heuristic algorithm and makes its best effort to search the set of target PMs and to find a optimal solution using energy consumption as a metric.

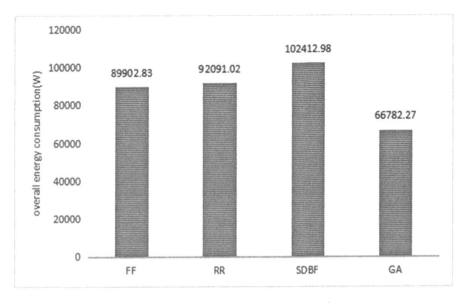

Fig. 1. overall energy consumption comparison

4.2.2 Comparison of Overall Resource Wastage

The second set of experiment aims at estimating the overall resource wastage after when the 2,000 VMs are allocated to the 1,024 PMs. The overall resource wastage is decided by memory and bandwidth.

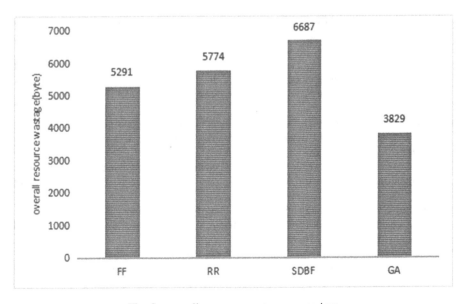

Fig. 2. overall resource wastage comparison

As depicted in Fig. 2, the experiment aims at estimating the overall resource wastage incurred due to the PMs used and the VMs hosted by these PMs. The experimental results indicate that SDBF has the most amount of the overall resource wastage. The reason is it can increase the resource misbalancing because resource in the cloud is multi-dimension (CPU, memory, bandwidth etc.). GA has the least amount of the overall resource wastage because in each iteration we use resource wastage as metric in mutation and selection stages.

5   Conclusions

The VM placement is one of the research problems in cloud infrastructure. Each of the virtual machine placement algorithms works well but only under certain specific conditions and have close relationship with the size of the problem [13–15]. So it is a critical task to choose a technique that is suitable for both the cloud user and cloud provider. Based on the experimental results, we can conclude that in addition to minimizing the overall energy consumption, GA minimizes the overall resource wastage at the same time coping with a set of parallel applications.

References

1. Wang, S., Zhou, A., Yang, F., Chang, R.: Towards network-aware service composition in the cloud. IEEE Trans. Cloud Comput. doi:10.1109/TCC.2016.2603504
2. Liu, J., Wang, S., Zhou, A., Kumar, S.A.P., Yang, F., Buyya, R.: Using proactive fault-tolerance approach to enhance cloud service reliability. IEEE Trans. Cloud Comput. (2016). doi: 10.1109/TCC.2016.2567392
3. Wang, S., Zhou, A., Hsu, C., Xiao, X., Yang, F.: Provision of data-intensive services through energy- and QoS-aware virtual machine placement in national cloud data centers. IEEE Trans. Emerg. Topics Comput. 2(4), 290–300 (2016)
4. Wang, S., Sun, Q., Zou, H., Yang, F.: Towards an accurate evaluation of quality of cloud service in service-oriented cloud computing. J. Intell. Manuf. 25(2), 283–291 (2014)
5. Zhang, G.W., He, R., Liu, Y.: The evolution based on cloud model. J. Comput. Mach. 7, 1233–1239 (2008)
6. Rodrigo, N., et al.: A heuristic for mapping virtual machines and links in emulation testbeds. In: Proceeding of 9th IEEE International Conference on Parallel Computing, pp. 518–525 (2009)
7. Gao, Y., Guan, H., Qi, Z., Hou, Y., Liu, L.: A multi-objective ant colony system algorithm for virtual machine placement in cloud computing. J. Comput. Syst. Sci. 79, 1230–1242 (2013)
8. Beloglazov, A., et al.: Energy efficient allocation of virtual machines in cloud data centers. In: Proceeding in 10th IEEE/ACM International Symposium on Cluster, Cloud and Grid Computing, pp. 577–578 (2010)
9. Zhou, A., Wang, S., Cheng, B., Zheng, Z., Yang, F., Chang, R.N., Lyu, M.R., Buyya, R.: Cloud service reliability enhancement via virtual machine placement optimization. IEEE Trans. Serv. Comput. PP(99), 1–14 (2016). doi:10.1109/TSC.2016.2519898

10. Chen, Y., Sun, Q., Zhou, A., Wang, S.: WebCloudSim: an open online cloud computing simulation tool for algorithm comparision. Serv. Trans. Cloud Comput. (STCC) **3**(2), 26–32 (2015)
11. Zhou, A., Wang, S., Zheng, Z., Hsu, C., Lyu, M., Yang, F.: On cloud service reliability enhancement with optimal resource usage. IEEE Trans. Cloud Comput. **PP**(99), 1 (2014)
12. Zhou, A., Wang, S., Yang, C., Sun, L., Sun, Q., Yang, F.: FTCloudSim: support for cloud service reliability enhancement simulation. Int. J. Web Grid Serv. **11**(4), 347–361 (2015)
13. Liu, Z., Wang, S., Sun, Q., Zou, H., Yang, F.: Cost-aware cloud service request scheduling for SaaS providers. Comput. J. **57**(2), 291–301 (2014)
14. Wang, S., Sun, Q., Zou, H., Yang, F.: Particle swarm optimization with skyline operator for fast cloud-based web service composition. Mobile Networks Appl. **18**(1), 116–121 (2013)
15. Zhou, A., Wang, S., Li, J., Sun, Q., Yang, F.: Optimal mobile device selection for mobile cloud service providing. J. Supercomputing **8**(72), 3222–3235 (2016)

Subspace Learning Based on Data Distribution for Face Recognition

Yong Ye[⊠]

State Grid Fujian Electric Power Company, Quanzhou, China
paperctding@126.com

Abstract. Over the past years, a large family of algorithms has been designed to provide different solutions to the problem of dimensionality reduction, such as discriminant neighborhood embedding (DNE), marginal fisher analysis (MFA) and double adjacency graphs-based discriminant neighborhood embedding (DAG-DNE). In this paper, we investigate the effect of data distribution for face recognition. We conduct three settings to investigate the performance when we have different numbers of the training samples. One is randomly select 20% samples as training set and the remaining face images are used for testing. One is randomly select 40% samples as training set and the last one is randomly select 60% samples as training set. In the end, we find as interesting observation is that when the training sample size is large enough to sufficiently characterize the data distribution, all algorithms we discussed in this work can achieve good performance.

Keywords: Discriminant neighborhood embedding · Marginal fisher analysis · DAG-DNE

1 Introduction

Dimensionality reduction has a wide range of applications in computer vision, and pattern recognition. In recent years, many supervised dimensionality reduction algorithms are proposed.

Classical supervised learning algorithms include linear discriminant analysis (LDA) [3,13], which aims at searching for the directions that are most effective for discrimination by minimizing the ration between the intraclass and interclass; discriminant neighborhood embedding (DNE) [14], which constructs an adjacency graph to preserve the local geometric structure (i.e., local intraclass and local interclass scatters); marginal fisher analysis (MFA) [12], which constructs two adjacency graphs (i.e., the intrinsic graph and the penalty graph, respectively) to preserve the local geometric structure; and double adjacency graphs-based discriminant neighborhood embedding (DAG-DNE) [1], also constructs two adjacency graphs to preserve the local geometric structure.

In this paper, we mainly focus on investigate the effect of data distribution for face recognition. Based on DNE, MFA and DAG-DNE, we conduct three settings to evaluate the effect. Experiment results illustrate that when the training

© Springer International Publishing AG 2016
C.-H. Hsu et al. (Eds.): IOV 2016, LNCS 10036, pp. 232–237, 2016.
DOI: 10.1007/978-3-319-51969-2_20

number size is large enough, all algorithms we discussed in this work can achieve good performance.

2 The Compared Algorithms

DNE, MFA and DAG-DNE are all classical subspace learning algorithms. Here, we introduce MFA as a representation.

2.1 Marginal Fisher Analysis

MFA proposed based on LDA can overcome some shortcomings of LDA (e.g., the data of each class is approximately Gaussian distributed). However, real-world data do not always satisfy a Gaussian distribution. MFA projects the data into a discriminative feature space in which the data is clearly separated and the data not have to satisfy a Gaussian distribution.

In MFA, we construct two adjacency graphs, the intrinsic graph and the penalty graph, respectively. In the intrinsic graph, for each sample $\mathbf{x}_i$, we set the intrinsic adjacency matrix $W_{ij}^w = W_{ji}^w = 1$ if and only if $\mathbf{x}_j$ is among the k-nearest neighbors of $\mathbf{x}_i$ in the same class, otherwise $W_{ij}^w = W_{ji}^w = 0$. In the penalty graph, for each sample $\mathbf{x}_i$, we set the intrinsic adjacency matrix $W_{ij}^b = W_{ji}^b = 1$ if and only if $\mathbf{x}_j$ is among the k-nearest neighbors of $\mathbf{x}_i$ in the different classes, otherwise $W_{ij}^b = W_{ji}^b = 0$.

MFA can finds the optimal projection directions via the following Marginal Fisher Criterion:

$$\min_{\mathbf{P}} \frac{\mathbf{P}^T \mathbf{X}(\mathbf{D}^{lw} - \mathbf{W}^{lw})\mathbf{X}^T \mathbf{P}}{\mathbf{P}^T \mathbf{X}(\mathbf{D}^{lb} - \mathbf{W}^{lb})\mathbf{X}^T \mathbf{P}} \tag{1}$$

where $tr(\cdot)$ is the trace of a matrix.

3 Experiments

In this section, we compared three algorithms (DNE, MFA and DAG-DNE) on UMIST dataset. In the following experiments, we use the Euclidean metric and one nearest classifier for classification due to its simplicity.

The UMIST face dataset consists of 564 images of 20 individuals, taking into account race, sex and appearance. Each subject is taken in a range of poses from profile to frontal views. The pre-cropped dataset is used and the size of each image is 112×92 pixels, with 256 gray levels per pixel. Each image is manually cropped and resized to 32×32 pixels. Note that the original images on UMIST database are normalized, so that two eyes are aligned at the same location. Figure 1 shows some image samples in the UMIST dataset. In this experiment, PCA is utilized to reduce dimensionality from 1024 to 100 and conducts three experimental settings (i.e., we randomly select 20%, 40% and 60% training images from each person and the remaining images are used for testing). Every experiment runs 10 times.

Fig. 1. Subject from the UMIST image dataset.

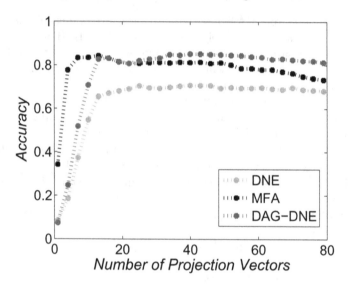

Fig. 2. Accuracy of three methods versus number of dimension on the UMIST dataset (20% training samples)

From Figs. 2, 3 and 4 and Table 1, we can see that:

(1) We can see that no matter what the number of training samples (i.e., 20%, 40% or 60%), MFA always goes up faster than DNE and DAG-DNE. However, with the increase of the numbers of projection vectors, DNE and DAG-DNE all can achieve good performance. From Figs. 2, 3 and 4 and Table 1, in the end, DAG-DNE in two cases even has a more higher accuracy than MFA (e.g., 20% training samples, MFA (85.14%), DAG-DNE (87.36%)).

(2) We also get a conclusion that when the training sample size is large enough to sufficiently characterize the data distribution, such as the case when number of training samples if 60% samples, all algorithms we discussed in this work can achieve good performance (e.g., DNE (97.30%), MFA (98.80%), DAG-DNE (98.35%)). This fact shows that, for a real-world application, it is critical to collect enough samples for all face images.

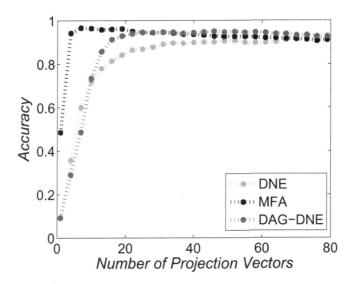

Fig. 3. Accuracy of three methods versus number of dimension on the UMIST dataset (40% training samples)

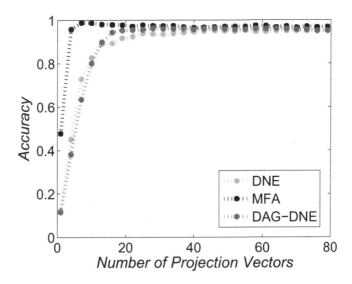

Fig. 4. Accuracy of three methods versus number of dimension on the UMIST dataset (60% training samples)

Table 1. Performance comparison of the methods on the UMIST face dataset with different training sample numbers

Method/Result	UMIST (20% training)			UMIST (40% training)			UMIST (60% training)		
	Mean	Best	Dim	Mean	Best	Dim	Mean	Best	Dim
DNE	0.8271	0.8381	100	0.9453	0.9552	98	0.9730	0.9820	53
MFA	0.8514	0.8714	14	0.9692	0.9821	6	0.9880	0.9910	7
DAG-DNE	0.8736	0.9113	42	0.9701	0.9851	27	0.9835	1	23

4   Conclusion

In this paper, we compare DNE, MFA and DAG-DNE methods and experiment them on UMIST face dataset with different settings (i.e., we randomly select 20%, 40% and 60% training images from each person and the remaining images are used for testing). When we conduct different settings, we find an interesting observation is that when the training sample size is large enough to sufficiently characterize the data distribution, all algorithms we discussed in this work can achieve good performance. Future work will consider our model in service computing environment and cloud computing system [2,4–11,15].

References

1. Ding, C., Zhang, L.: Double adjacency graphs-based discriminant neighborhood embedding. Pattern Recogn. **48**(5), 1734–1742 (2015)
2. Liu, Z., Wang, S., Sun, Q., Zou, H., Yang, F.: Cost-aware cloud service request scheduling for saas providers. Mob. Inf. Syst. **57**(2), 291–301 (2014)
3. Martinez, A.M., Kak, A.C.: Pca versus lda. IEEE Trans. Pattern Anal. Mach. Intell. **23**(2), 228–233 (2001)
4. Wang, S., Zhou, A., Hsu, C., Xiao, X., Yang, F.: Provision of data-intensive services through energy- and qos-aware virtual machine placement in national cloud data centers. IEEE Trans. Emerg. Topics Comput. **4**(2), 290–300 (2016)
5. Wang, S., Hsu, C.-H., Liang, Z., Sun, Q., Yang, F.: Multi-user web service selection based on multi-qos prediction. Mob. Inf. Syst. **16**(1), 143–152 (2014)
6. Wang, S., Sun, L., Sun, Q., Wei, J., Yang, F.: Reputation measurement of cloud services based on unstable feedback ratings. Int. J. Web Grid Serv. **11**(4), 362–376 (2015)
7. Wang, S., Sun, Q., Zou, H., Yang, F.: Towards an accurate evaluation of quality of cloud service in service-oriented cloud computing. J. Intell. Manufact. **25**(2), 283–291 (2014)
8. Wang, S., Sun, Q., Zou, H., Yang, F.: Towards an accurate evaluation of quality of cloud service in service-oriented cloud computing. Mob. Inf. Syst. **25**(2), 283–291 (2014)
9. Wang, S., Zheng, Z., Zhengping, W., Yang, F.: Context-aware mobile service adaptation via a co-evolution extended classifier system in mobile network environments. Mob. Inf. Syst. **10**(2), 197–215 (2014)

10. Wang, S., Zhu, X., Sun, Q., Zou, H., Yang, F.: Low-cost web service discovery based on distributed decision tree in P2P environments. Wirel. Pers. Commun. **73**(4), 1477–1493 (2013)
11. Wang, S., Zhu, X., Yang, F.: Efficient qos management for qos-aware web service composition. Int. J. Web Grid Serv. **10**(1), 1–23 (2014)
12. Yan, D., Xu, S.C., Zhang, B.Y., Zhang, H.J., Yang, Q.: Graph embedding and extensions: a general framework for dimensionality reduction. IEEE Trans. Pattern Anal. Mach. Intell. **29**(1), 40–51 (2007)
13. Yu, H., Yang, J.: A direct lda algorithm for high-dimensional data with application to face recognition. Pattern Recogn. **34**(10), 2067–2070 (2001)
14. Zhang, X.Y., Xue, W., Guo, Y.F.: Discriminant neighborhood embedding for classification. Pattern Recogn. **39**(11), 2240–2243 (2006)
15. Zhou, A., Wang, S., Li, J., Sun, Q., Yang, F.: Optimal mobile device selection for mobile cloud service providing. J. Supercomput. **72**(8), 3222–3235 (2016)

Multiple Classification Using Logistic Regression Model

Baoping Zou[✉]

State Grid Information & Telecommunication Group
Great Power Science and Technology Corporation, Quanzhou, China
zz20161025@163.com

Abstract. The traditional logistic regression model is always used binary classification tasks, such as a person's gender (male or female). In this paper, we introduce how to adapt the traditional logistic regression model to multiple classification task. To validate our proposed method, we conduct an experiment on a open dataset, and the experimental results show that our proposed method is promising in multiple classification task.

Keywords: Multiple classification task · Logistic regression · Binary classification task · Gradient descent

1 Introduction and Related Work

The traditional logistic regression model is always used binary classification tasks, such as a person's gender (male or female) [2,3]. However, in practical application scenarios, most of the classification tasks are multiple classification. For example, a guy's attitude towards the British voting to leave the European Union in 2016 is a three-type task, i.e. positive, negative or neutral. It can be decomposed into three binary-type tasks, i.e. whether a persons attitude is positive (negative or neutral) or not, and then we apply the traditional logistic regression model to perform these binary classification tasks. But this decomposition process is very boring. So the existing work in [2,3] is not enough.

Faced with this problem, in this paper, we introduce how to adapt the traditional logistic regression model to multiple classification task. To validate our proposed method, we conduct an experiment on a open dataset, and the experimental results show that our proposed method is promising in multiple classification task.

This article is organized by the following: in Sect. 2 we detail the constructing process of the proposed multiple classification using logistic regression model. In Sect. 3 we list the experiment setup and the experimental results. In Sect. 4, we conclude this article, and give the future directions.

The original version of this chapter was revised: Author's affiliation has been corrected. The erratum to this chapter is available at https://doi.org/10.1007/978-3-319-51969-2_23

© Springer International Publishing AG 2016
C.-H. Hsu et al. (Eds.): IOV 2016, LNCS 10036, pp. 238–243, 2016.
DOI: 10.1007/978-3-319-51969-2_21

2   Multiple Classification Using Logistic Regression Model

The traditional logistic regression model is always used binary classification tasks, such as a person's gender (male or female). In this section, we introduce how to adapt the traditional logistic regression model to multiple classification task.

Assume the label of a sample from the dataset takes value from set $\{1, 2, \cdots, K\}$, then the probability of each label for each coming sample can be written by the following:

$$P(y = k|\mathbf{x}) = \begin{cases} \frac{\exp(\mathbf{w}_k \cdot \mathbf{x})}{1 + \sum_{k=1}^{K-1} \exp(\mathbf{w}_k \cdot \mathbf{x})} & k = 1, 2, \cdots, K-1 \\ \frac{1}{1 + \sum_{k=1}^{K-1} \exp(\mathbf{w}_k \cdot \mathbf{x})} & k = K \end{cases} \tag{1}$$

Then the likelihood function can be written down as the product of all of the probabilities, as follows:

$$\prod_{i=1}^{N} \prod_{k=1}^{K} P(y_i = k|x_i)^{y_i^k}, \tag{2}$$

where $P(y_i = k|x_i)$ denotes the probability of label k for the input sample x_i, and y_i^k serves as indicator function, which takes value 1 when real label of x_i is equal to k otherwise 0.

Then we take the log of the likelihood function, we get this objective function as summarization of several items by the following:

$$\begin{aligned} L(w) &= -\frac{1}{N} \sum_{i=1}^{N} \sum_{k=1}^{K} y_i^k \log P(y_i = k|x_i) \\ &= -\frac{1}{N} \sum_{i=1}^{N} (\sum_{k=1}^{K-1} y_i^k \log \frac{\exp(\mathbf{w}_k \cdot \mathbf{x}_i)}{1 + \sum_{j=1}^{K-1} \exp(\mathbf{w}_j \cdot \mathbf{x}_i)} + y_i^K \log \frac{1}{1 + \sum_{j=1}^{K-1} \exp(\mathbf{w}_j \cdot \mathbf{x}_i)}) \\ &= -\frac{1}{N} \sum_{i=1}^{N} (\sum_{k=1}^{K-1} y_i^k (\mathbf{w}_k \cdot \mathbf{x}_i - \log(1 + \sum_{j=1}^{K-1} \exp(\mathbf{w}_j \cdot \mathbf{x}_i))) - y_i^K \log(1 + \sum_{j=1}^{K-1} \exp(\mathbf{w}_j \cdot \mathbf{x}_i))) \\ &= \frac{1}{N} \sum_{i=1}^{N} (\sum_{k=1}^{K} y_i^k \log(1 + \sum_{j=1}^{K-1} \exp(\mathbf{w}_j \cdot \mathbf{x}_i)) - \sum_{k=1}^{K-1} y_i^k \mathbf{w}_k \cdot \mathbf{x}_i) \end{aligned} \tag{3}$$

Note that to avoid overfitting, we must add at the tail of the objective function an item like this:

$$\sum_{k=1}^{K-1} \frac{|\mathbf{w}_k|^2}{2\sigma^2} \tag{4}$$

$$L(w) = \frac{1}{N} \sum_{i=1}^{N} (\sum_{k=1}^{K} y_i^k \log(1 + \sum_{j=1}^{K-1} \exp(\mathbf{w}_j \cdot \mathbf{x}_i)) - \sum_{k=1}^{K-1} y_i^k \mathbf{w}_k \cdot \mathbf{x}_i + \sum_{k=1}^{K-1} \frac{|\mathbf{w}_k|^2}{2\sigma^2} \tag{5}$$

Given the defined objective function of various parameters, we apply the gradient descent method to optimize this function to find the most appropriate parameters. The gradient of the objective function is as follows:

$$
\begin{aligned}
\frac{\partial L(w)}{\mathbf{w}_k} &= \frac{1}{N} \sum_{i=1}^{N} \frac{\exp(\mathbf{w}_k \cdot \mathbf{x}_i)}{1 + \sum_{k=1}^{K-1} \exp(\mathbf{w}_k \cdot \mathbf{x}_i)} \cdot \mathbf{x}_i - \frac{1}{N} \sum_{i=1}^{N} y_i^k \mathbf{x}_i + \frac{\mathbf{w}_k}{\sigma^2} \\
&= \frac{1}{N} \sum_{i=1}^{N} P(y_i = k | \mathbf{x}_i) \cdot \mathbf{x}_i - \frac{1}{N} \sum_{i=1}^{N} y_i^k \mathbf{x}_i + \frac{\mathbf{w}_k}{\sigma^2}
\end{aligned}
\tag{6}
$$

Given the objective function and the gradient of each parameter, we can use the gradient descent method to optimize this function to find the most appropriate parameters.

3   Experiments

3.1   Experiment Setup

We use an open dataset called Iris to validate our proposed model. The Iris flower data set or Fisher's Iris data set is a multivariate data set introduced by Ronald Fisher in his 1936 paper The use of multiple measurements in taxonomic problems as an example of linear discriminant analysis. It is sometimes called Anderson's Iris data set because Edgar Anderson collected the data to quantify the morphologic variation of Iris flowers of three related species. Two of the three species were collected from the same pasture, and picked on the same day and measured at the same time by the same person with the same apparatus.

Figure 1 shows the scatterplot of the data set, i.e. visualization of classification of the Iris data. The data set consists of 50 samples from each of three species of Iris (Iris setosa, Iris virginica and Iris versicolor). Four features were measured from each sample: the length and the width of the sepals and petals, in centimetres. Based on the combination of these four features, Fisher developed a linear discriminant model to distinguish the species from each other.

The majority of the code is implemented in Python, whereas the model training procedure of is written in C++ for the sake of training efficiency. The experiments are all performed on a server with a 16-core 2.6 GHz Intel Xeon processor with 32 GB of RAM.

3.2   Experimental Results

The performance at each iteration number during the training process is as shown in Fig. 2. Once the parameters are updated using the training set at each iteration number, we test the performance of the model with the test set. Figure 2 is plot with the experimental results of 300 iteration number. As we can see, in the first 100 iterations, the performance improves significantly; while after that, the performance will not change much. So in practical application scenarios, we

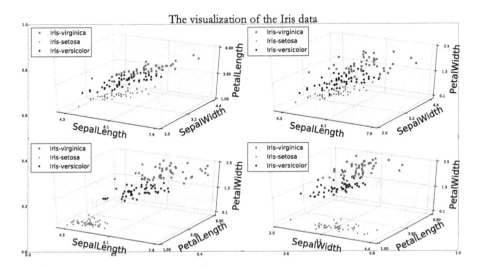

Fig. 1. The visualization of classification of the Iris data.

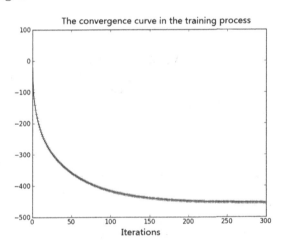

Fig. 2. The training process of multiple classification using logistic regression model.

must choose a appropriate iteration number to balance the performance and the cost. Simple though, the experiment results validate that our proposed method is promising in multiple classification using logistic regression model.

The final classification result is shown in the confusion matrix in Table 1. The confusion matrix contains information about actual and predicted classifications done by a classification system. As we can see, all of the 50 samples of the Iris-setosa are classified into the right category. While with Iris-versicolor and Iris-virginica, only 4 of 50 samples are judged wrong. That is to say, using our proposed method, most of the classification results are right. So, our experimental results validate are proposed method.

Table 1. The confusion matrix of the classification result

	Iris-setosa	Iris-versicolor	Iris-virginica
Iris-setosa	50	0	0
Iris-versicolor	0	46	4
Iris-virginica	0	4	46

4 Conclusion

In this paper, we proposed to utilize the inherent advantages of the traditional machine learning model, namely logistic regression model, and apply it to multiple classification task to get more accurate. The subsequent experiments are introduced to validate our proposed method.

In the future, we will study how to consider our model in service computing environment [1,4,6–10,12,13] and cloud computing system [5,11,14,15], which may bring about effectiveness and efficiency.

References

1. Li, J., Sun, Q., Yang, F., Zhou, A., Wang, S.: Optimal mobile device selection for mobile cloud service providing. J. Supercomput. **72**(8), 3222–3235 (2016)
2. Hosmer, D.W., Lemeshow, S.: Introduction to the logistic regression model. Applied Logistic Regression, 2nd edn, pp. 1–30. Prentice Hall, New York (2000)
3. Lemeshow, S., Hosmer, D.W.: A review of goodness of fit statistics for use in the development of logistic regression models. Am. J. Epidemiol. **115**(1), 92–106 (1982)
4. Liu, Z., Wang, S., Sun, Q., Zou, H., Yang, F.: Cost-aware cloud service request scheduling for SaaS providers. Mob. Infor. Syst. **57**(2), 291–301 (2014)
5. Wang, L., Sun, O., Wang, S., Ma, Y., Xu, J., Li, J.: Web service QoS prediction approach in mobile internet environments. In: 2014 IEEE International Conference on Data Mining Workshop (ICDMW), pp. 1239–1241. IEEE (2014)
6. Wang, S., Zhou, A., Hsu, C., Xiao, X., Yang, F.: Provision of data-intensive services through energy- and QoS-aware virtual machine placement in national cloud data centers. IEEE Trans. Emerg. Top. Comput. **4**(2), 290–300 (2016)
7. Wang, S., Hsu, C.-H., Liang, Z., Sun, Q., Yang, F.: Multi-user web service selection based on multi-QoS prediction. Mob. Inf. Syst. **16**(1), 143–152 (2014)
8. Wang, S., Sun, L., Sun, Q., Wei, J., Yang, F.: Reputation measurement of cloud services based on unstable feedback ratings. Int. J. Web Grid Serv. **11**(4), 362–376 (2015)
9. Wang, S., Sun, Q., Zou, H., Yang, F.: Towards an accurate evaluation of quality of cloud service in service-oriented cloud computing. J. Intell. Manufact. **25**(2), 283–291 (2014)
10. Wang, S., Sun, Q., Zou, H., Yang, F.: Towards an accurate evaluation of quality of cloud service in service-oriented cloud computing. Mob. Inf. Syst. **25**(2), 283–291 (2014)
11. Wang, S., Zheng, Z., Zhengping, W., Yang, F.: Context-aware mobile service adaptation via a co-evolution extended classifier system in mobile network environments. Mob. Inf. Syst. **10**(2), 197–215 (2014)

12. Wang, S., Zhu, X., Sun, Q., Zou, H., Yang, F.: Low-cost web service discovery based on distributed decision tree in P2P environments. Wirel. Pers. Commun. **73**(4), 1477–1493 (2013)

13. Wang, S., Zhu, X., Yang, F.: Efficient QoS management for QoS-aware web service composition. Int. J. Web Grid Serv. **10**(1), 1–23 (2014)

14. Xu, J., Wang, S., Su, S., Kumar, S.A.P., Chou, W.: Latent interest and topic mining on user-item bipartite networks. In: 2016 IEEE International Conference on Services Computing (SCC), pp. 778–781. IEEE (2016)

15. Xu, J., Zhou, A., Wang, S., Sun, Q., Li, J., Yang, F.: Machine status prediction for dynamic and heterogenous cloud environment. In: 2016 IEEE International Conference on Cluster Computing (CLUSTER), pp. 136–137. IEEE (2016)

Joint of Local and Global Structure for Clustering

Baoping Zou[✉]

State Grid Information & Telecommunication Group
Great Power Science and Technology Corporation, Quanzhou, China
zz20161025@163.com

Abstract. We consider the general problem of clustering from labeled and unlabeled data, which is often called semi-supervised learning or transductive inference. Most of existing works consider the intrinsic local or global structure of the dataset, which introduced poor clustering performance in real case scenarios. In this paper, we study the complementary relationship between local and global structure of a dataset, and proposed to obtain a better clustering performance via label propagation process. To validate our proposed method, we conduct experiment on the two-moon problem, and find that our method yields encouraging experimental results on a number of classification problems and demonstrates effective use of unlabeled data.

Keywords: Clustering · Local structure · Global structure · Joint training

1 Introduction and Related Work

Cluster analysis or clustering is the task of grouping a set of objects in such a way that objects in the same group (called a cluster) are more similar to each other than to those in other groups. It is a main task of exploratory data mining, and a common technique for statistical data analysis, used in many fields, including machine learning, pattern recognition, image analysis, information retrieval, bioinformatics, data compression, and computer graphics.

Traditional clustering methods are unsupervised, meaning that there is no outcome measure and nothing is known about the relationship between the observations in the data set. However, in many situations one may wish to perform cluster analysis even though an outcome variable exists or some preliminary information about the clusters is known. While in this paper, we consider the general problem of clustering from labeled and unlabeled data, which is often called semi-supervised learning or transductive inference, which has proved to have a wide range of potential applications.

The original version of this chapter was revised: Author's affiliation has been corrected. The erratum to this chapter is available at https://doi.org/10.1007/978-3-319-51969-2_23

© Springer International Publishing AG 2016
C.-H. Hsu et al. (Eds.): IOV 2016, LNCS 10036, pp. 244–248, 2016.
DOI: 10.1007/978-3-319-51969-2_22

Most of existing works consider the intrinsic local or global structure of the dataset, which introduced poor clustering performance in real case scenarios [2,15–17]. This is because the global structure and local structure of a dataset are complementary in clustering. Ignoring any of both is not enough for a good clustering result.

As a result, in this paper, we study the complementary relationship between local and global structure of a dataset, and proposed to obtain a better clustering performance via label propagation process. To validate our proposed method, we conduct experiment on the two-moon problem, and find that our method yields encouraging experimental results on a number of classification problems and demonstrates effective use of unlabeled data.

This article is organized by the following: in Sect. 2 we detail the constructing process of the proposed multiple classification using logistic regression model. In Sect. 3 we list the experiment setup and the experimental results. In Sect. 4, we conclude this article, and give the future directions.

2   A Clustering Method by Joint of Local and Global Structure

First we must identify the definition of the local and global structure respectively, by the following:

- We define the local structure as the relationship between a sample and its neighbors. For example, if an sample's label is already assigned, and in the next step, it will try to propagate its label to one or two or several of its neighbors. In general, it will select the nearest neighbor as the candidate. During this space, the already assigned sample only knows the information of its adjacent neighbors, without knows the remote samples' information. So we call this information as the local structure;
- The global structure means the global information of the dataset. For example, given a crowd of samples, we can find the number of the peaks, and the distance of each sample to these peaks, and the nearest peak for each sample. So during the propagation process of the labels, we can combine the global structure and local structure of dataset to assign a sample's label more scientifically.

Based on the above analysis, we can incept the basic thought into the existing clustering method in works [2,15–17], and proposed new method that can utilize the complementary relationship between local and global structure of a dataset to obtain a better clustering performance via label propagation process. Due to the space limit, we will not describe the implementation details of the method, but the readers can easily implement one.

3   Experiments

3.1   Experiment Setup

In order to firstly assess our approach, we consider a well-known synthetic datasets generated by two intertwining moon structures (see top of Fig. 1). This dataset is always used for testing the clustering performance of a innovative clustering method.

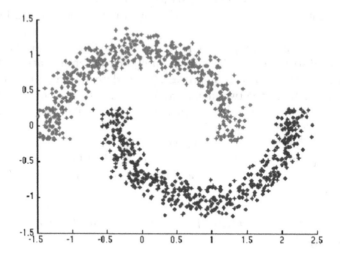

Fig. 1. Illustration of the famous two moon dataset, which is always used for testing a new clustering method.

The majority of the experimental codes are implemented in Python, whereas the core procedure of model training is written in C++ for the sake of training efficiency. The experiments are all performed on a computer with a 16-core 2.6 GHz Intel Xeon processor with 32 GB of RAM.

3.2 Experimental Results

The experimental results are shown in Fig. 2. Figure 2 contains 8 consecutive snapshots of the clustering process, which illustrates the performance of the proposed method that can join the intrinsic global and local structure of two moon dataset and apply this knowledge to propagate the label of samples appropriately.

As we can see, in Fig. 2(1), there are only several initial samples are assigned the labels. From Fig. 2(2)–(7), the labels propagate among the samples, and more and more samples are assigned the labels. However, during this process, quite a lot of samples are assigned the wrong labels. Nevertheless, the performance are becoming better and better as the adjacent samples are assigned the same labels, in the meanwhile sample pairs with a long distance are always assigned different labels. Figure 2(8) shows the final clustering result, which shows a sound clustering result like in the Fig. 1.

This result seems to confirm that the proposed approach is able to deal with an important issue of joint learning of global and local structure of dataset: the consistency, i.e. nearby points and points on the same structure are likely to have the same label.

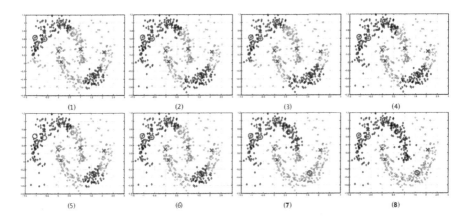

Fig. 2. Label transmission process via local and global structure.

4   Conclusion

In this paper, we study the complementary relationship between local and global structure of a dataset, and proposed to obtain a better clustering performance via label propagation process. To validate our proposed method, we conduct experiment on the two-moon problem, and find that our method yields encouraging experimental results on a number of classification problems and demonstrates effective use of unlabeled data.

In the future, we will study how to consider our model in service computing environment [1,3,5–9,11,12] and cloud computing system [4,10,13,14], which may bring about effectiveness and efficiency.

References

1. Li, J., Sun, Q., Yang, F., Zhou, A., Wang, S.: Optimal mobile device selection for mobile cloud service providing. J. Supercomput. **72**(8), 3222–3235 (2016)
2. Liu, W., He, J., Chang, S.-F.: Large graph construction for scalable semi-supervised learning. In: Proceedings of the 27th International Conference on Machine Learning (ICML 2010), pp. 679–686 (2010)
3. Liu, Z., Wang, S., Sun, Q., Zou, H., Yang, F.: Cost-aware cloud service request scheduling for saas providers. Mob. Inf. Syst. **57**(2), 291–301 (2014)
4. Wang, L., Sun, Q., Wang, S., Ma, Y., Xu, J., Li, J.: Web service qos prediction approach in mobile internet environments. In: 2014 IEEE International Conference on Data Mining Workshop (ICDMW), pp. 1239–1241. IEEE (2014)
5. Wang, S., Zhou, A., Hsu, C., Xiao, X., Yang, F.: Provision of data-intensive services through energy- and qos-aware virtual machine placement in national cloud data centers. IEEE Trans. Emerg. Top. Comput. **4**(2), 290–300 (2016)
6. Wang, S., Hsu, C.-H., Liang, Z., Sun, Q., Yang, F.: Multi-user web service selection based on multi-qos prediction. Mob. Inf. Syst. **16**(1), 143–152 (2014)

7. Wang, S., Sun, L., Sun, Q., Wei, J., Yang, F.: Reputation measurement of cloud services based on unstable feedback ratings. Int. J. Web Grid Serv. **11**(4), 362–376 (2015)
8. Wang, S., Sun, Q., Zou, H., Yang, F.: Towards an accurate evaluation of quality of cloud service in service-oriented cloud computing. J. Intell. Manufact. **25**(2), 283–291 (2014)
9. Wang, S., Sun, Q., Zou, H., Yang, F.: Towards an accurate evaluation of quality of cloud service in service-oriented cloud computing. Mob. Inf. Syst. **25**(2), 283–291 (2014)
10. Wang, S., Zheng, Z., Zhengping, W., Yang, F.: Context-aware mobile service adaptation via a co-evolution extended classifier system in mobile network environments. Mob. Inf. Syst. **10**(2), 197–215 (2014)
11. Wang, S., Zhu, X., Sun, Q., Zou, H., Yang, F.: Low-cost web service discovery based on distributed decision tree in P2P environments. Wirel. Pers. Commun. **73**(4), 1477–1493 (2013)
12. Wang, S., Zhu, X., Yang, F.: Efficient QoS management for QoS-aware web service composition. Int. J. Web Grid Serv. **10**(1), 1–23 (2014)
13. Xu, J., Wang, S., Su, S., Kumar, S.A.P., Chou, W.: Latent interest and topic mining on user-item bipartite networks. In: 2016 IEEE International Conference on Services Computing (SCC), pp. 778–781. IEEE (2016)
14. Xu, J., Wang, S., Zhou, A., Yang, F.: Machine status prediction for dynamic and heterogenous cloud environment. In: 2016 IEEE International Conference on Cluster Computing (CLUSTER), pp. 136–137. IEEE (2016)
15. Zhang, Z., Zhao, M., Chow, T.W.S.: Graph based constrained semi-supervised learning framework via label propagation over adaptive neighborhood. IEEE Trans. Knowl. Data Eng. **27**(9), 2362–2376 (2015)
16. Zhou, D., Bousquet, O., Lal, T.N., Weston, J., Schölkopf, B.: Learning with local and global consistency. Adv. Neural Inf. Process. Syst. **16**(16), 321–328 (2004)
17. Zhu, X., Ghahramani, Z., Lafferty, J., et al.: Semi-supervised learning using gaussian fields and harmonic functions. ICML **3**, 912–919 (2003)

Erratum to: Internet of Vehicles – Technologies and Services

Ching-Hsien Hsu[1(✉)], Shangguang Wang[2], Ao Zhou[2],
and Ali Shawkat[3]

[1] Department of Computer Science, Chung Hua University,
Hsinchu, Taiwan, Taiwan
chh@chu.edu.tw
[2] Beijing University of Posts and Telecommunications, Beijing, China
[3] The University of Fiji, Suva, Fiji

Erratum to:
C.-H. Hsu et al. (Eds.):
Internet of Vehicles – Technologies and Services, LNCS 10036,
https://doi.org/10.1007/978-3-319-51969-2

The affilation of the author Baoping Zou is not correct. The correct information is given below.

State Grid Information & Telecommunication Group Great Power Science and Technology Corporation, Quanzhou, China
zz20161025@163.com

The updated online version of this book can be found at
https://doi.org/10.1007/978-3-319-51969-2
https://doi.org/10.1007/978-3-319-51969-2_21
https://doi.org/10.1007/978-3-319-51969-2_22

C.-H. Hsu et al. (Eds.): IOV 2016, LNCS 10036, p. E1, 2016.
https://doi.org/10.1007/978-3-319-51969-2_23

Author Index

Printed in the United States
By Bookmasters